D0864865

The Participation
of the Soviet Union
in Universal International
Organizations

The Participation of the Soviet Union in Universal International Organizations

DR. CHRIS OSAKWE

Assistant Professor of Law and
Political Science
University of Notre Dame

A Political
and Legal Analysis
of Soviet Strategies and
Aspirations inside
ILO, UNESCO and WHO

A.W. SIJTHOFF LEIDEN 1972

ISBN 90 286 0002 7

Library of Congress Catalog Card Number: 73-182525
© A. W. Sijthoff International Publishing Company, N.V. 1972

Printed in the Netherlands

To my beloved Mother
with gratitude and
respect

FOREWORD

The classics of Marxist thought gave little guidance to the Soviet regime in the conduct of international relations. In the 1920's Soviet leaders and scholars debated whether the Soviet government should scorn the existing world legal order and appeal directly to the workers and peasants of other countries or whether it should attempt to transform the existing legal order and organizational structure from within to achieve its strategic and ideological goals. Statesmen of non-communist countries debated whether the Soviet threat they perceived could better be controlled by the containment of Soviet foreign policy within the structure of international organizations or by the exclusion of the Soviet representatives from those organizations.

Recent years have seen some accommodations in international organizations between the special interests of the U.S.S.R. and the interests of the other members, and accommodations have been reached affecting the legal structure and powers of these organizations. These developments have been parallelled by the development of a sophisticated Soviet theory of the legal nature of international organizations, a theory which not only helps to justify Soviet actions before world public opinion, but which also, to some extent, limits and guides Soviet policy.

Professor Osakwe comes well equipped to the task of interpreting Soviet theory and practice in the law and politics of international organizations. He spent eight years at Moscow State University, completing his work for the degree of Candidate of Legal Sciences in 1970 under the able guidance of Professor G. I. Tunkin, the leading Soviet authority on international law. The time spent as a student in Moscow have given him an acquaintance with the Soviet political process that few of his generation in the English speaking world have. We are privileged to share in his insights and interpretation.

Peter B. Maggs
Professor of Law
University of Illinois, College of Law

ACKNOWLEDGMENT

This book has long been in the process of preparation and during the period of time while it has been taking shape in my mind I have accumulated innumerable debts none of which can be adequately fulfilled and some of which, in fact, cannot be discharged.

Greatest of my debts goes to my Master in the law, Professor Peter B. Maggs of the College of Law of the University of Illinois who at all stages in the preparation of this book offered his most valuable assistance and cooperation. His suggestions proved most vital towards the outcome of this work. To him I am deeply grateful.

My deep gratitude also goes to Professor Chin Kim, Professor of Library Science and Assistant Law Librarian, Foreign and International Law Collection of the Law Library of the University of Illinois. He and his staff willingly came to my aid at those critical and sometimes frustrating moments when I took up a permanent seat in the Law Library.

Professor Robert F. Miller of the Department of Political Science of the University of Illinois offered me his most professional assistance throughout the time that I was working on the manuscript of this book. The experience I gained from taking over his class on Soviet Foreign Policy during his absence was not only pedagogical, but also intellectually stimulating. The exercise drew my attention to certain practical issues that are raised in the book. To him I express my deep gratitude.

I also wish to express my sincere gratitude to the Institutional Responses to Rapid Social Changes in Russia and Eastern Europe (IRRSCREE) Group of the Russian and East European Center of the University of Illinois at whose spring (1971) session I presented a portion of my study as a paper. The discussion of, and the constructive remarks on, my Report by members of the Group were most helpful in my final preparation of that section of this book. I am also very grateful to Professor Ralph T. Fisher Jr., Director of the Russian and East European Center of the University of Illinois who generously, through his office, funded the final phase of my work on this book. Without this crucial assistance from his Center the result of my research on this topic may not have been what it is today.

My gratitude also goes to the Curatorium of The Hague Academy of

International Law, personally to Miss N. M. Maarleveld of the Academy Secretariat, and to the authorities of the Peace Palace Library for having made it possible for me to spend the summer of 1971 at the Carnegie Library at The Hague while I was putting finishing touches to the final draft of this book.

I am equally grateful to Professor F. Kalshoven of the University of Leiden, Faculty of Laws for his painstaking efforts to read through the entire manuscript and for the very important corrections he made in the text. His suggestions for changes in the general structure of the book were highly appreciated.

And, finally, may I express my sincere gratitude to Miss E. S. Lightfoot of the Registry of the International Court of Justice at The Hague for her most valuable secretarial assistance and to the Editors of AJIL for the permission to use my article which originally appeared in that Journal (vol. 65 No. 3, July 1971, pp. 502-521).

While acknowledging all the valuable help rendered to me by all the individuals and groups mentioned above, I must accept that the final responsibility for any faults and weak points in this work remains entirely mine.

Peace Palace
The Hague, August 1971

C. O. Osakwe

PREFACE

Law as a social phenomenon, in contradistinction to coercion and morality, has suffered many definitions in the hands of various leading jurisprudents right from the time of John Austin and all these definitions have tended to show the law's many lives. This is not necessarily true of that amorphous body of norms commonly referred to as "International Law" for lack of a better term. If the saying "Lex est ancilla politicae" is true of domestic (national) law, it is even more so of international law.

Despite the many uncertainties surrounding the very nature of international law and its capacity to regulate effectively the behaviour of international entities, international organizations are founded and operate on the basis of international law. From the time the founding members of an international organization adopt a constituent instrument for their new organization, this not including the fact that the very process of treaty negotiation itself is regulated by the law of treaties, international law comes into full play in the relationship between these members "inter se" and also, as is often the case, in their relationship with third parties. It is no secret, of course, that behind this effort on the part of the member states of any particular international organization to cooperate with other states lie their closely guarded political interests. These interests not only lead states into accepting these legal forms of cooperation as provided by the international organizations, but also, to a considerable extent determine to what extent they shall be willing to carry out their obligations undertaken therefrom. Added to these two phenomena—law and politics—ideology comes into play as a yet more fundamental force in contemporary international relations.

Politics, by which expression we mean a form of power game, is founded on ideology and law in its turn is only an ancillary of politics. The principal purpose of this study, therefore, is to examine the mechanism of the close interplay of international law, international politics and ideology in the zig-zag process of Soviet participation in universal international organizations. Emphasis, however, is placed on the analysis of Soviet outlook on international politics and the ideological foundations of this outlook. Jurisprudential discussion about the nature of international law is only incidental to the key question.

We have tended to view international law as a dynamic process of conflict resolution rather than as a static body of rules. And it is in this capacity that international law should be seen as providing the necessary legal framework for the conduct of foreign policy of any particular nation. That this law is far from perfect is an understatement—a fact which should be borne in mind by the reader at all times.

As a final note to the reader I would like to mention that the "Footnotes" at the end of each chapter are generally substantive in character and parenthetical to the text.

TABLE OF CONTENTS

LIST OF ABBREVIATIONS

AFDI	Annuaire Français de Droit International
AFL-CIO	American Federation of Labour and Congress of Industrial Organizations. (A trade union movement established in December 1955 by the merger of the AFL and the CIO with a membership put at approximately 14.5 million.)
AJIL	American Journal of International Law
ANZUS	(Australia, New Zealand, and the United States) The tripartite security treaty concluded between the three countries at San Francisco on September 1, 1951
AUCCTU	All-Union Central Council of Trade Unions (Vsesoiuznyi Tsental'nyi Soviet Professional'nykh Soiuzov)
BYIL	British Yearbook of International Law
Can. YBIL	Canadian Yearbook of International Law
COMECON	Council of Mutual Economic Assistance
CPSU	Communist Party of the Soviet Union
ECOSOC	Economic and Social Council of the United Nations
FAO	Food and Agricultural Organization of the United Nations
FZMK	Fabrichnyi Zavodskoi Mestnyi Komitet Profsoiuza (The Factory Plant Local Committee of the Trade Union)
GA-UN	General Assembly of the United Nations
Hague Recueil	Recueil des Cours de l'Académie de Droit International de La Haye
HOLN	Health Organization of the League of Nations
IAEA	International Atomic Energy Agency
IBPH	International Bureau of Public Health
ICAO	International Civil Aviation Organization
ICJ Reports	International Court of Justice, Reports of Judgment, Advisory Opinions and Orders
ILO	International Labour Organization
IMCO	Inter-Governmental Maritime Consultative Organization
ITU	International Telecommunications Union

Kan. Jur.	Kandidat Iuridicheskykh Nauk (Candidate of Juridical Sciences)—considered the equivalent of the Ph.D. degree
KGB	Komitet Gosudarstvennoi Bezopasnosti (Committee on State Security)
LNTS	League of Nations Treaty Series
Mag. Jur.	Magistr Iuridicheskykh Nauk (Master of Juridical Sciences)—considered the equivalent of the LL.M degree
MGU	Moskovskii Gosudarstvennyi Universitet (Moscow State University)
PASIL	Proceedings of the American Society of International Law
SC-UN	Security Council of the United Nations Organization
SEMP	Sovetskii Ezhegodnik Mezhdunarodnogo Prava (Soviet Yearbook of International Law)—published by the Soviet Association of International Law
SGP	Sovetskoe Gosudarstvo i Pravo (Soviet State and Law)—published by the Institute of State and Law of the Soviet Academy of Sciences
TASS	Telegrafnoe Agentstvo Sovetskogo Soiuza (Telegraphic Agency of the Soviet Union)
UNCIO Docs.	United Nations Conference on International Organization—Documents
UNESCO	United Nations Educational, Scientific and Cultural Organization
UNTS	United Nations Treaty Series
WHO	World Health Organization

INTRODUCTION

One of the major by-products of the first world war was the precipitation of the Bolshevik Revolution of November 1917 which later swept across the full length and breadth of the entire Russian continental Empire. The events of November 1917 definitely marked a turning point in the history of Russia—they revolutionised the entire thinking of the Russian people, they sharply affected the attitude of Russia towards any schemes or ideas that were hatched outside its borders. Russia all of a sudden withdrew from its position as a great European power.[1] After the events of November 7, 1917 Russia gradually isolated herself from the rest of Europe and, in fact, from the rest of the world as a whole as she progressively built iron walls all along her borders to make her own citizens prisoners in their own country.

On the home front intellectual imprisonment progressively dawned upon the Russian intelligentsia. The revolutionary spirit of Bolshevism infiltrated into the spheres of art, science, and culture and this in its turn led to the new posture which was to be adopted by the emergent Soviet doctrine of international law—the posture of critical negativism towards traditional international legal concepts.[2] However, this new mental attitude adopted by Soviet international lawyers, like all forcibly imposed positions from above, has never been consistently presented. One only needs to take a glance at the historical development of Soviet international legal science to notice the frequent shift of positions within it.[3]

The creation of the League of Nations in 1919 within the framework of the Treaty of Versailles provided the first test for Soviet attitude towards a legal order hatched outside, and without the participation of, Soviet Russia. Soviet attitude towards the League of Nations was violently negative right from the outset, particularly between 1919-1934 and later on after 1939. By and large Soviet Russia saw the League of Nations as an anti-communist coalition aimed at destroying the new Soviet state, Soviet attitude towards the League demonstrates to its fullest the zig-zag development and neomachiavellism which has come to be closely associated with Soviet foreign policy be it under the leadership of V. I. Lenin, or under Joseph Stalin, or even under the direction of N. S. Khrushchev, not to talk of the present Kremlin troika.

1

Max Beloff, commenting on Soviet attitude towards the League of Nations at the time, stated: "From its foundation the League of Nations had been regarded with suspicion by the Soviet Union. It was denounced at the First Congress of the Communist International (COMINTERN) as the holy alliance of the bourgeoisie for the suppression of the proletarian revolution."[4] He further records that as late as 1928 the Manifesto of the Sixth Congress (of the COMINTERN) declared the League of Nations the product of Versailles and, therefore, the most shameless robber-treaty of the last decade which was an attempt to cloak the military aims of the members by working out projects for disarmament.[5]

Max Beloff, however, like all Western scholars, and to our mind justifiably too, refuses to share this Soviet view on the intentions of the founding fathers of the League of Nations. The League certainly was a very bold experiment in the international organization of a hitherto unorganized international community of nations and it is only to be regretted that the Soviet government attributed to this new institution the qualities of an anti-communist monster. Whatever reasoning compelled the Soviet Union to adopt such a negative attitude towards the League of Nations and its sister-institutions is undoubtedly very political.

It would be intellectually dishonest, however, for us not to attempt to analyse Russia's grievances against the League of Nations. The following reasons might suggest themselves as being responsible for Russia's initial hatred for the League of Nations:

1. France, one of the two leading members of the League helped Poland, another member of the League, in her war against Soviet Russia;

2. England, the other leading member of the League and the United States—one of the chief architects of the League but who later refused to join the Organization—nourished the same belief as the other states that were represented at the Paris Peace Conference, namely, that the League of Nations might aid the counter-revolutionaries by serving as an antidote to the "communist poison" posed by the Bolshevik revolution. All these events made Russia highly sceptical of the value of the League of Nations as an international organization for the maintenance of international peace and security. She naturally looked upon the League of Nations as an anti-Soviet coalition and as a bastion of counter-revolution. Various Soviet statesmen called the League of Nations by various names: "an alliance of world bandits against the proletariat", "a league of the capitalists against nations", "the shadow of the feast of the Supreme Allied Council", etc.[6]

However, Soviet foreign policy founded, like any other foreign policy of any state in the world, on Machiavellian principles, did not hesitate to reconsider its attitude towards the "imperialist League of Nations" when such a move was dictated by some superior political interests. This was exactly what happened in 1934 when the Soviet attitude towards the

League of Nations changed radically from a condemnation of its aims and objectives to that of co-operation with the Organization. The explanation for such a change of attitude is very clear to any student of international politics—in international politics like in national, there are no permanent friends nor are there permanent enemies, but only permanent interests and these interests are permanently served by a combination of alternating options and through constantly shifting alliances.

During the period immediately following 1934 Russia was afraid of the growing menace of Hitler's aggression. Russia was at this time, at least militarily, highly vulnerable and she knew that she could not stand a blow from fascist Germany. This fear was heightened by the fear of Japanese militarism from the East just as it was coupled with the internal vulnerability which Stalinist Russia faced from the gross discontent which dominated her domestic political scene. All these practical political considerations led Soviet Russia into a political re-appraisal of her attitude towards the League of Nations. In fact, Russia was of the impression that Germany withdrew from the League of Nations in order to prepare an attack against her.

One might begin to wonder how such a reasoning is compatible with the official Soviet position of viewing the League of Nations as being anti-communist. The fact is that, in the Soviet view, even though the League was seen as an instrument of anti-Soviet machinations, the Germans thought that the League was insufficiently anti-Soviet and was, therefore, constituting itself into an intolerable obstruction for the more radically anti-Soviet Nazi schemes. This led Germany to withdraw from the coalition.

In more specific terms one can say that a combination of the following factors pushed Russia into joining the League of Nations in 1934:

1. Soviet Russia had been feeling itself menaced from the East by Japan. This became all the more apparent when the aggressive military party gained almost complete control of the Japanese government.

2. The repeated statements of the Nazi leaders concerning their ambitions enhanced the Soviet fear of German design on the Ukraine. Prior to assuming power and much after that Hitler persistently condemned Bolshevism as an attempt by the Jews to obtain world power and he had been insisting that Germany needed to acquire more territory in order to feed its surplus population.[7]

In the light of the political events of 1931-1934, the Soviets came to believe that Japan and Germany had withdrawn from the League of Nations in order that they might have free hands for the strengthening of their imperialist power and dominance by planning a joint crusade on Russia—Japan was to strike from the East and Germany, from the West.

3. The Soviet Union's hesitancy to join the League of Nations increased the possibility of war. Political exigencies dictated to the USSR to join

the League and at least to parade itself as an exponent of complete disarmament and indivisible peace. War at this time would be injurious to the aspirations of Soviet foreign policy.

4. The launching of the first and second 5-year plans in 1928 and 1933 made Soviet Russia eager to obtain loans from European capitalists and she hoped that Geneva might prove a profitable meeting place as well as a platform for dexterous Soviet propaganda.[8]

In the light of all these circumstances Russia succumbed to a higher political interest—she settled for the maintenance of the "status quo" in Europe. Russia joined the camp of the major victorious powers of World War 1 and in May 1935 she signed Peace Treaties with France and Czechoslovakia for mutual defense against Germany. That these supposedly "peace treaties" were entered into by Russia at this time as a result of the Russian fear of a possible German attack cannot be denied.[9]

The political somersault on the part of Soviet Russia was, however, welcome inside the League circles, at least by the major powers. To avoid the necessity for a formal application by the Soviet Union to join the League, a procedure which would necessarily lead to a formal scrutiny of that government's qualification for League's membership, it was known by the beginning of September 1934 that the Assembly of the League would be asked to invite the Soviet Union to join the Organization. This simplified procedure of invitation had previously been used only in 1931 and 1932 for Mexico and Turkey for whose admission universal agreement was obtainable.

However, as was probably expected, a strong opposition came from Poland which objected to the granting of a permanent seat to the Soviet Union in the League Council since Poland itself was denied this seat. Furthermore, Poland felt that Russia would embarrass her by raising the question of Poland's treatment of her national minorities and therefore wished the Russians to bind themselves by a minorities treaty before entering the League. But the Russians prefered to give the Poles an assurance, on September 10, that they would deal with all questions arising between them on the basis of the Riga Treaty, the Polish-Soviet non-aggression pact, and the 1933 Convention for the Definition of Agression. There was also some opposition from some dissenting states which however was of no great political importance.[10]

On September 10, 1934 the Council of the League, meeting in a secret session, decided 'nemine contradicente', with two abstentions (Portugal and Argentina), in favour of the Soviet government being awarded a permanent seat on the Council.[11] The Soviet delegation appeared in the League Assembly for the first time on Sept. 17, 1934. Now the Soviet Union formally became a member of an "imperialist club with an anti-communist orientation". It must be noted, however, that the willingness of the Soviet Union to join the League of Nations at this time, at least in terms of 'Realpolitik' if nothing else, matched the equal determination of the League members to admit this "Bolshevik state" into an otherwise anti-Bolsehevik coalition. Anti-communist member states of the Organization suddenly found a tolerable political bedmate in a communist state.

Once inside the League the Soviet Union acted as a loyal and even enthusiastic member, but is was obviously no more willing than any other power to risk vital national interests for the sake of demonstrating its devotion to League principles.

The election of the Soviet Union to the League of Nations carried with it automatic membership of another sister-institution of the League—the International Labour Organization (ILO)[12] and in July 1935 the Russians were represented, though incompletely, at its 19th. Conference.[13]

The political marriage between the Soviet Union and the League of Nations lasted barely five years. In 1939 the League Council considered it necessary to expel the Soviet Union from the Organization after the Soviet Union attacked Finland. From the Soviet point of view the expulsion of the USSR from the League in 1939 was an act of political suicide on the part of the League itself. This act, in the Soviet view, was to be the first step towards the dissolution of the Organization. One can actually say that with the decision of the United States not to join the League and the League's subsequent expulsion of Russia from the Organization coupled with the blatant rejection of League principles by Germany and Italy, and the apparent impotence of England and France to keep the peace, the League remained a living corpse long before its formal dissolution in 1946.

A new era dawned on the Soviet attitude towards universal international organizations with the creation of the United Nations in 1945. At least at this time, unlike the case of the League before it, the Soviet Union took an active part in the creation of the UN. Whereas the Covenant of the League of Nations was an integral part of the Treaty of Versailles which, along with other peace treaties, ended the first world war, the UN Charter was an independent international act which stood completely outside the framework of any of the post-World-War-Two settlement agreements. Whereas the League of Nations initially adopted an anti-Soviet posture, the United Nations Organization, at least judging from the available evidence at both the Dumbarton-Oaks and San Francisco Conferences, was not intended to be anti-Soviet. All these factors contributed to the radical change in Soviet attitude towards the new Organization.

The Soviets, however, had not completely forgotten the bitter experiences of the League of Nations. At all stages leading to the creation of the UN Soviet spokesmen and legal scholars made it abundantly clear that the Soviet Union would not participate in any international organization that would be patterned after the defunct League of Nations. The Soviets demanded that the future international organization must be built on an agreement, unanimity and close cooperation of the great powers of the anti-German coalition.

The Treaty of Versailles, the Russians would maintain, in fact, strengthened the hands of Hitler due to its ineffectiveness and, therefore, the Soviets were sceptical of any international agreement that would repeat the mistakes of Versailles. German aggression had cost mankind too dearly to allow any future peace treaty to repeat the fatal errors of Versailles. Having learned the bitter lessons of recent history, the Soviets were prepared this time to settle only for a concert or balance of the Great Powers.

At the United Nations Conference on International Organization (UNCIO) in 1945[14] the Soviet delegate presented Soviet official policies as follows:

1. The principle of unanimity and accord between the permanent members of the Security Council was an indispensable prerequisite for the successful and fruitful operation of the projected international organization in the maintenance of international peace and security.

2. Theoretically, all sovereign states were juridically equal. Actually, the Great Powers alone possessed the manpower and the material resources to keep the peace.

Thus, as far as we can see, the Soviet Union not only joined the UN which she was instrumental in establishing, but she became one of the Organization's most active members. Does this mean that the Soviet Union was now prepared to cooperate fully with the rest of the world in the maintenance of international peace and security? Does it mean that the Soviet Union had ceased to look upon the "imperialist camp" as its arch-enemy and an adversary that must be annihilated at all costs? Evidently not. All it meant was that the Soviet Union found in the United Nations' machinery a suitable instrument for the execution of its foreign policy, a policy which in the very long run is aimed at Soviet Union's self-preservation. The fact that the Soviet Union hesitated to join most of the specialised agencies of the United Nations and, in fact, has not joined many of these agencies up till today,[15] points to the fact that political considerations play a major role in determining Soviet attitude towards these international organizations.

One might ask this question—what exactly is there in the nature of the United Nations and in those specialised agencies of the UN of which the USSR is a member that actually made them attractive to the Soviet Union? What has kept the Soviet Union out of those other five specialised agencies which she continues to keep at an arm's length up till today? We shall devote a greater portion of our analysis to examining each of these questions. We shall attempt to put together some of the major political considerations to which the Soviet Union gives prominence in her decision to join or not to join any given international organization.

6

As the title to this book suggests we are limiting our inquiry to only three of the existing thirteen UN specialised agencies, viz, the International Labour Organization (ILO), the World Health Organization (WHO), and the United Nations Educational Scientific and Cultural Organization (UNESCO). This choice is not intended to suggest that these three organizations are the most important of all the UN specialised agencies. Far from it. We decided upon these three merely because we feel that any analysis of Soviet participation in them will demonstrate to the possible fullest the general pattern of Soviet participation in universal international organizations.

We chose the ILO mainly because of its tripartite character and out of the understanding that this might enable us to focus attention on the role of the Soviet trade union organization—the All-Union Central Council of Trade Unions (AUCCTU)—in the conduct of Soviet foreign policy. It is probably a well known fact that the Soviet Union conducts its foreign policy today not only through the Soviet ministries of Foreign Affairs, Foreign Trade, Culture, and Higher Education, but also through such semi-governmental institutions like the AUCCTU, the various friendship and cultural organizations, and the numerous communist-front organizations, to mention just a few.

Since the Soviet trade union organization is a mass organization with the single largest membership in the Soviet Union, a fact which made Lenin refer to it as "the school of communism",[16] its role in both domestic and foreign policies of the Soviet Union cannot be exaggerated. When the Soviet trade union delegate walks up to the ILO to pose to represent the Soviet workers' union, we must realise that we are not dealing with a workers' representative in the regular sense of the word, but with a 'de facto' government delegate who represents a government-controlled labour union. In a society where the state is the only authorised employer of any significance, a representative of the employers' union is equally nothing but a government delegate.

The choice of the UNESCO is equally illustrative of our declared purpose here. The attitude of the Soviet Union towards the UNESCO is particularly interesting because this Organization is distinguished by the wide range of its activities and because the Soviet Union unexpectedly decided to join the UNESCO after a virtual boycott of nine years. Certain technical aspects of the UNESCO also give it an unusual position among international organizations. Furthermore, the UNESCO is very largely concerned with the area of international contacts which directly affect the Soviet system.

As the intensive post-war campaign against cosmopolitanism showed, the Soviet rulers consider "undirected" intellectual contact with Soviet intelligentsia a threat to their control; on the other hand, arguments and appeals addressed to intellectuals have formed an important weapon of communism ever since the days of Lenin. An examination of Soviet attitude towards the UNESCO may throw an additional light upon this ambivalent relationship—the protection of Soviet intelligentsia from any corrupting outside cultural influence and the reliance of the Soviet regime on the intelligentsia for the victory of communism.

The consideration of the Soviet attitude towards the WHO is most illuminating for our overall purpose. Art. 1 of the WHO Constitution defines the objective of the Organization as "the attainment by all peoples of the highest level of health" and by "health" the Preamble to the Constitution means "not merely the absence of disease" but also "a state of complete physical, mental, and social well-being" of all peoples. This certainly grants the World Health Organization, qua an international organization charged with the promotion of international public health, very much varied operational scope.

We hope that by analysing Soviet attitude towards these three organizations which we have discriminatingly handpicked we shall be able to evolve a general formula for determining Soviet participation in universal international organizations.

Finally, we might like to say a few words about some of the terms we shall be coming across in the course of our discussion—such terms like "universal", "international", and "organization". By the term "universal" we do not intend to mean "embracing all the states in the world", but rather by using it we mean an organization whose aims and objectives are of general interest to all states alike but which for one reason or the other has not attained an envisaged universal membership, stricto sensu. A more appropriate term in this context would probably be "universalist" which better describes this temporary short-coming in the membership structure. Strictly speaking there are no universal international organizations anywhere today. Rather there are universalist international organizations like the United Nations and its family organizations.

Secondly, the term "international" as applied to most institutions of international law is a notorious misnomer for "inter-state" or, as many may interject, for "inter-entity". Traditionally, the terms "international" and "inter-governmental" have been freely, though inaccurately, interchanged for "inter-state".[17] By "international" in this context we mean to refer to an organization the membership of which is primarily, though not exclusively, open to states. Other corporate entities may be members of such an international organization but this does not derogate from the original fact that the organization in question was primarily intended for states. The distinction between "inter-state" and "inter-governmental" has lost its essence today as most international organizations officially designated as "inter-governmental" are, in actual fact, inter-state in character.[18]

The term "organization" in contradistinction to any other institutional set-up, e.g. an international conference or any other ad hoc international

8

arrangement, presupposes some degree of permanence and separate legal identity. An international organization is not just a mechanical totality of its member-entities, but rather a "corpus separatum", a constitutional outgrowth from the original conglomeration of states participating therein.

These limitations, in effect, mean that our findings are not intended for application to regional international organizations, international conferences, universal, or, if one prefers, universalist, non-governmental international organizations and any such others. No doubt Soviet participation in these categories of international institutions is given substantial importance in foreign policy considerations but space will definitely not permit any such all-embracing study.

We would equally like to draw attention to the fact that in our analysis of Soviet doctrine of international law much emphasis is placed on the works of very few outstanding Soviet scholars rather than undertake an impossible task of checking the writing of all Soviet authors on the topic. Such an approach is based on the fact that in a society where the very process of thinking and the entire intellectual activity of its citizens are based on semi-military regimentation, it stands to reason to try to study the intellectual trend of the given society by examining the "very source" of all knowledge within the order.

The writings of Professor G. I. Tunkin to us serve as the "fountainhead" of all contemporary Soviet doctrines and concepts of present day international law[19] and, therefore, his role in the formulation of Soviet doctrines on international law cannot be overemphasised. However, where possible we have singled out other contemporary Soviet scholars for detailed analysis particularly so if such individuals are generally recognised within the Soviet caste of international lawyers as "expert" on a particular international organization that we may be investigating.

We might like to add that all references to Soviet doctrinal authorities in this study shall be limited to only contemporary authors. It is certainly true that a historical approach would have been helpful but we decided to focus attention on contemporary Soviet doctrine for two basic reasons: in the first place, there are already very many excellent works by both American and other Western scholars on the historical development of Soviet legal doctrine[20] and duplicating such efforts is hardly desirable here; and secondly, our inquiry is specifically intended to analyse contemporary Soviet theory and practice with an eye on predicting what future Soviet practice might be, given certain political constants and variables.

Soviet specialised research works on international organizations are a relatively new phenomenon. As a matter of fact Professor E. A. Korovin was perhaps the single Soviet expert on international law whose work was available[21] until the new breed of Soviet international legal scholars of the Krilov-Koretskii-Kozhevnikov-Tunkin generation emerged. Thus, while drawing heavily on the past and present Soviet government practices for our purpose, we can only take up contemporary Soviet doctrinal expositions on the subject.

However, before going on to discussing Soviet participation in the ILO, the WHO, and the UNESCO respectively in chapters two, three and four, we have thought it necessary to present in a very brief form, first, the fundamental principles of Soviet doctrinal international law on the juridical nature of universal international organizations and, second, the ideological contents and the political foundations of the much-talked-of principle of peaceful coexistence. We do hope that this short re-statement of the relevant sections of Soviet international legal doctrine in chapter one will lay the required theoretical foundation from which to approach the subsequent chapters. Thus, whereas chapter one is purely theoretical in its approach, the subsequent chapters are essentially analytical of contemporary Soviet practices in universal international organizations. In other words Chapter one is intended to provide the theoretical foundations and the ideological skeleton for the attempted political applications which follow in chapters two, three and four. An effort to synthesise the relevant Soviet theory and practice is made in the short concluding portion of our study.

We would like to conclude this Introduction with the caveat that the analysis which follows borrows heavily from Soviet political theory. Only secondarily do we present its international legal positions which in their turn are founded in international politics. Where appropriate we have attempted to supply the social origins of any of the political theories and legal positions exposed therein. This inter-disciplinary approach raises a question as to whether our efforts here can be considered an essay in international law, political science or political sociology. Without attempting to designate it as any of these, we can only say that all we have tried to do is to present the Soviet (communist) theory of international law—a science, or art depending on what one prefers to call it, which leaves no Western scholar with any doubts as to its dominant foundations in politics.

NOTES

1. Cf. the role of Russia in convening the Congress of Vienna of 1815, the Hague Conferences of 1899 and 1907, its role in bringing about the Concert of Europe, etc.

2. One of the principal tasks of Soviet international lawyers of the early period was to try to interprete international law in the light of Marxism-Leninism. This original role fell upon Pashukanis and Korovin who for quite some length of time remained Russia's leading Marxist international lawyers. For a fuller detail on the gradual development of Soviet international legal doctrine after the Bolshevik Revolution of 1917, see K. Grzybowski, Soviet Public International Law—Doctrines and Practices, Leyden, Durham N.C. 1970, pp. 1-25.

3. Very often one finds the same author refuting himself or, in communist terminology, "making open confessions and self-criticisms" as soon as he finds that his point of view falls out of favour with the political authority. The late Professor E. A. Korovin was perhaps the best example of such "intellectual acrobat". See W. W. Kulski, The Soviet Interpretation of International Law, 49 AJIL 1955, No. 4 at pp. 518-534.

For some of E. A. Korovin's open confessions see his letter of May 5, 1935, 4 SGP 1935 at p. 71; See also E. A. Korovin i Ratner L., Programma po Mezhdunarodnomu Publichnomu Pravu, Moskva 1936, at p. 12.

4. Max Beloff: The Foreign Policy of Soviet Russia, (2 vols.), vol. 1 N.Y. 1947 at p. 42.

5. See 'Manifest Shestogo S'ezda Kominterna', Materiali Shestogo S'ezda, Moskva 1928.

6. See L. N. Ivanov: Liga Natsii, Moskva 1929; also O. Afanasieva: Kratkaia Istoriia Ligi Natsii, Moskva 1945.

7. See Adolf Hitler: Mein Kampf, (English Translation by Ralph Manheim), Sentry Edition, Boston 1943.

8. It should be mentioned that even though the United States was not a member of the League of Nations, having refused to join the Organization she had helped to create, the signing of a diplomatic relations agreement between Soviet Russia and the United States in 1933 contributed a great deal towards changing Soviet attitude towards the West as a whole. The view according to which Russia's primary goal in wooing Geneva was to obtain the much needed capital for development at home is also shared by Max Beloff. See: op. cit.

9. See A. Rudzinski: "Soviet Peace Offensives", 40 International Conciliation, April 1953, at pp. 177-225.

10. For example, opposition to Soviet admission to the LN came from the self-styled exiled Ukrainian government in Lvov, etc. This, however, did not make any serious impact on the determination of the League members to admit the Soviet Union into the Organization.

11. When the question of the admission of the Soviet Union formally came before the League Assembly on Sept. 18, 1934, 39 members voted in favour of her admission. Switzerland, Belgium, Cuba, Luxemburg, Panama, and Venezuela abstained. On the same day a Soviet delegation headed by Foreign Affairs Commissar Litvinov took its seat in the Council of the League.

12. Soviet international lawyers, however, refuse to accept the interpretation of Soviet admission into the LN as conferring automatic membership of the ILO on Russia. For fuller details on the arguments advanced on both sides of this thorny issue and for a fuller discussion of Soviet attitude towards the ILO, see chapter two.

13. The Soviet delegation had only government representatives on it thus leaving

11

out representatives of the Employers and Workers as demanded by Art. 3 of the ILO Constitution.

14. Vide UNCIO Docs. vols. 1-15, San Francisco 1945.

15. Of the existing 13 Specialised Agencies the Soviet Union is a member of only 8: the International Labour Organization; the United Nations Educational, Scientific and Cultural Organization; the Universal Postal Union; the International Telecommunications Union; the World Health Organization; the Inter-governmental Maritime Consultative Organization; the World Meteorological Organization; and the International Civil Aviation Organization. She has persistently refused to join any of the Bretton-Woods Institutions—the International Monetary Fund, the International Bank for Reconstruction and Development, the International Finance Corporation, and the International Development Association as well as the Food and Agricultural Organization of the United Nations. The Soviet Union is, however, an active member of the International Atomic Energy Agency, the United Nations Conference on Trade and Development, and the United Nations International Development Organization all of which are related agencies of the UN.

Professor K. Grzybowski reports on page 357 of his "Soviet Public International Law—Doctrines and Practices", Leyden Durham NC 1970 that the Soviet Union is not a member of the IMCO as of 1970 when the book was published. We would like to assume that this was a misprint because the Soviet Union joined the IMCO as far back as 1958, i.e. from the time the IMCO Covention came into force. The IMCO Convention was drawn up at the UN Maritime Conference held at Geneva from 19 February to 6 March 1948 but came into force only on March 17, 1958. See UNTS vol. 289, p. 48. The USSR deposited its Instrument of Acceptance of the IMCO Convention with the UN Secretary General, in accordance with Art. 57 of the Convention, on December 24, 1958. See UNTS vol. 317 at p. 359. Professor K. Grzybowski understandably could not have recorded the fact of Soviet membership of the ICAO as the Soviets joined this Organization at a much later date.

16. In communist catch-phrases the trade union is referred to as "the school of communism", the Komsomol Organization—as "the university of communism", and the CPSU—as the conductor of the entire Soviet orchestra.

17. See, for example, E. A. Shibaeva: Spetsializirovannye Uchrezhdeniia OON, Moskva 1966 at p. 32; see also G. I. Tunkin: The Legal Nature of the UN, 119 Hague Recueil 1966-III, at pp. 1, 22; G. I. Morozov: Mezhdunarodnye Organizatsii, Moskva 1969, chpt. 3.

18. See Art. 57 of the UN Charter.

19. The pronouncements of late Professor E. A. Korovin—Stalin's ideological watch-dog on the international legal front—today are considered highly embarrassing to the Soviet government and, therefore, are less often cited by Soviet diplomats, military experts, or even by legal scholars. See Hans Kelsen, The Communist Theory of Law, London, 1955.

20. See J. N. Hazard: Cleansing Soviet International Law of anti-Marxist theories, 32 AJIL, 244-252, Apr. 1938; also by the same author, The Soviet Union and International Law, Soviet Studies, vol. 1; T. A. Taracouzio, The Soviet Union and International Law, N.Y. 1935; A. Patkin, The Soviet Union in International Law, Proceedings of the Australian and New Zealand Society of International Law (Melbourne) 1935, vol. 1; Rudolph Schlesinger, Soviet Theories of International Law, Soviet Studies, vol. 4, No. 3 (1953); Joseph Florin, La Théorie Bolsheviste de Droit International Public, Revue International de la Théorie du Droit, XII (1938); Jean-Ives Calvez, Droit International et Souveraineté en USSR, Cahiers de la Fondation Nationale des Sciences Politiques, 48, Paris 1953; Rudolph Schlesinger, Soviet Legal Theory—Its Social Background and Development, London 1945.

21. The earliest works by E. A. Korovin on the questions of International Law include: Mezhdunarodnoe Pravo Perekhodnogo Vremeni, Moskva 1924; Sovremennoe Mezhdunarodnoe Publichnoe Pravo, Moskva 1926. Both works had little or nothing to say about the relatively new science of the Law of International Organizations.

Chapter One

CONTEMPORARY SOVIET DOCTRINE ON THE JURIDICAL
NATURE OF UNIVERSAL INTERNATIONAL ORGANIZATIONS

Introductory Remarks

Whether or not we agree with the statement that international law is
nothing but "international public morality" or, what amounts to the
same thing, that international law is "primitive law" as compared with
its municipal counterpart, we are more likely to agree on the question
that Soviet doctrinal international law[1] is nothing but a mirror reflection of official Soviet government and party policies.[2] Under the Marxist theory law, like politics and ideology, constitutes the superstruc-
ture (nadstroika) over the economic substructure (bazis) from which it necessarily takes its roots. Law is seen as an instrument in the hands of the
economically dominant class in any society and used by that class for
the purpose of maintaining political power, a factor which enables it to
perpetrate its economic dominance over the propertyless class. Just as
there were no governments in the classless society, so there could not be
law without classes according to marxist theory. Furthermore, there is no
law without a centralised instrumentality for coercing its observation. If
these features are present in all municipal legal systems, then one would
entertain serious doubts as to the nature of international law. To avoid
this dilemma communist legal theoreticians have often tried to find a
different justification for the existence of international law.[3] They have
come to look upon international law not as law proper in the sense of
municipal law, but rather as law 'sui generis', a different system of law
which cannot be evaluated with the same criteria we use in character-
ising municipal law. Nevertheless, as the Marxist theory would maintain, international law is essentially a class-law, an inter-class law, the
class nature of which manifests itself not in the same form as under municipal law, but through the official government positions of different
states, the latter being a compromise between the divergent class interests within the given society.[4] Under these circumstances Soviet doctrine
of international law cannot be anything else other than an instrument for
international politics.

Soviet doctrinal international law is essentially a "fighting international law" as opposed to a thinking international law.[5] In a society where

14

political considerations permeate all spheres of human endeavours, in a society where such supposedly objective sciences like biology and medicine are reconditioned to toe the official party line, international legal science, like all other social and humanitarian sciences within the Soviet society, cannot lay claims to any exemption. Soviet doctrinal international law, by which expression we mean the presentation of the theory of international law by Soviet scholars, law schools and official state organs, is a highly politicised science which is characterised by its unmistakable party and class ideological approach.[6]

It should be pointed out, however, that when different Soviet authors postulate different doctrines on certain questions of international law they are acting under the genuine conviction that they are reflecting the real Marxist approach to the subject. This was the case, for example, when Korovin postulated the concept of "international law of a transition period", or when he referred to Marx, Engels and Stalin as the "only true sources of international law", or when Pashukanis regarded international law as nothing but "inter-class law". Similarly, Vyshinskii was acting in good faith when he sought to look upon international law as "external state law", just as Korovin was trying to be a good Marxist international lawyer when he came up with his "tripartite international law" formula, or when he asserted that subjects of international law included such entities like the Communist International (COMINTERN) and the various proletarian organizations.

In all such cases of theoretical disagreements among Soviet writers on questions of international law the Soviet government always remained the final arbiter as to which of the theoretical positions best served the foreign policy interests of the Soviet state.

The current Soviet doctrinal international law position on the juridical nature of universal international organizations is certainly not without some dissenting voices from within Soviet international legal circles. In the analysis which follows we shall restrict ourself to the dominant majority opinion and only where and when necessary shall we present the minority positions on the subject.

A leading Soviet scholar, Professor G. I. Tunkin, is perhaps the most authoritative exponent of contemporary Soviet doctrine. In one of his latest books—Ideological Struggle and International Law—[7] he arrives at the not un-expected conclusion that international law is nothing but a peaceful weapon for the conduct of a far-from-peaceful ideological warfare between the communist and the imperialist camps, an intellectual instrument for the pursuance of cold war between the East and the West. "In our era," writes Professor G. I. Tunkin, "international law has become worldwide. Subsequently, international relations, (ideological) struggle and the cooperation of states on a worldwide scale determine its existence and development. In this global system of international

15

relations, we find a reflection of the existence in the present time of the dichotomy between the economic systems, state structures, legal systems, and the ideologies of the different states. . . It would be incorrect to close our eyes to the fact that under such circumstances . . . cooperation intermingles with struggle, including ideological. Ideological struggle in international relations and international law is a reality, more so, a natural expectation."[8]

With these general remarks on the Soviet attitude towards international law in particular and law in general we can safely go on to examine in some greater detail contemporary Soviet doctrine on the juridical nature of universal international organizations, bearing in mind that the latter is nothing but a re-statement of the current Soviet negotiating positions in the perennial intellectual battle that rages over the nature of these corporate entities which, for lack of a better term, are referred to as "international organizations".[9]

Par. 1. *International Organizations as secondary (derived) subjects of*

international law

A. *General Remarks on the Current Western position on the International Personality of International Organizations*

Under classical international law only states were regarded as subjects of international law to the complete exclusion of any other entities, international or national. This in effect meant that only states could take part in international law-creating processes. This position was maintained mainly because there were no international organizations at the time that could convincingly assert any serious claims to such personality and, partially, because the individuals that mattered—the sovereigns—were in effect equated to the states they represented.

But with the emergence of relatively strong international organizations, e.g. the League of Nations in 1919 and with the subsequent proliferation of permanent institutions particularly after 1945, the entire notion of international personality underwent a most radical change. It is now generally accepted among Western scholars that inter-governmental organizations do possess a certain degree of international legal personality. But whereas some authors would argue that this personality is objective, i.e. that this personality is inherently present in all international organizations unless it is expressly revoked or limited by the founding fathers in the constituent instruments of the organizations in question, others would contend that such personality is limited to those powers that are granted under the charter of the organization. The latter theory, generally known as the theory of implied competence does concede the fact that the powers granted under the constituent instrument of an international organization could be expanded and extended through necessary inference from those powers expressed in the charter. A third school of thought is that commonly referred to as the doctrine of teleological constitutionalism according to which an organization, once created, grows and develops on its own not dependent on the wishes of the founding fathers, but rather in accordance with the teleological principles which govern any institutional development. This third school maintains that any international organization is a social organism and ought to grow in accordance with the laws of the society in which it finds itself, irrespective of any line of development which its creators may have set up for it.[9a]

On the international personality of individuals in general international law there is no unanimity among Western scholars today. Whereas some authors maintain that individuals possess international personality, others deny such attribute to physical persons.[9b]

Another aspect of this question that is worth mentioning at this point is the problem of the international personality of national or multinational corporations with transnational operational networks. The question of the juridical nature of private corporations today is so unsettled that it still remains a question of international law 'de lege ferenda'.[9c] With this general review of the present situation in Western literature on the question of international personality as a whole, we can now move over to a closer examination of the Soviet position on the question, in particular, of the international legal personality of international organizations.

B. *The Soviet Derived Personality Concept*

The academic debate over the juridical nature of international organizations is closely linked with the more general questions of international personality in general international law. On the latter question there are two leading schools of thought in Soviet doctrinal international law.

The first is grouped around Professor G. I. Tunkin's position that in contemporary general international law a subject of international law is not just an entity possessive of international rights and obligations, but rather an entity which not only possesses these rights and obligations, but also actively participates in international law-creating processes.[10]

This position further goes on to state that "there is no generally accepted norm which defines the legal status of all international organizations. . . At the same time international law does not contain any norm which precludes the granting of certain elements of international personality to this or that international organization. The scope of such personality shall be determined, in the case of each such organization, by the provisions of the constituent instrument."[11]

This in effect means, as G. I. Tunkin would argue, that sovereign states no longer possess a monopoly over international personality as the latter attribute has come to be extended to certain, but definitely not to all, inter-state organizations. This point of view is shared by G. I. Morozov,[12] R.L. Bobrov,[13] E.A. Shibaeva,[14] and a host of others. It would be correct to say that this represents a majority opinion in Soviet doctrine today.[15]

It should be pointed out, however, that all G. I. Tunkin did in 1956 was to popularise an already existing point of view in Soviet doctrine. In a textbook of international law which was published in 1946 by a veteran Soviet international lawyer, the first Soviet judge at the International Court of Justice, Professor S. B. Krylov, it was stated that international organs "cannot be placed on equal terms with states that created them— the full subjects of international law although some of them are granted some measure of international personality."[16]

This position was reiterated in 1947 by Professor F. I. Kozhevnikov, the successor to S. B. Krylov at the International Court of Justice.[17] He then asserted that "the United Nations on its own, even though it is not a subject of international law in the traditional sense of this word, is, according to its Charter, granted certain fairly general and conventional rights which enable it to operate on the international scene directly and independently."[18]

In the same year Professor D. B. Levin, perhaps the most prolific writer of all Soviet international legal experts,[19] posed the question as to whether international organizations can rightly be considered subjects of international law. His answer was: "Undoubtedly, they can be [so considered], if such organizations, on the basis of their constituent instruments, possess some measure of individual rights and obligations vis-à-vis states especially the right to conduct their external relations independently", and in his view such organizations include, in the first place, the United Nations. He sees the international personality of international organizations as being founded on the fact that these organizations promote the common interests of member-states in the sphere of maintenance of international peace and security and the development of inter-state cooperation. In his opinion these organizations "possess the right to take independent actions within the limits of these interests."[20]

Thus we find that the present concept according to which international organizations possess some measure of international personality which today occupies a dominant position in contemporary Soviet doctrine was first promulgated in the years between 1946 and 1947 principally by S. B. Krylov, F. I. Kozhevnikov, and D. B. Levin.

Reviewing the evolution and progressive development of Soviet doctrine on the international legal status of universal international organizations, Professor R. L. Bobrov of Leningrad University recognises the innovative nature of the contribution of these three authors during these creative years, but he openly regrets the fact that whereas these authors pointed out that international organizations possess some measure of international personality, they nevertheless failed to emphasise the "derived and non-sovereign character of such personality as compared to the personality of the real subjects of international law-states."[21]

As if summarising the salient points of this school of thought in contemporary Soviet doctrine, R. L. Bobrov, ex abundante cautela, writes: ". . . the United Nations [qua international organization] is a secondary, derived (non-typical) subject of contemporary international law, created by the expressed will of sovereign states—the principal and real subjects of this law. Created as a center for the coordination of the actions of states in the name of peace and development of international cooperation based on democratic grounds, the UN is granted a certain measure of international personality which is essential and necessary if she is to execute her functions properly. The significant characteristics of the international legal personality of the UN are interdependent and in their totality constitute a specific legal personality which is founded on such legal grounds that are different from these upon which the legal personality of states is founded. The capacity of the UN is strictly limited to those powers granted under its Charter. . ."[22]

A minority opinion on the question of international personality in general and on the juridical personality of international organizations in particular is held by Professor L. A. Modzhorian, Professor V. M. Shurshalov, and a host of other Soviet writers. This opinion, in contradistinction to the former, grants a monopoly of international personality to sovereign states[23] to the complete exclusion of all international organizations including the United Nations.

Professor L. A. Modzhorian maintains that the possession of sovereignty is a 'conditio sine qua non' for any international person and as long as international organizations are not sovereign entities, they are ipso facto, not subjects of international law.[24] In conclusion, she writes that "a necessary attribute for any subject of international law is the capacity to be represented on the international plane by a supreme authority which is capable of participating in law-creating processes, capable of undertaking international legal obligations and of fulfilling them and also capable of taking part in measures aimed at the enforcement of the observations of norms of international law by other subjects . . . all subjects of international law are sovereign and, ipso facto, have equal rights."[25] To her mind, any attempts to grant any measure of international personality to international organizations would not only undermine state sovereignty, but would also result in a fundamental "perversion of international reality."[26]

The same point of view is held by Professor V. M. Shurshalov who, while denying that international organizations are international persons

19

on the ground that they are fundamentally different from states, however, concedes to these entities some degree of international rights.[27]

Recent Soviet textbooks on International Law have, as a matter of course, consistently granted to international organizations some measure of international personality[28] with the only embarrassing exception of the most recent poorly coordinated six-volume Treatise on International Law which comes dangerously close to granting objective international personality to international organizations.[29]

For example, discussing the international legal personality of the United Nations, qua international organization, the authors of a 1964 textbook on international law stated that "the United Nations, within the limits spelled out in its Charter, possesses some specific measure of international personality as is deemed necessary for the execution of its functions. The specificity of the legal personality of the United Nations is to be seen, first and foremost, in its strictly limited scope as compared to the legal personality possessed by states. The scope of the personality of the Organization is determined by the Charter of the UN in a totality of all its provisions and in particular in Art. 105 of the Charter."[30]

Similarly, in a textbook of International Law published by a rival Soviet law publisher—Izdatel'stvo Iuridicheskaia Lituratura—the UN is considered as "a special subject of contemporary international law which is devoid of any sovereignty, territorial supremacy, or any other such qualities generally accorded to the fundamental subjects of International Law-states."[31] This, at least, is the dominant position today in contemporary Soviet doctrine of International Law.

But having defined a subject of international law as "an entity participating or capable of participating in international legal relations," the authors of the most recent Treatise on International Law (Kurs Mezhdunarodnogo Prava) had this to say on the legal personality of international organizations: "On the international legal personality of international organizations we can only talk of the personality of such international organizations that were not only legally constituted, but also function legally. The rights and obligations which can be granted to international organizations by their founding-states must remain in strict accordance with the generally binding principles and norms of international law . . . we can assert that any international organization whose existence is legally justifiable is a subject of international law so long as its constituent instrument compulsorily regulates relations between the organization and its member-states. . ."[32]

The various opinions cited above represent the general trend in Soviet doctrinal international law with regard to the general question of the international legal personality of international organizations. We may move on from this general position to a closer examination of certain particular component elements of this international personality and try to see what current Soviet doctrine has to offer on each of the selected items.

Any analysis of contemporary Soviet doctrine on the juridical nature of universal international organizations should be able to reflect Soviet attitudes on the following cardinal questions: does an international organization possess a distinct individual will of its own in contradistinction to the political wills of its member-entities; if so, to what extent is this individual will dependent upon, and/or distinguishable from the individual wills of its member-entities, or from a mere mechanical totality of the separate wills of these member-entities; is this individual will necessarily a supreme will vis-à-vis the individual wills of the member-entities or is it just a common will of the member-entities in which case it is a reflection of full agreement among the members; or is it the coordinated will of the member-entities based on politically motivated half-hearted compromise and incapable of any superior enforcement; must an international organization have permanent organs to qualify it for any international rights and obligations; can an international organization exercise an individual responsibility over its actions or should it be looked upon as a mere agent acting on behalf of its member-entities and thereby introducing the principal-agent relationship between an international organization and its member-entities; how many entities must have to come together before we can talk of an international organization having been established; must these entities necessarily be uniform in their legal character, i.e. must they all be states; and finally, must any formal international agreement between the member-states constitute the operational basis for this international organization; and where such an agreement exists must it go to the extent of enumerating the powers of such an organization; if the answer to the latter question is in the negative then the question arises as to what extent we can readily infer such powers that are not enumerated in the constitution of the relevant international organization. We shall begin by examining the first question in this series—the question of individual will for an international organization.

Individual will and individual responsibility of international organizations

Defining a "general international organization" as an international organization the membership of which is open to states from both ideological camps—imperialist and communist—Professor G. I. Morozov goes on to state that the individual wills of these various states cannot under any circumstances merge into one common will. He maintains that Leninist principles do not permit any measure of compromise with the imperialist camp in the sphere of ideology and that this basic position of Marxist-Leninist philosophy equally applies to international organizations.[33] "The deep dichotomy in the different class interests rules out any possibility of any such synthesis of wills about which bourgeois international lawyers write. . . . An international organization, created as a result of a voluntary union of states from different social systems cannot create any supreme common will of its participants. At the same time, however, such an organization is not an arithmetical totality of its members."[34]

Reading between these lines by G. I. Morozov, one gets the unmistakable impression that the author has not really made up his mind about whether or not an international organization possesses an individual will of its own. On the other hand the author asserts that an international organization is "not an arithmetical totality" of its member-states—an assertion which would lead one to expect, at least, that the author would concede to these organizations some sort of corporate personality, the possession of a single individual will. But then he goes on to say that so long as these organizations are made up of states representing opposing ideological camps it is impossible to arrive at any given common will for this organization.

Professor E. A. Shibaeva probably went a step further when, in her doctoral dissertation, she stated that "the recognition of international organizations as subjects of international law obligates us to recognise the possession by such entities of an autonomous (but not sovereign) will, a will that is distinct from the wills of the member-states and which the international organization freely expresses and manifests in an international legal act."[35]

The "autonomous but not sovereign will" formula propounded by E. A. Shibaeva raises very serious interpretative problems. If by the expression "autonomous will" she means a will which can be exercised freely and independently of any legally constituted external control, then the difference between sovereign and autonomous in this context is only one of semantics. Even the sovereign will of a state does not confer any absolute right on the state itself. Its exercise shall be subject to such restrictions as shall be imposed on it by general international law.[36]

Similarly, one would expect that the autonomous will of an international organization shall be subjected to certain legal and/or political control, for example, it shall be exercised subject to legal restrictions 'ratione temporis', 'ratione materiae' and 'ratione personae'. In the same manner the political foundations of international law in general, and of the law of international organizations in particular pose enough political restrictions on the exercise of this will. This does not in any way derogate from the legal independence which such a will enjoys with regard to the various individual wills of the member-entities of such an international organization.

If on the other hand E. A. Shibaeva means by "autonomous will" such will that shall be exercised only after prior consultation with the member-states, or only on the basis of a general authorization for such exercise then we find ourselves coming back to the old concept of principal-agent relationship in the ties between an international organization and the member-states. It is our belief that E. A. Shibaeva did not intend this latter interpretation. She most probably meant a legally independent individual will exercisable within the framework of the derived personality which we understand her to concede to such international organizations. Her choice of the formula "autonomous but not sovereign" was probably dictated by political considerations bearing in mind that this point of view still had to go through the official political censorship by state organs.[37]

It is most interesting to note that this concept of "autonomous but not sovereign will" was voiced by E. A. Shibaeva for the first time only in 1969. In her previous research works on the subject she, for reasons that are not exactly known to us, chose to sidetrack the entire question of individual will for international organizations.[38]

The most recent and perhaps the most authoritative pronouncement on the subject by a Soviet scholar is the opinion expressed by Professor G. I. Tunkin in his most recent work—Teoria Mezhdunarodnogo Prava[39]—in which he states, inter alia, "In international practice treaties concluded by international organizations take their special place as treaties by which international organizations acquire rights and take upon themselves certain obligations. International organizations are created by states; they are brought into being by states but the actions of international organizations are not in any way, de facto or de jure, to be equated to the actions of states."[40]

In this passage Professor G. I. Tunkin openly acknowledges the fact that international organizations possess individual will and, subsequently, in their actions they are not acting as agents for their member-states. Obviously Professor G. I. Tunkin had no particular international organization in mind at this point. The reference was a general one and, therefore, was apt to be less politically motivated.

But when he came to direct his mind to a particular international organization, we immediately notice a shift in his position. In his lecture at The Hague Academy of International Law on "The Legal Nature of the United Nations" he strongly criticised Sir Gerald Fitzmaurice for the latter's statement that "the personality and the capacities of the [United Nations] Organization have their origin in an instrument contractual in form, but once created and established they come to assume an objective, self-existent character for all the world."[41]

Disagreeing with the above statement, Professor G. I. Tunkin goes on to state his point of view in the following words: "the legal personality of an international organization is on the contrary based on its constituent instrument. And with regard to the statutes of International organizations it should be stated that there is practically none which would contain carte-blanche provisions concerning the legal personality of a particular international organization. The case is actually the converse. A constituent instrument of an international organization provides for certain rights and capacities of the organization which lead to the conclusion that the organization possesses a certain degree of international legal personality... The important organs of the UN having the power of decision such as the General Assembly, the Security Council, etc., are composed of the representatives of states who act according to their governments' instructions, expressing the wills of their respective states... It is, therefore, inaccurate to assume that the United Nations is an entity independent of its member states."[42]

Professor G. I. Tunkin, therefore, finds it difficult to see how a decision which is conceived and born out of a heated political debate within the organ of an international organization can justly lay claim to any legal independence of those various wills which, in the long analysis, led to its creation. In other words, the distinction between the political dependence (which constitutes the procedural aspect of this will) and the subsequent legal independence (i.e. the substantive aspect of the will) of the individual will of an international organization is unacceptable to G. I. Tunkin.

One finds it difficult to connect these two positions expressed by Professor G. I. Tunkin. Our belief, however, is that G. I. Tunkin himself would grant priority to his statement of 1966, i.e. in effect, that international organizations do not and cannot possess any individual will independent of those of their member-states. To him such a will is necessarily dependent upon the wills of the member-states of the organizations from the point of view both of its contents and its subsequent exercise.

This is as far as the first school of thought goes.[43] The second school of thought as represented by Professor L. A. Modzhorian and Professor V. M. Shurshalov in most categorical terms denies to all international organizations any degree of individual will. In the opinion of the authors, international organizations are nothing but mere agents of the various states which participate therein. As far back as 1948 Professor L. A. Modzhorian presented this position[44] only to be repeated in greater details in 1958.[45] In her view, all international agreements concluded by the United Nations Organization "precipitate obligations and rights not for the UN qua international organization, but for the member-states of the UN."[46] However, "the activities of the UN, as well as of the Specialised Agencies, as strictly determined by the member-states, precipitate rights and obligations only for such states that are members of the Organization."[47]

Thus, we find that whereas the Tunkin school in contemporary Soviet doctrine would concede to public international organizations some measure of international personality, it insists on emphasising the derivative

24

nature and the non-sovereign and secondary character of this personality. While conceding to public international organizations the limited capacity to conclude treaties in their own name, the Tunkin school quickly adds that this treaty-making power is a manifestation of powers originally delegated to these international organizations by the original subjects of international law—states.

Summing up the basic position of this school of thought Professor F. I. Kozhevnikov states, ex abundante cautela, that "subjects of an international treaty are, first and foremost, states. International organs can conclude international agreements within the limits of their powers as prescribed by their constituent instruments. However, in these treaties are expressed the delegated powers from the states themselves representing the principal subjects of international law."[48]

On the other hand, the Modzhorian-Shurshalov school, as if feeling that it is being overtaken by the events of time, seems to be showing some signs of a half-hearted departure from its basic tenets, particularly on the question of the capacity of international organizations to conclude treaties in thier own name. In a most recent article on 'Sub'ekty Mezhdunarodno-pravovoi Otvetstvennosti' (Subjects of International Legal Responsibility), Professor L. A. Modzhorian gives one the impression that she is prepared to modify her minority opinion on this subject. She states, inter alia, that: "To bear international legal responsibility means to answer for ones actions and in certain cases, also for the actions of others. Therefore, to be able to bear international legal responsibility an entity needs to possess the relevant legal capacity, i.e. international personality . . . the question of the international legal responsibility of international organizations cannot but be decided in close association with their international personality. The highly limited and conditional personality which member-states grant to international organizations must serve, in our opinion, as the basis for the determination of the international legal responsibility of this organization."[49]

For the first time L. A. Modzhorian concedes to international organizations some degree of what she terms "highly limited and conditional [international] personality". However, such a miserly concession on the part of L. A. Modzhorian is not sufficient to lead us into believing that she is now prepared to grant the fact that some international organizations possess an individual will that is independent of the wills of the member-states of such organizations.

The general conclusion one can reach from such analysis is that Soviet doctrinal international law, for the most part, refuses to concede to any universal international organization an individual will that is independent of the wills of the member-states. This will is seen as being not only derived from, and limited by, but also as being wholly dependent upon the wills of the member-states. The "autonomous but not sovereign will" concept raises more questions of interpretation than it ever resolves and until it is fully developed and elaborated upon by its author it should not be taken as truly representative of any liberal trend in Soviet doctrinal international law on the subject.

The question of permanent organs for international organizations

One would suppose that Soviet doctrinal international law is almost unanimous on the question of a permanent organ being necessary for the establishment of an international organization. Professor G. I. Tunkin refers to international organizations as "permanent bodies", created by states "to handle matters entrusted to them".[50] This is quite understandable because an international institution without permanent organs will not be much different from an ad hoc international institution, e.g. from an international conference or an international congress.

In the light of this general assumption one is immediately surprised to find that Professor G. I. Morozov classifies international organizations into what he calls "permanent" and "ad hoc".[51] This, in our opinion, looks like a misapplication of terms because what he terms "ad hoc international organizations", e.g. international conferences, consultations, congresses, etc. are nothing but ad hoc international institutions, and his subsequent reference to "permanent international organizations" is tautological. An organization is, by definition, a permanent institution. Permanence in this context does not mean, of course, that it is intended to last for ever or that all its organs are permanently in operation. All it means is that some of its organs are set up in such a manner as to make it possible for them to function continuously, e.g. the secretariat and, as in the case of the United Nations, the Security Council as well.

Membership of International Organizations

Traditionally, an international organization, if it is to be distinguished from a mere bilateral agreement, must comprise at least three member-entities.[52] Once an international organization with three or more member-entities fulfils the other criteria to be found in our analysis there is no inherent reason why it cannot justly lay claim to international personality, except if this is specifically denied in its constituent instrument.[53] The assumption, therefore, is that membership of an international organization, so long as it exceeds two, shall not act as a hindrance to granting international personality to an international organization.

The Soviet approach to this basic concept is slightly different. One tends to get the impression that the Soviet doctrine of international law directly subjects the entire question of international personality or at least its scope to some quantitative and qualitative membership considerations. Some of the membership criteria generally voiced in Soviet international legal literature include: inter-state character and universality of such membership.

Professor I. I. Lukaskuk, enumerating the demands which, in his view, must be satisfied by any international organization which lays claim to international personality writes that the members of such an organization must be states, duly represented by their governments and, secondly, a treaty between states must lay at the foundation of such an organization.[54]

E. A. Shibaeva, commenting in 1966 on the subject stressed that "From our point of view one can point to the following four criteria which must be satisfied by any international organization which is laying claims to the status of international personality: first, inter-state (intergovernmental) character[55] of the organization; secondly, universal membership; . . . thirdly, specific charter provision granting it legal capacity for certain international rights and obligations; and, fourthly, compatability of its aims and objectives with the generally recognised principles and norms of general international law."[56]

One can conveniently say that the first demand—the interstate membership criterium—is common to all Soviet scholars.[57] One hardly sees how this is consistent with contemporary international practice. There exist today many international organizations the membership of which is not strictly limited to states, e.g. parag. 3, Art. 11 of the Constitution of UNESCO grants associate membership to "territories or groupings of territories which are not responsible for the conduct of their international relations." This is also the case with the ITU,[58] and the WHO,[59] to mention just a few. It could be acceptable if the contention was that the granting of associate membership to these dependent territories does not in any way alter the basic interstate character of these organizations. After all it could be argued that these organizations were initially set up by states and only subsequently were partial membership rights extended to these non-sovereign territorial entities.

This argument, however, is immediately countered by a stronger one— the fact that today we have an example of an entity which is neither a state, nor a sovereign territorial unit, nor a combination of both of these, but rather an international organization and yet is not just an ordinary member, but an original member of another tertiary international organization. The example we have in mind here is the agreement between the International Atomic Energy Agency (IAEA), qua international organization, and certain Arab states for the setting up of a Regional Center for Radio Isotopes in Cairo. In this tertiary international organization the IAEA enjoys the full rights of membership including active and passive voting rights.[60]

The Soviet argument that only inter-state organizations can lay claims to international personality perhaps stems from the traditional Soviet concept that only states are "the original subjects of international law" and consequently only states are capable of delegating international personality to what the Soviet doctrine terms "secondary subjects" or "derived subjects" of international law.

The second demand by E. A. Shibaeva that any international organization in order to lay claim to international personality must of necessity be universal is, to say the least, absurd. The Soviet Union itself is a member of many regional international organizations, e.g. the COMECON, the Warsaw Pact, etc. These are international organizations which by any stretch of the imagination cannot be described as universal and yet it has not occurred to any Soviet scholar to deny to any of these organizations the crucial element of international personality. It is quite possible to conceive the fact that when E. A. Shibaeva wrote these lines quoted above, she intended them to apply specifically to universal international organizations to the exclusion of their regional counterparts. If this were so then it would have been appropriate for her to say so.

Professor G. I. Tunkin tends to suggest that the scope of this international personality to be granted to international organizations varies directly with the quantitative aspects of their membership—in other words, the more members there are in an international organization, the wider scope of the international personality which it can lay claim to. In his own words "The participation of all states in this or that international organization, possessive of international personality, or the recognition of the personality of such an organization not only by its members but also by all other states, converts such an international organization into a generally recognised subject of international law, a subject 'erga omnes'. Such subjects of international law, or what might be near to it, are the United Nations and a majority of the UN Specialised Agencies."[61]

One does not find much difficulty in understanding this quantitative-qualitative Soviet approach to the entire question of international personality for international organizations. The quantitative criterion—the insistence on the need for universal membership—is obviously intended to guarantee to the socialist camp adequate representation in these organizations and thereby enhance the chances of victory for the socialist camp in its declared political warfare against the West. For the conduct of such a tactical warfare against the West, or what is sometimes very vaguely referred to as the policy of "peaceful coexistence", there is no better place than the forum which these international organizations provide.

Reviewing the development of contemporary international organizations in an article dedicated to the memory of Professor Antonio de Luna, Professor G. I. Tunkin stated: "The nature of contemporary international organizations is to a very great extent determined by the existence of states belonging to different socio-economic systems and the inevitable struggle between them. That is why peaceful coexistence is now the basic condition of the development of general international organization. . ."[62]

Thus, any international organization which does not embrace member-states of the socialist camp, or to be more specific, if it does not have the Soviet Union on its membership roster, is immediately suspect. This was the case with the League of Nations between 1919 and 1934 and from 1939 until 1946 when it was officially dissolved. This also was the case with the International Labor Organization between 1919 and 1934 and from 1939 until 1954, as was the case until recently with the International Civil Aviaton Organization, and is still the case with the Food and Agricultural Organization, and the Bretton-Woods Institutions. To the Soviet legal mind these organizations at the various stages represented or still represent an international plot against the Soviet Union itself or against her political, economic, or ideological interests.

On the other hand, the insistence on qualitative considerations, i.e. the demand that only states shall be members of such international organizations is actually intended to keep out from such participation such entities as the various international business consortiums as well as physical persons. The participation of these entities in an international organization alongside with states is considered incompatible with the sovereign status of such member-states. The Soviet doctrine remains impervious to the revolutionary changes which have taken place in international law since the days when states were considered the only subjects of this law. Up till today Soviet doctrine still refuses to recognise non-governmental international legal entities or physical persons as possible subjects of international law even though contemporary international practice shows the former category of international entities has been enjoying some measure of ad hoc international personality. There is no doubt, of course, that the decision to deny to all private international entities and to physical persons any measure of international personality by contemporary Soviet doctrine is a political move and we can only hope that this Soviet position will be eroded or at least modified as time goes on.

The constituent instruments of international organizations as the operational basis of all international organizations

The basic Soviet concept on the role of the constituent instruments of international organizations, first, with regard to the establishment of these organizations and secondly, in the determination of the scope of their international personality can be summarised as follows: First, the conclusion of an international agreement is essential[63] for the establishment of an international organization.[64] The constituent instrument of an inter-

29

national organization, like all other treaties and international agreements, is the result of the coordination of the wills of the contracting states.[65] "Any contemporary international organization (inter-governmental) is created by states by means of concluding an international treaty for the purpose. A treaty creating an international organization, usually called charter, statute, etc., like any other international treaty is the result and an expression of the coordinated will of the participating states."[66] This in effect means that the process of coordination of these wills does not result in any perfect (complete) elimination of all the original antagonisms to be found in these wills. In other words, the constituent instruments of international organizations while on the one hand being regarded as the coordinated will of the founding members, are equally considered as an embodiment of some uneliminated antagonisms between the contracting powers.[67]

Second, the constituent instrument of an international organization stipulates not just the aims and objectives of the organization, but also the methods for achieving such aims. In the words of Professor G. I. Tunkin, "The United Nations is an inter-state organization; states have created it for certain purposes, they have prescribed certain means for the realization of its objectives, and the organization may not go beyond these limits without their consent."[68]

The international personality of an international organization shall to a great extent be limited to those powers which the founding fathers found necessary to incorporate into its constituent instrument. This is the widely acknowledged Soviet concept of secondary international personality for international organizations. In other words, Soviet doctrine of international law would contend that the international personality of an international organization is derived from, and restricted by, the provisions of its charter. Whereas a state is a primary subject of international law by the very fact of its objective existence, international organizations are secondary or derived subjects of this law only by virtue of those powers enumerated in their constituent instruments. This amounts to saying that "if under general international law a state is a subject of international law possessing certain rights and obligations, the position of international organizations is different. The legal personality of an international organization is, on the contrary, based on its constituent instrument."[69]

Under certain circumstances the scope of such personality may extend to those powers which may directly be inferred from the enumerated powers. But powers not enumerated cannot be freely inferred. As if driving home the Soviet concept of implied competence for international organizations G. I. Tunkin states with great caution that "Of course, practice has abundantly shown that no statute of an international organization, and especially of such a multi-functional organization like the UN, can contain specific provisions for all its activities. When drafting a statute of an international organization representatives of states always assume that some secondary problems which may arise in the course of its functioning will be settled later on on the basis of the statute. Thus we may speak of an implied competence. The implied competence is not a rule of general international law; it is a problem of interpretation of the statute of a particular international organization... So the implied competence of an international organization may be admitted in each particular case only to the extent to which it may be considered as actually implied in the provisions of the statute of the organization but not on the basis of a specific rule of international law on implied competence."[70]

On the basis of these contentions Soviet international legal doctrine, in its majority opinion,[71] helds that international organizations, to a varying degree, depending on quantitative membership criterion and functional latitude, possesses some measure of international personality. That the UN and some of the Specialised Agencies of the UN possess some measure of international personality is undisputed.

Similarly, the fact that the UN possesses the widest scope of international personality as compared with the various specialised agencies of the UN is equally undisputed. On the question of the component elements of the international personality which Soviet doctrine would grant to international organizations one would include, among other things, the power to make treaties, to enter into private contracts, the international legal capacity to claim reparation for injuries caused to it, and a host of other capacities.[72]

Elaborating on the treaty-making powers of international organizations Professor G. I. Tunkin writes: "It is well known that many international organizations are endowed on the basis of their constituent instruments, with the right to conclude agreements with other international organizations as well as with states... These agreements establish international rights and obligations... The granting to international organizations, however, of this capacity to enter into international agreements does not mean that these agreements can be placed on equal footing with agreements concluded by states inter se, nor does it mean that we can automatically extend to the former the application of norms of international law which are intended to regulate inter-state agreements."[73] In other words, while conceding to international organizations the capacity to make treaties, Professor G. I. Tunkin insists on drawing a distinction between such treaties that are concluded by international organizations either 'inter se' or with states, and those treaties that are concluded by states strictly 'inter se'.[74]

In the light of the above analysis one finds it extremely difficult to subscribe to the interpretation granted to Tunkin's position on the question of the treaty-making power of international organizations as given by Professor Kazimierz Grzybowski. Commenting on Soviet public international law, Professor K. Grzybowski stated that "Mr. Tunkin ... in the discussion on the Draft Convention on the Law of Treaties ... has rejected the idea of the right of an international organization to make treaties... A year later he confirmed his earlier opinion. In 1965 he was still firm in this view that no international treaties could be made by international organizations."[75]

The fact remains, as it seems to us, that as far back as 1962[76] Professor G. I. Tunkin granted to international organizations the limited and "derived" capacity to enter into treaties. But he asserted then, just as he did in 1966[77] and still maintains today[78] that treaties to which international organizations are parties ought to be separated from all such treaties to which only states are parties and it was on this basis that he vigourously argued at the sessions of the International Law Commission that separate conventions ought to be drafted to regulate these basically different types of treaties. This statement in itself, at least as it stands, does not mean a complete rejection by Professor G. I. Tunkin of the capacity of international organizations to conclude treaties.

The final question to be discussed by us in our attempt to present a general analysis of contemporary Soviet doctrine on the juridical nature of universal international organizations is the problem of the legal effect, if any, of the international personality of international organizations on third parties. Granted that Soviet doctrine concedes to certain international organizations some measure of international personality, does this mean that the application of this personality shall indiscriminately extend to states that are not members of such organizations and have not shown any intention of recognising the application of such personality to themselves? The readily ascertainable answer is no. Soviet doctrine would argue that whereas states are subjects of international law 'erga omnes', international organizations are only subjects 'sui generis'. Thus, whereas the international personality of primary subjects of international law—states—is exercisable irrespective of the recognition of such a state by other subjects of this law, the international personality of derived subjects of international law—international organizations—shall apply only to members of such organizations or to any such non-member states which have accepted to accord recognition to such an entity, e.g. Switzerland vis-à-vis the United Nations.

However, Soviet doctrine does not seem to hesitate to lift the UN Charter to a lofty height within the hierarchy of norms of general international law. "It should be borne in mind," wrote G. I. Tunkin, "that the Charter of the United Nations stands out among statutes of international organizations as an instrument of the highest authority. It is a statute of an international organization which has been put up by states in a predominant position with regard to all other international organizations... The Charter put the UN in a superior position with regard to regional organizations of collective security and gives it wide powers over actions of these agencies especially as to the use of force. The Charter is above all other treaties concluded by the members of the United Nations."[79]

While Professor G. I. Tunkin openly grants to the UN Charter a supreme status vis-à-vis all other existing treaties to which UN member-states are parties, he, like most Soviet scholars, still regards the UN Charter essentially as a treaty and like all other treaties its application extends only to its member-states or to those states who directly or indirectly, expressly or tacitly, grant their recognition to such an instrument.

One other aspect of the UN Charter, perhaps, is that it embodies some fundamental principles of general international law in which case it would be binding, by virtue of this fact, on even those non-member states that have not expressly or even tacitly submitted themselves to be bound by the UN Charter. Under such circumstances the binding force of these UN principles on such states should be traced back to the fact that the UN Charter itself is only a restatement of the general principles of general international law which otherwise, under the principle of 'jus cogens', would be binding on such states.

In conclusion we might say that contemporary Soviet doctrine on the juridical nature of universal international organizations was formulated under the impact of the creation of the United Nations. It began building up in the era of the great debates over the juridical nature of the United Nations, i.e. during the crucial years from 1946-1947. It is interesting to note that the establishment of the LN in 1919, despite the fact that this was a real revolution in the organization of the international community of nations, did not stimulate the Soviet legal mind into inquiring about the legal status of such an international organization.

If, therefore, the creation of the UN in 1945 was the single most influential factor in the evolution of contemporary Soviet doctrine on the juridical nature of universal international organizations, the establishment of a network of UN related agencies, especially the specialised agencies, was another factor that propelled the Soviet writers to think seriously about this problem. After all if the Soviet Union was to participate in some of these agencies, as she showed she was prepared to do, her scholars had first to work out a legal doctrine to be included in the ideological baggage which all Soviet diplomats carry along with them to the sessions of these organizations.

Despite this remarkable development of Soviet legal thinking on this question since 1946, one must note that the Soviet doctrine still has a long way to go before it can be convinced to accept some of the "ideologically abhorrent" and "politically bankrupt" concepts which are being brandished by contemporary Western scholars on the question of the international legal personality of universal international organizations.

For example, contemporary Soviet doctrine has a long way to go before it can accept the basic contentions of the Western theory of objective personality for international organizations according to which an international organization, once created, acquires an objective personality of its own, irrespective of the intentions of its creators, so long as the latter does not expressly deny the organization such quality.[79a]

Similarly, much water still has to flow under the bridge before the Soviets can accept in any form the doctrine of teleological constitutionalism according to which the capacities of an international organization once created develops along teleological lines, i.e. the original capacity conferred upon the organization expands in scope and depth in the light of experience and current demands and it shall not be necessary to seek any express authority from the members of such organization before the exercise of such capacities because the capacities are deemed to be inherent in or inferrable from the original powers granted in the constituent instrument of the organization.

Finally, it will need a mental revolution before Soviet writers can accept the basic Western contention that, besides the purely formal aspects of the question, there is practically no substantive difference between an international agreement contracted either by a state or by an international organization. In other words, it will take a long time before Soviet writers can abandon their present position of categorising subjects of international law into primary and secondary—the latter being the term used to define the international legal personality of public international organizations.

We do hope, however, that the same sophisticated Soviet legal minds that promulgated the concept of "limited and non-sovereign" international personality for international organizations will one day concede to these same "international bodies corporate" full personality only to be limited, as in the case of states, by such restrictions as may be imposed by general international law. The problem, however, is not as simple as it seems. It touches upon a highly sensitive aspect of Soviet foreign policy—the manipulation of international organizations to reach certain set ends. After all, what is international law if not a convenient vehicle placed at the generous disposal of the foreign office. We do not intend by such a distinction, however, to absolutise the basic differences between the dominant Soviet and Western positions on the juridical nature of universal international organizations. Just as there is no unanimity among Western scholars on the subject so also, at least in relative terms, is unanimity lacking on the subject within the Soviet camp. Besides, our analysis above shows that Soviet positions have changed radically since 1945. But since it would be unrealistic at this stage to expect a complete convergence of both Soviet and Western positions on the subject, in view of the wide differences in the ideological climate under which writers of both camps operate, it would be fair to expect that the Soviets would gradually shift their position in the light of the increasing impact of international organizations on international affairs in general and on international law-creating processes in particular.

This final note naturally leads us into the discussion of yet another of those ideological weapons which all Soviet diplomats are equipped with —the concept of peaceful coexistence. What exactly do we mean when we say that Soviet-U.S. relations are based on the principle of peaceful coexistence? What are the historical origins and the political foundations of this multi-faced Soviet principle of peaceful coexistence? These and other closely related questions will occupy us in the next paragraph of this Chapter.

Par. 2. *The Mechanics of the Policy of Peaceful Coexistence—the Political and Philosophical Foundations of Soviet Strategy Inside UN Specialised Agencies*

Law, like politics, is the product of social interactions in any given society. International organizations, for their part, are not only conceived in law and politics but also are the result of social evolution. The organization of the international society of nations is a process. The creation of international organizations marks a stage in this process. Thus, just as the birth of a human being is clouded in biological secrets, so the creation of an international organization remains a secret of sociology. It is sad as it is ironical to note that statesmen and international lawyers have always given thought to the creation of international organizations of peace only after the shock of a major war. For example, if the Treaty of Westphalia of 1648 which ended the thirty years' war failed to put forward any concrete plans for the creation of an international organization of post-war cooperation, the Congress of Vienna of 1815 which brought peace after the Napoleonic war laid the foundation stones for the creation of the Holy Alliance—an alliance which marked the first, though an unsuccessful attempt to create an international organization. Similarly, the by-now famous institutions of Versailles—the League of Nations, the International Labour Organization, and the Permanent Court of International Justice—were the products of the 1914-1918 war; whereas it is by now a truism that it was the war-time cooperation between the allied powers that eventually led to the creation of the Institutions of San-Francisco—the United Nations, and the International Court of Justice.

But as is by now the general pattern, the war-time exigencies which call for a post-war determination to "save the succeeding generations from the scourge of war which twice in our lifetime has brought untold sorrow to mankind" are almost immediately replaced by cold-war considerations. War-time cooperation gives way to post-war suspicion of one state by the other, law gives way to politics and the one-time "united nations" become as dis-united as they probably were before the outbreak of the war. When this happens the laws of the "power game" take over and the vicious circle continues all over again, for where law ends, anarchy begins.

It is probably true that in international politics there are no permanent friends but rather there are permanent interests. It is this perennial power game, this inevitable effort to introduce Machiavellism into the realm of International Law—a law which, of course, in itself is the immediate product of international politics—that is posing a difficult problem before international lawyers, lawyers who, in the final analysis, are themselves political animals of the Aristotlean traditions.

In the highly sensitive area of foreign policy isolationism is not the best strategy. Subsequently, states endeavour to enter into frequent intercourse 'inter se' despite the political hazards that such international comingling might entail. This need to enter into direct relations with foreign nations and the opposing desire to prevent foreign ideas from "corrupting" the domestic scene is a permanent conflict which foreign policy makers always have to battle with, particularly in "iron curtain countries" where the urge to "give out" to others is greater than the reciprocal demand to "take in" from others. In order to minimize such dangers to themselves states work out political doctrines to govern their relationship with other states.

If permanent isolationism is a bad foreign policy for any state to adopt, the policy of positive negativism[80] is equally bad if not worse. Temporarily rejecting both these principles as the corner stone of its foreign policy, the Soviet Union, thinking along such military lines that "offense is a better form of defense", evolved the principle of peaceful coexistence—a fighting ideology which the Soviet Union employs in the various offensive and defensive manoeuvres which its foreign policy generally stages.

The principle of peaceful coexistence—a principle by which the Soviet Union purports to coexist with states holding ideologically different viewpoints—forms but one of the three fundamental principles[81] of Soviet foreign policy. The other two are: socialist internationalism which regulates Soviet relationship with the "fraternal nations" of the Socialist Commonwealth;[82] and proletarian internationalism—a principle which provides the blueprint for the Soviet relationship with other communist and proletariat (workers') parties outside the socialist camp.

Thus, the relationship between the Soviet government and the government of the United States or Great Britain, France, West Germany or any other Western nation for that matter revolves around the policy of peaceful coexistence; whereas the relationships between the Kremlin and the governments in Prague, Warsaw, Sofia, Bucharest, Budapest, or East Berlin are founded on the principle of socialist internationalism. By inference one would assume that the relationship between the Soviet government and the various governments of nations of the third world is founded on the policy of peaceful coexistence, whereas the relationship between the CPSU on the one hand and, for example, the Communist Parties of Italy, France, the United States or the Socialist Workers' and Farmers' Party of Nigeria or the Communist Parties of India or Burma is founded on the principle of proletarian internationalism.

Whereas it is probably possible to determine the legal theory and the political lines of development of these principles it should be pointed out, however, that they are highly unpredictable in practice, they are extremely amorphous in form and extremely malleable.

For example, the historical fact that the Soviet Union, first as Soviet Russia, continuously flirted around the League of Nations' membership, played hot and cold with a sister-institution of the League—the International Labour Organization—and today is still very selective of those universal international organizations whose membership it is prepared to accept, and what is more, all of these in the name of peaceful coexistence, makes one wonder what exactly is meant by this policy of peaceful coexistence[83] which has hitherto served as one of the most effective instruments of Soviet foreign policy. For us to come to any closer understanding of the significance which Soviet foreign policy makers attach to this slogan[84] we ought, for the purpose of our analysis, to examine some of the current pronouncements by contemporary Soviet legal scholars on the subject.

Reviewing the progress of general international law since the forty years of the existence of Soviet Russia, Professor G. I. Tunkin in 1958 stated that contemporary international law is nothing but the law of peaceful coexistence—the law which presupposes the peaceful cooperation on the one hand and ideological struggle on the other hand between states belonging to the opposing ideological camps.[84a] Thus, while prepared to enter into some half-hearted forms of peaceful cooperation with the West, Soviet Russia has refused to abandon the persuit of its major aim— the imposition of communist ideology over the entire world.

The most elaborate re-statement of the communist position on the concept of peaceful coexistence[85] was undertaken by Professor G. I. Tunkin in 1967 in his fundamental work entitled "Ideological Struggle and International Law".[86] In this work he stated, inter alia, "From the point of view of the general tendency in social development, peaceful coexistence of states representing the two different social systems is a specific form of class struggle between socialism and capitalism. It presupposes the struggle and cooperation[87] of states belonging to these two systems... Under this situation of peaceful coexistence socialist and capitalist states experience economic, political, and ideological struggle. This struggle is inevitable. What is more, it is necessary... A characteristic feature of this ideological struggle is that in it there cannot be any compromises or agreements. Socialist and bourgeois ideologies are incompatible."[88]

The Program of the CPSU categorically states, "Peaceful coexistence of states with different social structure does not mean the slackening of ideological struggle. The Communist Party shall in the future (as before) continue to expose the anti-popular and reactionary contents of capitalism and all attempts to whitewash the capitalist society... The communist ideology [is] the most humane ideology. Its ideals are the establishment of real human interaction between individuals, between nations, the emancipation of mankind from the threats of destructive wars, the establishment on earth of general peace, and free and happy life for all men."[89]

Professor A. N. Talalaev in a most familiar fashion stated: "Between capitalist and socialist states there exists political, economic, and ideological struggle. Imperialist powers will never give up their plans to unleash a new world war against member-states of the socialist commonwealth. As long as imperialism survives, there still remains the economic basis for, and the danger of, starting new wars. This fatal inevitability of wars under contemporary international situations has been considerably tempered by the existence of socialist and non-alligned states. A global war can be averted and peaceful coexistence can be finally guaranteed. [However], peaceful coexistence does not mean just the state of peace or the absence of contacts or the isolation of states of the different systems. It is a special form of class struggle..."[90]

Professor R. L. Bobrov polemicizes with both what he calls "malicious bourgeois" and "uninformed Soviet" distortions of Lenin's concept of peaceful coexistence by criticising the points of view expressed by Warren Lerner[91] and Leon Lipson[92] on the one hand, and the ignorant exposition of Lenin's theory on the subject by another Soviet theorist, Professor H. M. Minasian.[93]

R. L. Bobrov goes on to the conclusion that "Lenin's theory of peaceful coexistence and its practical accomplishment by the world commonwealth of socialist countries has nothing in common with the reactionary idea of the abandonment "for the sake of peaceful coexistence" of class struggle, an idea which is being propagated by many bourgeois ideologists and, on the other hand, is being maliciously pedalled by Maoist agents against the executors of Leninist foreign policy."[94]

Probably, the most erratic exponent, from the majority Soviet point of view, of the theory of peaceful coexistence is Professor H. M. Minasian who violently disagrees with both R. L. Bobrov[95] and G. I. Tunkin[96] on certain details of this concept as laid down by Lenin. The central point of disagreement here is the statement by G. I. Tunkin, and supported by most other Soviet commentators on the subject, that "V. I. Lenin made room for the possibility of wars between states of the two systems and even considered such wars inevitable but not because, as is often contended by the enemies of communism, a socialist state is determined to spread socialism by force" but because the ruling classes of capitalist states attempted to destroy "the newly emerged socialist state . . . which had opened up an era of socialist revolutions."[97]

H. M. Minasian considers this a distortion of Lenin's original thesis and goes on to state his own interpretation of Lenin's position as follows: "Lenin deeply believed in the possibility of peaceful coexistence, in the development of exclusively peaceful relations between states with different social structure."[98] In other words, H. M. Minasian holds the point of view that Lenin intended peaceful coexistence to mean the development of exclusively peaceful relations with the West, thus eliminating absolutely any possibility of war between the opposing ideological camps.

It is highly interesting to find these disciples of Lenin arguing over what Lenin meant by his doctrine of peaceful coexistence—an utterly amorphous concept which is capable of a wide range of interpretations. Without necessarily taking part with any of the parties in the above intra-ideological conflict as regards what they consider the central point of the Leninist principle of peaceful coexistence, one can certainly say that even those who once interpreted Lenin to mean the strict inevitability of war between communist and capitalist states have come to modify their stand on the issue. With the entrenchment of the socialist camp in a one-third portion of the world, the resolution of the military question of "who (shall destroy) whom", in other words, with the gradual elimination of the initial military imbalance between the capitalist and the communist camps, they now talk no longer of the fatalistic inevitability of such a war, but just of its possibility. The word "necessary" seems to have given way to the word "possible".

If we try to evaluate Soviet participation in universal international organizations in terms of these avowed aims of its foreign policy, we inevitably come to the conclusion that any such participation is half-hearted. The Soviet Union cannot, by definition, take upon itself the full membership obligation of any such universal international organization to keep the peace because such an obligation will sharply conflict with its dedication to the concepts of "the inevitability of ideological class warfare" and "the possibility of (hot) war between the East and the West". True to its policy of peaceful coexistence, the Soviet Union carefully selects those organizations the membership of which shall only further its general aims while she continues to fight shy of any such organizations the membership of which shall, to say the least, be detrimental to the cause of world revolution.[99]

The United Nations is definitely an ideal platform from which to launch its ideological offensive against the West and there is no doubt at all that the Soviet Union is making use of this facility to its maximum capacity.

Richard N. Gardner in his evaluation of Soviet participation in the UN had the following to say: "When we look at the record of the Soviet Union in the United Nations we see a striking contrast between word and deed, between communist ideology and Charter principles. In a word, the Soviet Union has often found it expedient to support the UN . . . (but) the Soviets have hardly lived up to these words. . . Putting it bluntly, the ideological 'baggage' which the Soviet Union brought with it into the UN has made it difficult, if not impossible (for her) to accept full obligations of membership. Indeed it is hard to escape the conclusion that there is a fundamental incompatibility at almost every point between traditional communist doctrine and the principles of the UN Charter".[100]

Turning to other international organizations we find that the Soviet Union had developed a very strange relationship with the ILO. Having re-examined her original grievances against the International Labour Organization, the Soviet Union has come to look upon this creation of the "imperialist" Treaty of Versailles as a favourable ground for meeting workers' representatives from all parts of the globe. Soviet participation in the ILO conceivably grants her official access to the minds of the world's proletarian aristocracy.

Next in the Soviet hierarchy of "acceptable" international organizations comes UNESCO which affords the Soviet Union the unique opportunity to demonstrate to the entire world "the superiority of socialist culture over its Western counterpart", to show to the world youth "the excellence of the Soviet educational system and its grandiose achievements within a relatively short period of its existence".

Thus we find that while the Soviet Union concentrates its political offensives in New York, it launches its labour and cultural attacks from Geneva and Paris respectively. Geneva is still to prove itself to be an effective launching pad from which the Soviet Union can demonstrate to the entire world the popularity of Soviet medical and health services—the achievements of Soviet socialist medicine in the field of public health and sanitation. When the World Health Organization was established in 1946 the Soviet Union was a founding member but after barely one year of membership in an Organization which she had helped to create the Soviet Union pulled out only to return to it when such a move was dictated by the demands of peaceful coexistence.

The Soviet Union participates in all these Organizations and in a host of other international organizations in the name of "peaceful coexistence". It is the same peaceful coexistence policy that provides the official Soviet justification for non-participation in many other international organizations. Soviet exponents of peaceful coexistence would readily argue that the voting arrangements in the Financial Institutions of Bretton-Woods—the International Monetary Fund, the International Bank for Reconstruction and Development (the World Bank), the International Finance Corporation, and the International Development Association—

make them un-acceptable to the Soviet Union because accepting such terms might mean acquiescing in the fact that the U.S. dollar is superior to the Russian ruble and this would be harmful to the cause of the global revolution which Soviet "ruble diplomacy" is out to achieve. Soviet deep respect for the territorial sovereignty over her air space made it difficult, for quite a long time, for the Soviet Union to reconcile itself with the very broad terms of the 1944 Chicago Convention on International Air Traffic Regulation. The Soviet Union finally joined the ICAO in 1970 after very painful and protracted heart-searching. The Food and Agricultural Organization of the United Nations (FAO) still has a long way to go before it can recommend itself to any possible Soviet membership.

Let us for a moment attempt a political evaluation of the Soviet doctrine of peaceful coexistence. What can we say are the probable impacts of this Soviet doctrine on the general development of contemporary international law today? For one thing it would be incorrect to assert that the policy of peaceful coexistence as evolved in 1920, or as many might interject in 1917, and as practiced today by the Soviet Union has had no impacts whatsoever on the general international atmosphere. It certainly has had some impacts on the latter be these impacts positive or negative depending on the way one views them.

One of such impacts is that the Soviet Union has quietly carved out for itself, with the tacit consent of the Western powers, a considerable portion of the European continent as its political domain. The whole of the European continent has come to be accepted as being divided into two spheres of influence—the Soviet and the American (even though the United States is fast loosing its grasp over Western Europe). The Western powers certainly played the game of "peaceful coexistence" when they viewed the invasion of Czechoslovakia by Soviet-controlled Warsaw Pact forces as a purely "domestic" affair of the communist countries. Through such repeated acts of tacit acquiescence on the part of the Western powers the Soviet Union has, through a political application of the principle of acquisitive prescription, come to regard itself as the un-challenged master of that portion of Europe generally referred to as "the Peoples' Democracies".

Secondly, certain principles of peaceful coexistence, e.g. the consent of states being necessary for the creation of norms of general international law,[101] the prohibition of wars as an instrument of foreign policy,[102] etc. have come to characterise post-war international law. The pre-war doctrine of 'jus ad bellum' quietly gave way to the doctrine of non-violent, peaceful coexistence of ideologically incompatible political camps.

Thirdly, the principle of peaceful coexistence has so penetrated into the minds of contemporary international lawyers, both Western and communist, that an international organization that does not seat the Soviet Union and some of its East European allies is no longer considered as being truly representative of the new international structure. In the past it was enough to create a 'de facto' club of metropolitan states and call it a universal international organization, for example, the League of Nations. But today such creations will only pass as "partisan" and will be generally ineffective. The fashion today is for an international organization that purports to have the general welfare of all mankind in mind to fight to qualify for the title of "organization of peaceful coexistence".[102a] This was the case with the ILO from 1919-1934 and from 1939 to 1954. This is the case today with most other UN Specialised Agencies in which the Soviet Union does not retain any membership.

The negative impact of the principle of peaceful coexistence most probably is that it has placed an impediment on the path of the historical development of mankind towards greater integration. Peaceful coexistence instead of emphasising the common bonds that link all nations together, tends rather to play upon their differences. This, however, does not make the disciples of peaceful coexistence less mondialist than some contemporary Western power politicians. Instead the former preach Marxist mondialism. It is this internal contradiction that is highly intriguing about peaceful coexistence—it preaches "mondialism" through "extreme nationalism". In the succeeding chapters we shall try to analyse the rules of this highly dexterous game of peaceful coexistence as conducted by the Soviet Union within the confines of selected universal international organizations.[103]

Another disquieting impact, though a less obvious one, of the principle of peaceful coexistence on the general pattern of universal international organizations today is that there is a general drift toward establishing the hegemony of one of the two super powers over some specialised agencies[104] of the United Nations. It is an established fact that all the Financial Institutions of Bretton-Woods are de facto "functionaries" of the United States—the US holds lion's shares in them, controls the voting machine in these Organizations, and almost holds a monopoly of appointments to top executive offices in each of these Organizations. The fact that all these Organizations have their head offices in the United States dramatises this whole situation. The absence of any Soviet participation in any of these financial arrangements leaves the United States as the supreme captain of the activities of all these Organizations.

On the other hand the Soviet Union is gradually but surely asserting its position, though yet far from that of supreme leadership, over some other UN specialised agencies. For example, even though she is a late comer to the International Labour Organization, there is every reason to believe that her subsequent dynamic and well-manipulated participation therein is not only calculated to squeeze the United States out of her position of partial leadership or even out of the Organization should the US over-react to such Soviet moves, but is also intended to build up for the Soviets an image as a potential leader of the Organization in some not too remote future. Similarly, the impact of the Soviet Union on the UNESCO and the WHO is tremendous.

Under an ideal situation of international cooperation no international organization should come under the direct domination of any one particular state or group of states. An international organization in order to be truly international should serve the interests of all its members without showing any signs of overcommitment to the policy goals of any of the members. However, whether such an ideal is politically attainable is a question which falls outside the ambit of our immediate objective in this book.

NOTES

1. By the term "doctrinal Soviet international law" we mean the exposition of the theoretical foundations of contemporary international law by Soviet legal scholars based on the theory of Marxism-Leninism. In this chapter, however, it is not our intention to exhaust all available Soviet doctrinal sources such as the positions taken by Soviet lawyers in the International Law Commission, in the International Court of Justice, or in any other international bodies. We shall subsequently base our study principally on the writings of some of the most authoritative contemporary Soviet jurists.

2. This assertion, however, does not rule out the fact that sometimes among Soviet legal writers there are theoretical disagreements as to certain problems in international law. The open disagreements among Soviet scholars, for example, as to what entities should be considered subjects of international law, or as to the substantive contents of the principle of peaceful coexistence are discussed below.

3. For a vivid account of the classical Marxist (Soviet) doctrine on the question of the juridical nature of contemporary international law see Hans Kelsen: The Communist Theory of Law, London 1955.

4. See G. I. Tunkin: Ideologicheskaia Bor'ba i Mezhdunarodnoe Pravo, Moskva 1967; also his, Teoriia Mezhdunarodnogo Prava, Moskva 1970; see also R. L. Bobrov: Osnovnye Problemy Teorii Mezhdunarodnogo Prava, Moskva 1968.

5. This notion runs through all the works by one Soviet Union's most authoritative exponent of this doctrine—Professor G. I. Tunkin, Ideologicheskaia Bor'ba i Mezhdunarodnoe Pravo, Moskva 1967; 'Sorok Let Sosushchestvovaniia i Mezhdunarodnoe Pravo', SEMP 1958; Teoriia Mezhdunarodnogo Prava, Moskva 1970.

6. See Sovetskoe Gosudarstvo i Mezhdunarodnoe Pravo (ed. by F. I. Kozhevnikov), Moskva (IMO) 1967.

7. G. I. Tunkin: Ideologicheskaia Bor'ba i Mezhdunarodnoe Pravo, Moskva 1967; also by the same author, 'Sorok Let Sosushchestvovaniia i Mezhdunarodnoe Pravo', SEMP 1958; Teoriia Mezhdunarodnogo Prava, Moskva 1970. The fact that Tunkin gave his book the title 'Ideologicheskaia Bor'ba i Mezhdunarodnoe Pravo' and not 'Mezhdunarodnoe Pravo i Ideologicheskaia Bor'ba' demonstrates the prominence which he grants to 'Ideologicheskaia Bor'ba' over 'Mezhdunarodnoe Pravo'. Such an arrangement is definitely not a slip of the pen on the part of the author as the contents of the book vividly show.

8. G. I. Tunkin: Ideologicheskaia Bor'ba i Mezhdunarodnoe Pravo, Moskva 1967, at pp. 3 and 175.

9. On the origins of the term 'international organizations" see Potter: 39 AJIL 1945, pp. 803-806.

9a. It should be pointed out, however, that this enumeration is by no means exhaustive of the current trends in contemporary Western literature on the international legal personality of international organizations. There are so many diversified views on the subject among Western scholars that it is, perhaps, impractical and futile to attempt a full coverage of them. We do hope, however, that the few schools of thought mentioned above will give the reader a general idea of the contemporary development in this field. For sources on the international legal personality of international organizations, see, inter alia: C. Wilfred Jenks, The Proper Law of International Organizations, London 1962; The Injuries Case, ICJ Reports 1949; Certain Expenses Case, ICJ Reports 1962; Clive Parry, The treaty-making power of the United Nations, BYIL 1949, 108; W. Friedmann, The Changing Structure of International Law, 1964; Bowett, The Law of International Institutions, 1963; Finn Seyersted, International personality of International Organizations, Indian Journal of International Law, 1964, No. 1; Sir Gerald

Fitzmaurice, The Law and procedure of the ICJ—International Organizations and Tribunals, 29 BYIL 1952.

9b. For further details see: Jessup, A Modern Law of Nations, Macmillan 1948; H. Lauterpacht, International Law and Human Rights, Stephens 1950; Jurisdiction of the Courts in Danzig, PCIJ Adv. Op. No. 15, Ser. B, No. 15 (1928); Mavromatis Palestine Concessions (Jurisdiction) Case, PCIJ 1924, Ser. A. No. 2; Lauterpacht, The Universal Declaration of Human Rights (1948) BYIL, 354; Kunz, The UN Declaration of Human Rights, 43 AJIL, 316 (1949); Drost, Human Rights as Legal Rights (1951); Green, The UN and Human Rights, 1956.

9c. On the international legal personality of transnational corporations see, inter alia: Adam, Société Européene pour le Financement du Materiel Ferroviare (Eurofima), 3 European Yearbook 70, 1957; Colino, Intelsat: Doing Business in Outer Space, 6 Columbia Journal of Transnational Law 17 (1967); McNair, The national character and status of corporations (1923-1924) BYIL, 44.

10. G. I. Tunkin: Osnovy Sovremennogo Mezhdunarodnogo Prava, Moskva 1956.

11. G. I. Tunkin: Ibid. at pp. 17-18.

12. See G. I. Morozov: Organizatsiia Ob'edinennykh Natsii, Moskva 1962, p. 198.

13. See R. L. Bobrov: Osnovnye Problemy Teorii Mezhdunarodnogo Prava, Moskva 1968; also his, "Iuridicheskaia Priroda OON", SEMP 1959.

14. See E. A. Shibaeva: Spetsializirovannye Uchrezhdeniia OON, Moskva 1966 at p. 32.

15. In the twilight days of the evolution of Soviet international legal doctrine Eugene B. Pashukanis and Eugene A. Korovin were engaged in a highly ideological debate over the nature, the sources and the subjects of international law, with E. A. Korovin alternately holding the position that international organizations were and were not subjects of international law on the basis of reasons which were more political than legal. We do not consider it appropriate to recall the basic positions in these early debates as they do not seem to make any significant contribution to our present analysis. However, for a textual documentation of these debates, see Hans Kelsen, The Communist Theory of Law, London 1955; see also John Hazard, "Cleansing Soviet International Law of anti-Marxist Theories", 32 AJIL 1938 at pp. 244-252.

16. V. N. Durdenevskii and S. B. Krylov: Mezhdunarodnoe Pravo—Uchebnik, Vypusk I, Moskva 1946 at p. 31.

17. S. B. Krylov served as the first Soviet judge at the ICJ from 1946 to 1952 and was briefly succeded by S. A. Golunskii (1952-1953). The latter died in office and was replaced by Professor F. I. Kozhevnikov from 1953-1961.

18. F. I. Kozhevnikov: Uchebnik Publichnogo Mezhdunarodnogo Prava, Moskva (Iurizdat) 1947, at p. 54.

19. As of December 1967 when he celebrated his 60th. birthday he had published over 160 scientific works on various aspects of international law ranging from the responsibility of states for aggression and war crimes, problems of war and peace, the law of international organizations, the problems of diplomatic immunity, etc. See 'Personaliia' on D. B. Levin in SEMP 1968 at pp. 336-337.

20. See D. B. Levin: 'O poniatii i sisteme sovremennogo mezhdunarodnogo prava', 5 SGP 197 at pp. 11-12. For a current restatement of this view, see by the same author: Osnovnye Problemy Teorii Mezhdunarodnogo Prava, Moskva 1958 at p. 85.

21. R. L. Bobrov: 'Iuridicheskaia Priroda Organizatsii Ob'edinennykh Natsii', SEMP 1959 at pp. 233-234. R. L. Bobrov, however, concedes the fact that the credit for introducing this new element of "derived and limited personality" for international organizations goes to Professor D. B. Levin who first made this distinction in his book: Osnovnye Problemy Sovremennogo Prava, Moskva 1958 at p. 85.

In 1955 Professor V. N. Durdenevskii in a Preface to the Russian edition of Labeyrie-Menahem's Des Institutions Specialisées—Problèmes Juridiques et Diplomatiques de l'Administration Internationale, Paris 1953 briefly stated that the specialised agencies of the UN "cannot lay claims to equal status with states as sovereign subjects of International Law". See p. 5 of the Russian edition of this book published in Moscow by Izdatel'stvo Innostrannaia Literatura.

22. R. L. Bobrov: 'Iuridicheskaia Priroda OON', SEMP 1959, pp. 239-240.

23. The attribute of international personality is partially granted to what is vaguely referred to as "belligerent nations" and also to national-liberation fronts. See L. A. Modzhorian: Sub'ekty Mezhdunarodnogo Prava, Moskva 1958.

24. L. A. Modzhorian: Sub'ekty Mezhdunarodnogo Prava, Moskva 1958.

25. Ibid. at p. 17.

26. Ibid. at p. 8; see also by the same author: 'O Sub'ektakh Mezhdunarodnogo Prava', 6 SGP 1956 at pp. 95-97.

27. See V. M. Shurshalov: Osnovnye Voprosy Teorii Mezhdunarodnogo Dogovora, Moskva 1959. Similarly, Professor G. P. Zadorozhnyi maintains that whereas only "sovereign entities", an expression which he uses to mean only states and nations, "are subjects of international law, such entities like international organizations, juridical persons and physical persons are, at best, only subjects of international legal relations and not of international law". See SEMP 1968 at pp. 364-365.

28. See Mezhdunarodnogo Pravo—Uchebnik, Moskva (IMO) 1964; see also the revised edition of the same textbook issued in 1966: Mezhdunarodnoe Pravo—Uchebnik dlia Iuridicheskikh Vuzov published by the Izdatel'stvo Iuridicheskaia Literatura, Moskva 1964.

29. Volume 1 of this six-volume Kurs Mezhdunarodnogo Prava (Moskva 1967) at p. 159 openly grants international personality to "all legally existing international organizations"—a concept which if accepted would convey, except for the interjection of the word "legally", the same meaning as does the theory of objective international personality which is strongly condemned by Soviet doctrine.

However, an interview with Professor G. I. Tunkin, himself a member of the Editorial Committee which was appointed to edit this Treatise, reveals some poor coordination among the Committee members. He specifically mentioned that the Committee did not edit this particular section of the Treatise before it was sent out to the publishers and, subsequently, is not representative of Soviet doctrine on the issue raised therein. Professor N. A. Ushakov, the present Soviet member of the International Law Commission of the United Nations and Head of the International Law Section of the Institute of State and Law of the Soviet Academy of Sciences is supposed to be the author of the controversial passage from the Treatise.

30. Uchebnik Mezhdunarodnogo Prava (edited by F. I. Kozhevnikov), Moskva (IMO) 1964 at p. 450. This point of view is repeated in the 1966 edition of the same textbook at pp. 438-440.

31. Mezhdunarodnoe Pravo—Uchebnik dlia Iuridicheskikh Vuzov (edited by D. B. Levin), Moskva, Iuridicheskaia Literatira, 1964 at p. 292.

32. Kurs Mezhdunarodnogo Prava, Izdatel'stvo 'Nauka', Moskva 1967, vol. 1 at pp. 146-159.

33. See G. I. Morozov: Mezhdunarodnye Organizatsii, Moskva 1969, at pp. 110 etc.

34. G. I. Morozov: Ibid. at p. 110.

35. See E. A. Shibaeva: Iuridicheskaia Priroda i Pravovoe Polozhenie Spetsializirovannykh Uchrezhdenii OON (Avtoreferat Doktorskoi Dissertatsii) Iuridicheskii Fakul'tet, MGU, Moskva 1969 at p. 16.

36. Cf. the concept of Jus Cogens in general International Law.

37. See E. A. Shibaeva: Spetsializirovannye Uchrezhdeniia OON, Moskva 1962; see also by the same author: Spetsializirovannye Uchrezhdeniia OON (enlarged and revised edition) Moskva 1966.

38. At the 'publichnaia zashchita' of this dissertation at the Faculty of Laws of the Moscow State University this formula was violently attacked by Professor L. A. Modzhorian and Professor V. M. Shurshalov who both tried to read into it some meaning which, from their point of view, "was alien to the Soviet doctrine of International law" and only intended by the author, knowingly or unknowingly, "to grant support to the dominant bourgeois concept" on the question. See Stenograficheskii Otchet of the proceedings of the publichnaia zashchita of the dissertation, Iuridicheskii Fakul'tet MGU, December 1969.

39. G. I. Tunkin: Teoriia Mezhdunarodnogo Prava, Moskva 1970.

40. G. I. Tunkin: Ibid. at pp. 124-125.

41. Sir Gerald Fitzmaurice, The Law and Procedure of the ICJ—International Organizations and Tribunals, 29 BYIL 1952, at p. 14.

42. G. I. Tunkin: The Legal Nature of the UN, 119 Hague Recueil 1966-III at pp. 31, 32.

43. Vide supra for a presentation of the basic concepts of the two rival schools of thought.

44. See L. A. Modzhorian: O Sub'ektakh Mezhdunarodnogo Prava, Moskva 1948 at pp. 13-14.

45. L. A. Modzhorian: Sub'ekty Mezhdunarodnogo Prava, Moskva 1958.

46. L. A. Modzhorian: Ibid. at p. 33.

47. Ibid. at pp. 33-34.

48. Mezhdunarodnoe Pravo—Uchebnik dliia Iuridicheskikh Vuzov, Moskva 1966 at p. 327.

49. L. A. Modzhorian: 'Sub'ekty Mezhdunarodno-pravovoi Otvetstvennosti', 12 SGP 1969 at pp. 122, 124.

50. G. I. Tunkin: 119 Hague Recueil 1966-III.

51. G. I. Morozov: Mezhdunarodnye Organizatsii, Moskva 1969 at p. 70. Attention should, however, be drawn to the enumeration of "international organizations without permanent organs" cited at the bottom of p. 62 in Morozov's Mezhdunarodnye Organizatsii, Ibid.

52. For example, the ANZUS. See also G. I. Morozov, Mezhdunarodnye Organizatsii at p. 62.

53. Cf. The Bank for International Settlements.

54. I. I. Lukashuk: 'Mezhdunarodnaia Organizatsiia kak Storona v Mezhdunarodnykh Dogovorakh', SEMP 1960 at p. 148.

55. Curious attention should be drawn to the fact that E. A. Shibaeva does not seem to distinguish between the "inter-state" and the "intergovernmental" criterion in the classification of international organizations—a position which certainly looks inconsistent to a Western reader.
This free interchange of the terms "inter-state" and "intergovernmental" is also to be noticed in the writings of many other Soviet authors. Cf. G. I. Tunkin: The Legal Nature of the United Nations, 119 Hague Recueil 1966-III at pp. 1 and 22; see also G. I. Morozov: Mezhdunarodnye Organizatsii, Moskva 1969, chapter 3.

56. E. A. Shibaeva: Spetsializirovannye Uchrezhdeniia OON, Moskva 1966 at p. 32.

57. Except, of course, those who deny any measure of international personality to international organizations as a whole. Vide supra.

58. See also Art. 1. parag. 3 of the Consitution of the ITU.

59. See Art. 8 of the WHO Constitution.

60. Vide UNTS vol. 494 at p. 220. On the regional level we have the example of four international organizations teaming up with the Inter-American Development Bank to create a new 'corpus separatum'—the Inter-American Committee on Agricultural Development. For fuller details see G. I. Morozov, Mezhdunarodnye Organizatsii, Moskva 1969 at p. 65.

61. G. I. Tunkin: Teoriia Mezhdunarodnogo Prava, Moskva 1970 at pp. 410–411. The reference to "a majority of the UN Specialised Agencies" in this passage obviously means those specialised agencies of the UN of which the Soviet Union and/or at least some of her East European allies are members—a fact which would lead one to wonder if the author intends direct Soviet participation as one of the requirements for granting international personality to such universal international organizations.

Unfortunately, the scantiness of available Soviet literature on the legal nature of those specialised agencies in which the Soviet Union does not participate, e.g. the Financial Institutions of Bretton-Woods, makes it difficult for us to reach any conclusion on this question. The prevalent academic disinterest of Soviet scholars in the international organizations in which the Soviet Union does not participate is demonstrated not only by the scanty references to these organizations in major Soviet works devoted to international organizations (see Spetsializirovannye Uchrezhdeniia OON, edited by G. I. Morozov, Moskva 1967; E. A. Shibaeva: Spetsializirovannye Uchrezhdeniia OON, Moskva 1966), but also most vividly by the fact courses in international organizations in Soviet Law Schools hardly cover at all the League of Nations, the Permanent Court of International Justice, the Bretton-Woods Institutions, etc. See Programma po Mezhdunarodnomu Pravu dlia Iuridicheskikh Vuzov issued by the Ministerstvo Vysshego i Spetsial'nogo Obrazovannia SSSR, Moskva 1967.

62. G. I. Tunkin: "Remarks on the Normative Function of Specialised Agencies", Instituto Francisco de Vitoria De Derecho Internacional, Madrid, 1969, p. 11.

63. See E. A. Shibaeva: Spetsializirovannye Uchrezhdeniia OON, Moskva 1966; see also I. I. Lukashuk, 'Mezhdunarodnaia Organizatsiia kak Storona v Mezhdunarodnykh Dogovorakh', SEMP 1960.

64. It is interesting to note, however, that G. I. Morozov in his definition of an international organization relegates only to a secondary position the question of having a constituent instrument or not. Vide G. I. Morozov, Mezhdunarodnye Organizatsii, Moskva 1969 at p. 62.

The fact that the COMECON, a socialist international organization which was founded in January 1949 at the Moscow Economic Conference of East European States existed for 11 years (until December 1959) without a formally concluded constituent instrument lends support to this thesis. Cf. also the Pan-American Union which existed prior to the adoption of the Bogotá Charter in 1948 which formally set up the OAS.

65. See G. I. Tunkin: Ideologicheskaia Bor'ba i Mezhdunarodnoe Pravo, Moskva 1967; see also by the same author, Teoriia Mezhdunarodnogo Prava, Moskva 1970; see also R. L. Bobrov, Osnovnye Problemy Teorii Mezhdunarodnogo Prava, Moskva 1968; D. B. Levin, Osnovnye Problemy Sovremennogo Mezhdunarodnogo Prava, Moskva 1958.

66. G. I. Tunkin: 'The Legal Nature of the UN", 119 Hague Recueil 1966-III at p. 7.

67. A. N. Talalaev: Iuridicheskaia Priroda Mezhdunarodnogo Dogovora, Moskva 1963.

68. G. I. Tunkin: 119 Hague Recueil 1966-III, p. 22.

69. G. I. Tunkin: Ibid. at pp. 30-31.

70. G. I. Tunkin: 119 Hague Recueil 1966-III, pp. 23, 25.

71. With the insignificant exception of the Modzhorian-Shurshalov school of thought which denies to all international organizations including even the UN and its specialised agencies any degree of international personality. Vide supra.

72. E. A. Shibaeva: Spetsializirovannye Uchrezhdeniia OON, Moskva 1966; see also R. L. Bobrov, 'O Iuridicheskoi Prirode OON', SEMP 1959; see also G. I. Morozov: Mezhdunarodnye Organizatsii, Moskva 1969.

73. G. I. Tunkin: Voprosy Teorii Mezhdunarodnogo Prava, Moskva 1962 at p. 82. See also by the same author: Teoriia Mezhdunarodnogo Prava, Moskva 1970.

74. As a matter of fact this position eventually gained the upper hand inside the International Law Commission as is evidenced by its adoption of the Vienna Convention on the Law of Treaties which is specifically intended to be applied to treaties between states. See Art. 1 of the Vienna Convention on the Law of Treaties adopted at the Vienna Conference on May 23, 1969.

75. See Kozimierz Grzybowski: Soviet Public International Law—Doctrines and Diplomatic Practice, Leyden 1970 at p. 363.

76. Vide supra.

77. Vide 119 Hague Recueil 1966-III.

78. See G. I. Tunkin: Teoriia Mezhdunarodnogo Prava, Moskva 1970.

79. G. I. Tunkin: "The Legal Nature of the United Nations", 119 Hague Recueil 1966-III, pp. 18-19.

79a. As has been pointed out above this doctrine of objective personality is not universally accepted even among Western Scholars. Vide supra.

80. By "positive negativism" as a line of foreign policy we mean the declared policy of combating the proliferation, or the containment of another phenomenon which, from the point of view of the state pursuing such policy, is evil; for example, the policy of anti-communism without offering something new merely seeks to restrict communism to those areas which are already under its grip.

81. Of these three inter-dependent principles of Soviet foreign policy we shall concentrate our analysis on just one—peaceful coexistence.

82. Soviet political scientists and legal theoreticians have often tended to look upon this principle of "socialist internationalism" as providing the political background and the legal framework upon which the "Brezhnev Doctrine" is founded. It was under the banner of this doctrine that the Soviets staged a counter-revolution in Hungary in 1956 and the Warsaw Pact troops marched into Czechoslovakia in 1968. It is also on this platform that the Soviet Union is conducting its undeclared policy of "sovietization" of Eastern Europe today.

83. The term "peaceful coexistence" as much as has been found in Soviet literature dates back to 1920. Contemporary Soviet writers, notably Professor G. I. Tunkin and Professor R. L. Bobrov attribute to Lenin the origin of the idea of peaceful coexistence. But Lenin himself does not seem to have used this term at any instance. Soviet Party historians so far have not succeeded in implanting this term into one of the continuously revised editions of Lenin's Complete Works.

Western scholars have recalled that the term was first used by the Soviet Foreign Affairs Commissar Chicherin when he referred to the Peace Treaty with Estonia in 1920 as the first "experiment in peaceful coexistence with bourgeois states". But twenty years later the bourgeois state of Estonia having been "rescued" by Soviet forces, it became un-necessary to co-exist with her anymore. Thus, the first experiment in peaceful coexistence has been unilaterally successful.

84. For a fuller detail on the evolution, development, and practice of this doctrine of peaceful coexistence see W. Lerner: "The Historical Origins of the Soviet Doctrine of Peaceful Coexistence", in The Soviet Impact on International Law (edited by Hans W. Baade), Oceana N.Y. 1965; see also in the same book an article by Leon Lipson: "Peaceful Coexistence"; Bernard A. Ramundo: Peaceful Coexistence—International Law in Building of Communism, Johns Hopkins Press, Baltimore, 1967;

49

Edward McWhinney: Peaceful Coexistence and Soviet-Western International Law, Leyden 1964; T. A. Taracouzio: The Soviet Union and International Law, N.Y. 1935; American Bar Association: Peaceful Coexistence, A Communist Blueprint for Victory, Chicago 1964; Kazimierz Grzybowski: Soviet Public International Law, Leyden 1970; Bernard A. Ramundo: The (Soviet) Socialist Theory of International Law, Washington D.C., Institute of Sino-Soviet Studies, The George Washington University 1964.

84a. G. I. Tunkin: 'Sorok Let Sosushchestvovaniia i Mezhdunarodnoe Pravo', (Forty Years of Coexistence and International Law), SEMP 1958.

85. Most exponents of the theoretical basis of Soviet foreign policy regard this Decree which was issued and signed by V. I. Lenin himself as the first promulgation of the contemporary Soviet foreign policy of peaceful coexistence of countries with divergent socio-economic structures. See G. I. Tunkin: 'Sorok Let Sosushchestvovaniia i Mezhdunarodnoe Pravo', SEMP 1958.

However, Professor R. L. Bobrov, while reaching the conclusion that the Peace Decree of 1917 formally established the foundation stones of the future Bolshevik foreign policy of peaceful coexistence, does state that "in the pre-October (1917) period Leninist principles of foreign policy of the new Bolshevik state contained in themselves an approach to the principle of peaceful coexistence of socially incompatible states (which was to lay at the basis of the relations of the future socialist state with the peoples of other countries)".

This, in other words, means that the guiding principles of the doctrine of peaceful coexistence had long been set out by Lenin before its official promulgation in the Peace Decree of November 7, 1917. See R. L. Bobrov: Osnovnye Problemy Teorii Mezhdunarodnogo Prava, Moskva 1968, at pp. 92-93.

However, most political historians in the West would attribute the commencement of a serious pursuit of the doctrine of peaceful coexistence to the failure of the Red Army in Poland in 1921 rather than to the Peace Decree of 1917. See W. Lerner, Ibid. at p. 24.

86. G. I. Tunkin: Ideologicheskaia Bor'ba i Mezhdunarodnoe Pravo, Moskva 1967.

87. Note the emphasis placed on "struggle" (bor'ba) and the secondary role assigned to "cooperation" (sotrudnichestvo). This trend is equally noticed in Tunkin's book title. Vide supra.

88. G. I. Tunkin: Ideologicheskaia Bor'ba i Mezhdunarodnoe Pravo, Moskva 1967 at pp. 3-5. Consistent reiteration of this concept is to be found in the later works of G. I. Tunkin.

89. Programma Kommunisticheskoi Partii Sovetskogo Soiuza, Moskva (Politizdat) 1965 at p. 122.

90. A. N. Talalaev: Iuridicheskaia Priroda Mezhdunarodnogo Dogovora, Moskva 1963 at p. 5.

91. See: The Soviet Impact on International Law (edited by Hans W. Baade) Oceana N.Y. 1965.

92. See also: The Soviet Impact on International Law, N.Y. 1965.

93. Vide infra.

94. R. L. Bobrov: Osnovnye Problemy Teorii Mezhdunarodnogo Prava, Moskva 1968 at p. 111. Chapters 4 and 5 of this book are devoted to a re-statement of Lenin's theory of peaceful coexistence—its evolution, development and component elements. Ibid., pp. 89-168.

95. For a fuller narrative of the polemic between R. L. Bobrov and H. M. Minasian on the correct interpretation of Lenin's basic theory of peaceful coexistence, see R. L. Bobrov, Osnovnye Problemy Teorii Mezhdunarodnogo Prava, Moskva 1968 at pp. 104-106.

96. For H. M. Minasian's points of disagreement with G. I. Tunkin, see H. M.

Minasian, Pravo Mirnogo Sosushchestvovaniia, Izdatel'stvo Rostovskogo Universiteta, 1966 at pp. 19 etc.

97. G. I. Tunkin: "Printsip Mirnogo Sosushchestvovaniia—General'naia Liniia Vneshnepoliticheskoi Deiatel'nosti KPSS i Sovetskogo Gosudarstva,' 7 SGP 1963 at p. 27.

98. H. M. Minasian: Pravo Mirnogo Sosushchestvovaniia, at p. 19.

99. In the concluding paragraph on the interaction of the twin doctrines of peaceful coexistence and world revolution in Soviet foreign policy, W. Lerner has this to say: "More serious reflection will indicate that be it under Khrushchev, Stalin or Lenin, peaceful coexistence has been adopted by the Soviet Union as a pragmatic measure and not as an inherent belief. World revolution on the other hand is inherent in communist doctrine; and should the international situation offer new opportunities, it might again supplant peaceful coexistence as it has in the past". W. Lerner, "The Historical Origins of the Soviet Doctrine of Peaceful Coexistence", Ibid. at p. 26.

100. Richard N. Gardner: "The Soviet Union and the United Nations", The Soviet Impact on International Law, Oceana N.Y. 1965 at p. 1.

101. It would be correct, however, to note that prior to the evolution of contemporary Soviet "will theory" as the basis for obligation in international law there had existed in Western jurisprudence the concept which required the consent of the parties to any international agreement before an international obligation could be assumed to have been created. But unlike the hitherto predominant "will theory" the Soviet "will theory" places much emphasis on the coordination of these divergent and sometimes even antagonistic wills of the various participating states in any international agreements.

102. Prior to 1917 the right of states to resort to war in order to resolve their differences (jus ad bellum) was an accepted feature of classical international law. As the Soviets would argue Lenin's "Peace Decree" of 1917 was the first act, though national in character, to denounce this 'jus ad bellum'. The international rejection of the idea of 'jus ad bellum', the Soviet argument continues, was partially incorporated into the Covenant of the LN in 1919, in the Paris Agreement of 1928, and was fully unwrapped in the UN Charter of 1945.

102a. The term "international organization of peaceful coexistence" just like the term "international law of peaceful coexistence"—both founded in communist usage—have so far failed to gain the recognition of Western scholars. W. Friedmann and O. Lissitzyn, would rather prefer the term "law of international cooperation" or the "international law of cooperation" to describe contemporary international law, the difference being, perhaps, that the former (the international law of peaceful coexistence) emphasises the society aspects of contemporary international law as against the community aspects which the Friedmann-Lissitzyn phrase stresses. See W. Friedmann, The Changing Structure of International Law, 1964; O. Lissitzyn, International Law Today and Tomorrow, 1965.

103. We have so far attempted a political analysis of the aims and objectives of the doctrine of peaceful coexistence as applied in Soviet foreign policy particularly vis-à-vis universal international organizations. For a legal examination of the contents of peaceful coexistence see: Leon Lipson, "Peaceful Coexistence", The Soviet Impact on International Law, at pp. 27 etc. We do not find it necessary to duplicate the excellent job that has already been done by L. Lipson in that passage.

104. It is expected however that the decision of the UN-GA to grant the Chinese seat in the Organization to Peking—a fact which has generated similar actions in many UN Specialised Agencies—may upset the effective implementation of this unholy alliance between Washington and Moscow to carve the various agencies into their spheres of influence.

Chapter Two

THE SOVIET UNION AND THE INTERNATIONAL LABOUR ORGANIZATION (ILO)

Introductory Remarks

The International Labour Organization, qua international organization, was set up primarily as an international instrument for the attainment of universal and lasting peace based upon social justice. Some of the fundamental principles of the Organization include the recognition of the principle of freedom of association and expression as being essential to sustained progress, the idea that the war against want requires to be carried on with unrelenting vigour within each nation and by continuous and concerted effort in which the representative of workers and employers, enjoying equal status with those of governments, join with them in free discussion and democratic decision with a view to the promotion of the common welfare of all. The Organization was conceived as a tripartite body in which representatives of the three corners of any national economy—government, employers, and employees—were to meet and discuss in a free atmosphere the general welfare of all involved. Accordingly, the roles of the employers' and workers' unions within the framework of the Organization were not to be undermined. It will, therefore, be impossible for us to appraise Soviet (government) attitude towards the ILO without first inquiring into the state of its organized labour unions. We shall then begin our examination of the Soviet-ILO relationship with a short survey of the trade union situation inside the Soviet Union today—a question that has created some measure of concern even for the ILO itself.

Par. 1. Trade Union Situation in the Soviet Union and ILO Tripartism— a preliminary survey

A factual survey relating to the freedom of association in the Soviet Union was undertaken by the ILO in 1959 at the invitation of the government of the USSR.[1] The survey was carried out by a Mission[2] from the International Labour Office which was in the Soviet Union from the end of August until the end of October of that year. Previously a similar mission had been carried out in the United States.

As was pointed out in the Report on "Trade Union Situation in the United States",[3] a great deal of attention had already been paid to the subject of freedom of association by the ILO for many years. The decision to undertake on-the-spot surveys in the member-countries was the latest step in the long series of actions which had included the adoption of the Freedom of Association and Protection of the Rights to Organize Convention (1948, No. 87), the Right to Organize and Collective Bargaining Convention (1949, No. 98), and certain other conventions and recommendations.[4]

Other steps have involved the creation of a Fact-Finding and Conciliation Commission in 1950, and the appointment of an ILO Governing Body Committee on Freedom of Association in 1952—which had investigated a large number of complaints concerning alleged infringements of the principle of freedom of association and the preparation of a report concerning the extent of the freedom of employers' and workers' organizations from government domination or control (the McNair Report) which was circulated to the members of the Governing Body at the 131st Session (Geneva, March 1956).[5]

When the McNair Report was discussed by the Governing Body at the 133rd Session (Geneva, November 1956) the Workers' Group of the Governing Body proposed that: ". . . a machinery be set up to obtain not just the legal, but the real facts about conditions in each member-state. The factual inquiry envisaged will be broader in scope than the reporting under the Convention procedure in the Constitution, and broader than the work of the Governing Body Committee on Freedom of Association, although it might draw upon both these sources for information." This proposal was adopted by the Governing Body at its 138th Session (Geneva, March 1958).

The fundamental idea behind the whole project was clearly expressed by the Governing Body in the introduction to the Report of a similar Mission sent out by the ILO to study the situation of the trade unions in the United States[6] in the following words: "The purpose of the factual survey—which was in effect to be a series of national surveys—as understood by the Governing Body, was to provide a full picture of the actual conditions in each country which affect the extent to which freedom of association is respected. For the factual survey in a country to yield realistic results it was agreed that its scope should be wide enough to cover all aspects of national life relevant to freedom of association. It was also agreed that to be fully factual, comprehensive and authentic, such a survey should not be limited to official and other documentary sources but should include the possibility of studying the situation on the spot in the different countries. It will be noted that the procedure for the factual surveys was completely separated from that for dealing with allegations. The surveys were designed to elicit the facts in an objective manner and not to investigate disputes, and they were entrusted to the ILO in general rather than to any Committee inside or outside the Organization."

Debates on freedom of association have taken place both in the International Labour Conference and in the Governing Body of the ILO. These discussions took on a particularly acute form after the USSR had joined, or as some might interject, rejoined[7] the ILO in 1954 and two points in particular have aroused considerable controversy. In the first place, the Employers' Group in the Governing Body and in various ILO Conferences and meetings has contended that delegates appointed as employers to represent the USSR were not free employers in the generally accepted sense of the word but were rather officials who were obliged to carry out the policies of their government.

Secondly, some members of the Government, Employers' and Workers' Groups have maintained that the trade unions in the USSR were not freely constituted organizations set up by the workers themselves but were merely bodies for ensuring that the orders of the government were carried out by the workers. On this latter point a specific complaint was submitted to the ILO by the International Confederation of Free Trade Unions and investigated by the Governing Body Committee on Freedom of Association. The reports of the Committee on this subject contain an analysis of the complaint, the observations of the Soviet government and extracts from the relevant documents.[8]

From all available accounts one would say that the Mission directed its inquiry at three cardinal questions with regard to the status of trade unions within the Soviet society—one, whether the workers in the Soviet Union are free to join trade unions; two, whether they can set up any unions they please; and three, whether the unions are completely independent of any forms of governmental control.

It may be said that the prime functions of trade unions in traditional Western societies is to protect and improve the wages and working conditions of their members through collective actions, whether by bargaining with the employers or by promoting legislation on these lines. In fact, historically, one of the principal reasons for setting up trade unions was to enable workers and employees to acquire a combined strength which would enable them to bargain more effectively with the employers and to replace the individual contracts with a collective bargain. To find out whether Soviet trade unions fitted into these traditional Western patterns was the primary task of the ILO Mission.

But then we must not forget, just as the ILO Mission realised, that the background[9] or "national circumstances" surrounding Soviet trade unions are radically different from those that obtain in any traditional Western society. We must also remember that the special position now enjoyed by Soviet trade unions was not achieved at a single stroke but is the result of a historical process which had already started at the beginning of the present century. We have no cause to believe that this gradual evolutionary process has halted completely in the Soviet Union.

The Constitution of the USSR, as adopted in 1936 and subsequently amended, brings out certain points which throw some light on the position of the workers and the trade unions in the Soviet Union today: these include the abolition of private ownership of the means of production and distribution, the elimination of "the exploitation of man by man", the institutionalization of the socialist system as the predominant form of economy in the USSR, and the determination and direction of the economic life of the state through a closely coordinated state plan. The Soviet official view is that under such circumstances the worker is not engaged in producing a return on capital invested by private individuals but is considered to be taking part in a national effort to promote the welfare of the entire population. Whether he is employed in the factory or on the land, in mining or in forestry, on the railways or in the air, in an office or in the shop, in education, science, or in culture, he is either working on, or making use of, property which belongs to the whole people (obshchenarodnaia sobstvennost'). The percentage of persons engaged in "small private economy" is extremely small and even for them economic activities must not include "the exploitation of the labour of others". Every worker in the Soviet Union—and this means practically the whole population apart from the armed services—is therefore held to be participating in the common effort to raise the standard of living for everybody including himself. His private interests and the sectional interests of his enterprise and locality are subordinated to the overall interests of the entire Soviet fatherland and of the Soviet population as a whole.

Soviet trade unions are organized on the basis of production units rather than on professional principles. This, in effect, means that membership of any one given trade union embraces all the workers and employees no matter what their professions are, and even sometimes membership of such trade unions is extended to individuals who do not belong to any of the above categories but who, perhaps, have some sort of affiliation with the given functional-territorial unit, e.g. the trade union organization of the Moscow State University which is considered a functional-territorial unit incorporates not only the entire service personnel of the University, and this includes the cleaners, door-keepers, hostel wardens, security guards and all others, but also its entire faculty members and even the students. There is certainly no common professional denominator between a university professor and a janitor to warrant their being members of the same professional union. But to the Soviet mind there seems to be.

Another specific feature of Soviet trade unions is that they are all affiliated to a single central body—the All-Union Central Council of Trade Unions (AUCCTU)—which has its Headquarters in Moscow. This central organ exercises vertical control over all local chapters of these mass organizations throughout the Soviet Union in accordance with the principle of "democratic centralism". The relationship between the Trade Union Organization of the USSR and the Soviet Communist Party is defined in the Preamble to the Rules of the Trade Unions of the USSR adopted in March 1959 in the following passage: "The Soviet trade unions which are mass non-party public organizations unite, on a voluntary basis, workers and other employees of all occupations, irrespective of race, nationality, sex, or religious beliefs.

The Soviet trade unions conduct all their activities under the guidance of the Communist Party of the Soviet Union, the organizing and directing force of Soviet society. The trade unions of the USSR rally the masses of workers and other employees around the Party and mobilise them for the struggle to build a communist society."[10] Since the Communist Party is virtually the dominant political force in the Soviet society the use of such phrase as "guidance of the Communist Party" in the above passage actually means the imposition of party dictatorship over the trade union organization. In this context the Soviet trade union organization is to be seen as a mere executive instrument of the Communist Party. Unless we constantly bear in mind this Trade Union-Communist Party relationship in the Soviet Union we can never come near to understanding the role of Soviet trade unions within that society.

"With a membership of millions of workers, the trade unions acting as a school of communism have become the leading organizers, and the active participants in the building, of socialism, the pillars of the dictatorship of the working class and the faithful explainers of the policy of the Communist Party to the toiling masses. They serve as a link between the Party and the masses, first and foremost at the production level."[11]

The theory that the trade unions had an educational part to play in the building of a communist society and that they should act as a transmission belt between the Party and the masses has survived unchanged until today.[12]

In a similar manner the Soviet trade union is so involved in the day-to-day government of the society that one can hardly conceive of any measure of political independence of the former from the actual government itself. However, this is not the same thing as saying that the trade unions are an integral part of the Soviet government. The actual situation today is that the trade union organization of the Soviet Union stands between the Party and the government, while remaining distinct from each of these other organizations in order to be able to perform certain tasks which fall to it during the transition period from capitalism to communism. The trade unions are essential for the purpose of building socialism and subsequently, as the state withers away, they will remain as the "educational organization, an enlisting and training organization . . .

a school of administration, a school of management, a school of communism."[13]

Having attempted a socio-political survey of the place and role of trade unions within the Soviet society today we might now direct our attention towards a legal analysis of their status.

The Legal Status of Soviet Trade Unions: the right to organize or strike

In 1865, four years after the abolition of serfdom in Russia, the tsarist government enacted legislation under which strikes were declared acts of sedition; in 1886 the Penal Code was amended to make striking a crime and to lay down heavy penalties for persons promoting or taking part in strikes and for employers who provoked strikes by violating the existing labour legislation. In December 1905 another law was passed prohibiting strikes on the railways, in telephone companies and in all undertakings where the security of the state could be affected.

Thus, until 1905 the Russian workers were prohibited by law from organizing into trade unions. Instead they found outlets for their desire to organize in such groups like mutual benefit, aid, benevolent, burial and sickness societies as these served as the only channels through which the revolutionary political parties reached the masses of the workers. Later on the government-controlled police union formed by Zubatov, Chief of the Moscow Secret Police, in 1901 served as the meeting ground for Russian workers.

The Russian workers finding no better alternatives were forced to join this Police Union in great numbers and through it initiated extensive strikes. As an aftermath to the 1905 Revolution in Russia the first trade unions were formed throughout Russia. But as soon as the revolution was crushed by the tsarist government all labour organizations were exterminated, trade unions were once again prohibited by law, their funds confiscated, and their leaders ruthlessly destroyed. The workers thereupon formed underground unions which conducted their activities in spite of the law.[14]

The tsarist government attitude towards trade unions and strikes in Russia was virtually inherited by the Bolshevik regime which was swept into power after the 1917 Revolution. The Constitution of the Russian Federation which was promulgated on July 10, 1918, the first Labour Code of the Russian Federation which was adopted on December 10, 1918, and the second Labour Code of the Russian Federation which was adopted on November 9, 1922—all had provisions regulating the rights of trade unions.

On June 23, 1933 all the various agencies of the People's Commissariat of Labour were amalgamated with the Central and local organizations of the AUCCTU of the USSR and their functions were taken over

57

by the latter body.[15] Other instruments regulating the rights of trade unions in the USSR include: the Federal Constitution of December 5, 1936, the Federal Decree of July 15, 1958 which was adopted by the Presidium of the Supreme Soviet of the Soviet Union. The Decree sought to lay down the rights of the Factory and Local trade union committees.

Art. 126 of the Federal Constitution of the USSR guarantees to all citizens the right to organize into trade unions.[16]

The article reads: "In conformity with the interests of the working people, and in order to develop the initiative and political activity of the masses of the people, citizens of the USSR are guaranteed the right to unite in mass organizations—trade unions, cooperative societies, youth organizations, sporting and defence organizations, cultural, technical and scientific societies; and the most active and politically conscious citizens in the ranks of the working class, working peasants and working intelligentsia voluntarily unite in the Communist Party of the Soviet Union, which is the vanguard of the working people in their struggle to build a communist society and is the leading core of all organizations of the working people, both governmental and non-governmental."

This constitutional right is re-echoed in Art. 151 of the RSFSR Labour Code. Before they were last amended, the Federal Constitution and the Rules of the Trade Unions of the USSR stated that "membership of the trade union is open to all citizens of the USSR" (Art. 1). Although the Preamble to the Rules declared that the Soviet trade unions united workers and other employees without distinction as to race or nationality,[17] this did not exclude the requirement that no person might join the trade union organization in the USSR unless he is a citizen of that country. However, at the 12th Congress of the AUCCTU held in March 1959 this provision was struck out thus enabling aliens to join Soviet trade unions.[18]

Any professional organization, in order to be able to style itself a trade union, must be registered with an inter-union body under Art. 152 of the 1922 RSFSR Labour Code.[19] Thus, unlike the non-occupational organizations inside the Soviet Union, the trade unions, instead of having to register with a state organ, are required to register with, and affiliate themselves to, an inter-union organization. The most recent revised edition of the Soviet Fundamental Principles of Labour Legislation in the USSR states in Art. 95 that "Trade Unions shall operate on the basis of a Constitution adopted by the Unions themselves and such (constitutions) shall not be subject to registration with any state organ."[20]

In principle, all Soviet trade unions must be industrial in character, i.e. they are organized vertically and there should not be more than one trade union organization in any one given enterprise. Art. 14 of the Rules adopted by the Congress of the AUCCTU stipulates that "all persons employed in the same factory or office belong to the same union; each

58

trade union comprises the employees of one branch or several branches of the national economy." Under Art. 56 of these Rules this principle has to be accepted by all trade unions registered with the AUCCTU. Under these circumstances it is difficult to conceive of any possibility of the parallel existence of more than one union in any one given industrial enterprise.

Art. 13 of the Civil Code of the RSFSR regulates the rights and duties of trade unions as juridical persons. This provision, however, does not grant these trade unions a "carte blanche" authorization to engage in any activities they might wish to carry out because under Art. 18 of the Civil Code of the Russian Federation "the existence of a legal entity may be terminated by the proper organ of government authority, if the legal entity deviates from the purpose defined by its Charter or contract or, if the activities of organs of the legal entity (its general meeting or management) deviate in a direction which is contrary to the interests of the state." Thus, it does appear that a trade union may be dissolved by a government organ because a trade union is both a legal entity as well as a public organization. Art. 18 of the Civil Code of the Russian Federation does talk also of the possibility of self-dissolution of these legal entities as an alternative to dissolution from above.

At no time has Soviet legislation expressly prohibited workers' recourse to strikes,[21] but there was a provision in the Federal decree of Jan. 23, 1929[22] protecting strike funds, which seemed to imply that the right to strike existed.

In the history of industrial relations in the USSR reference has been made more than once to the question of strikes both in doctrine and in trade union resolutions. The attitude of both theorists and trade unionists on the subject has varied. For example, in the first important collective agreement concluded in the Soviet Union immediately after the Revolution, striking as a means of trade union action was renounced. The attitude of the workers in accepting this clause was typical of the early years. Even where the right to strike was accepted in principle, i.e. in private employment, every attempt was made to avoid using it. In public industries striking was considered foolish and criminal because it would constitute an act of violence by the workers against themselves as socialist part-owners of the means of production and distribution. This attitude does not mean, however, that in practice direct action was never employed.[23]

When the New Economic Policy (NEP) and its system of mixed economy were introduced in 1921 the trade unions openly admitted the possibility of strikes in state-owned as well as in private undertakings. "Previously it was the trade unions themselves which established the conditions of labour, the executive authorities confining themselves to purely formal ratifications of the method adopted. Now, however, these conditions are laid down, in state as well as in private undertakings, by agreements between the two parties concerned. And the existence of an agreement naturally presupposes the possibility of a disagreement or dispute.[24]

All along there have been decrees issued by the state which touched upon the right of workers to be absent from work or to go on strike[25] but the act of December 25, 1958 probably comes nearest to answering our questions as to the legality of strike actions in the USSR. Art. 6 of the Decree states that "an act of commission or ommission aimed at undermining industry, transport, agriculture, the monetary system, trade or some other branch of national economy or the activity of a state agency or public organization for the purpose of weakening the Soviet state, if such an act was commited by utilising a state or public institution, enterprise or organization or by hindering its normal work, is punished by deprivation of freedom for a period of eight to fifteen years and confiscation of property."[26] If strike actions are interpreted as coming under the meaning of the term "act of commission" aimed at disrupting or undermining national industry, transport or agriculture, then our conclusion that workers' strikes are proscribed in the Soviet Union will be correct.

An analogous provision is to be found in the revised version of the Criminal Code of the Russian Federation. On September 16, 1966 the Presidium of the Supreme Soviet of the Russian Federation issued a Decree "On the adoption of an additional provision to the Criminal Code of the RSFSR"[27] and this additional provision later became Arts. 190-1, 190-2, and 190-3 of the Criminal Code. We are directly interested in the provision of Art. 190-3 which carries the caption "Organization or active participation in any group actions in breach of public order." This article specifically states: "Any organization, as well as any active participation in group actions rudely breaching public order or accompanied by any blatant refusal to abide by the legal demands of representatives of state authority, or culminating in the obstruction of the (normal) operation of (public) transport, state, social enterprise or production plant shall be punished by a deprivation of freedom for a term of up to three years or by corrective labour for a period of up to one year or by a fine of up to one-hundred rubles." The penalty imposed by this recent law is probably less severe than the one imposed by the 1958 Federal law but they both have a striking similarity in the sense that they both incorporate any possible definition of strike actions. What is a strike if not an organised group action aimed at the temporary disruption of the production process with a view to pressurizing the employer or, in the Soviet case, the administration, into meeting some of the demands of the strikers? One can only guess the legislative intention behind these laws cited above but one thing is certainly clear—they were either specifically intended to cover strike actions or at best they have come to reach such strike actions through their legislative overbreadth. The clear possibility of these laws being interpreted to reach strike actions and the inevitable prophylactic effect they are bound to produce on any potential strikers in the Soviet Union are certainly enough to make us reach the conclusion that they represent a prohibitive regulation of strikes in the Soviet Union.

It is interesting to note, however, that when the ILO Mission to the Soviet Union in 1959 questioned Soviet labour officials as to whether the provisions of the 1958 law could be interpreted to reach strike actions, "the Mission was told that this act was intended to apply to criminal offences and that it would not be used in the case of strikes."[28] Such an answer is hardly convincing even if we decide to grant it some degree of good faith.

If we move on from this inductive reasoning into a possible deductive approach we find that we shall arrive at practically the same conclusion. All Soviet experts on the labour law of "bourgeois countries"[29] are unanimous in their appraisal of strikes in capitalist countries. To the authors of a Soviet textbook on labour law[30]—a textbook which is widely used in Soviet Law Schools—strikes represent "one of the basic forms of struggle of the working class in capitalist countries for their political and economic interests." The social and economic roots of strikes they see in the operation of private ownership of the means of production and distribution and the subsequent division of the society into the "haves" and the "have-nots", into those who possess the means of production and distribution and therefore are in the position to employ human labour to operate them and those who are forced by economic exigencies to sell their man-power. In other words this social setting is essential before strike actions can become a "social necessity". But since the Soviet society is practically rid of this antagonistic dichotomy, the authors would argue, there is no social necessity for strikes in the Soviet society and therefore strikes should not be granted any legislative protection in a "state of all the people."[31]

No doubt this was the reasoning behind the minds of the authors of the two legislations cited above. They, however, refused to spell it out in clear-cut terms that they intended to place a ban on all strike actions because such overt regulation of strikes would in itself be tantamount to a tacit recognition of the fact that strikes are even possible in the Soviet society—a conclusion which would be contradictory to the "government of all the people" theory in contemporary Soviet marxism.[32]

All this leads us to the overall conclusion that the Soviet Union, while desisting from placing any outright ban on strikes in view of the fact that such an open prohibition of strikes will be embarrassing has, nevertheless, opted for an indirect method of attaining the much desired ban—by passing amorphous laws which through judicial interpretation can be construed to reach strike actions.

The Soviet trade union organization is the most massive organization in the Soviet Union today. It embraces workers of all categories and even students of higher and vocational schools. Available figures put the proportion of workers who were members of the union at well over 90 percent of the working population. It has actually been estimated that the average union membership for all industries is 93 percent.[33]

In law membership of these unions is on a voluntary basis but in actual practice the social pressure brought to bear upon non-members is so great that the voluntary nature of such membership has become a farce.[34]

We can summarise our brief study of the contemporary trade union situation in the Soviet Union into the following major points:

1. The close institutional interaction between the trade union organization, the Soviet government and the communist party is a reality of the contemporary Soviet political system. None of these three institutions actually incorporates the other. They are all complementary to one another with the communist party as the unchallenged director of the affairs of the entire nation. Membership of these institutions interlocks and in fact, past trade union leaders have often found their way into top government and party posts.[35] The Soviet trade union organization, a highly centralised organization at that, is not and cannot justly lay claim to any independence from the communist party. It is rather an appendage of the party and serves as the latter's specialised labour relations agency.

2. Membership of Soviet trade union organization is allegedly voluntary[36] but certain practices both inside and outside these unions lead one to the inevitable conclusion that such membership is at best non-voluntary.[37]

3. Soviet legislation does not in any express terms prohibit recourse to strikes. On the other hand it does not appear to give them any protection either. The practical truth is that strikes in the Soviet Union are politically undesirable, socially abhorrent, ideologically unimaginable and, subsequently, legally unprotected. The fact that Soviet authorities resort to the enactment of laws which are extremely amorphous in their wordings and which could be judicially construed to reach strike actions, as was the case in the Federal Law of 1958 and the 1966 amendments to the Criminal Code of the Russian Federation, gives one the impression that the Soviet government obviously is interested in legally keeping out any forms of strikes in its production processes, but on the other hand it prefers not to legislate on such matters in any direct form. Any such direct legislation by the Soviet government will not only be inherently self-contradicting but also embarrassing. The Soviets therefore would argue—why legislate directly on any issue when you can conveniently reach the same result through an indirect regulation? Such reasoning represents not only some political wisdom but also resourcefullness in judicial draftsmanship.

4. Official party and government policy reserves for the trade union organization the role of an eventual replacement for the traditional government machinery in the field of economic organization of the Soviet society. The past, present, and future roles of the Soviet trade union organization do not seem to provide us with sufficient grounds for reaching the conclusion that Soviet trade unions are trade unions at all. In fact, the qualitative differences between Soviet trade unions and traditional Western trade unions are so great that the former can hardly qualify to be grouped into the genus of trade unions, or even to be classified as trade unions 'sui generis'. They are camouflaged government economic functionaries. They are "a school of administration and economic management, a school of communism".[38]

But then the question remains as to whether Art. 3 of the ILO Constitution envisaged only such trade unions that are virtually free from all government control. In fact, is there any such thing as "an independent trade union organization", meaning independent of all forms of government control, in a highly complex and closely interdependent industrialised society of today? We shall be discussing these and other related questions when we come to appraise Soviet impact on the ILO.

With this brief survey of the trade union situation in the Soviet Union we can now go on to examine the relationship which existed between the Soviet Union and the International Labour Organization between 1919 and 1934, i.e. from the time the Organization was set up until the time the Soviet Union was, if nothing else, technically admitted into it.

Par. 2A. *The hostile boycott. 1919-1934*

The Treaty of Versailles of June 28, 1919 is perhaps one of the most important post-first-world-war peace treaties which sought to consolidate the 'status quo post bellum' in Europe. This treaty is to be remembered not just as a peace treaty which it was, but more so because it incorporated the constituent instruments of three organizations which were later to constitute a landmark in the history of the organization of the international society of nations—the Covenant of the League of Nations, the Statute of the Permanent Court of International Justice, and the Constitution of the International Labour Organization. These three "Institutions of Versailles" each in its own way created a precedent in international organization—the first, in the political organization of a highly polarised international society, the second, in the highly sensitive field of international adjudication and the peaceful settlement of international disputes, and the ILO in the sphere of organised international labour and industrial relations. The adoption of the Constitution of the ILO set the stage for the first ever international experiment in the field of international labour legislation.

The original text of the ILO Constitution formed part XIII of the Treaty of Versailles[39] and it states in its Art. 387 that "A permanent organization is hereby established for the promotion of the objects set forth in the Preamble. The original members of the League of Nations shall be the original members of this Organization, and hereafter membership of the League of Nations shall carry with it membership of the said Organization." It was this latter phrase that was to be construed later as confering automatic membership of the International Labour Organization on the Soviet Union when the latter was subsequently admitted into the League of Nations in 1934—an interpretation which has consistently been challenged by all Soviet commentators.[40]

From its very inception the League of Nations had been regarded with deep suspicion by the Soviet Union. It had come to be regarded not only as an anti-revolutionary organization, but also as being directed primarily against Soviet Russia.[41] This original Soviet hatred or suspicion for the League of Nations and the Treaty of Versailles as a whole was extended to all sister-institutions of the League—to the ILO and the PCIJ alike.

A close examination of Soviet foreign policy objectives at this time shows that the Soviet Union consistently flirted around the League of Nations—she sporadically unleashed virulent attacks against the League while at the same time keeping the doors open for a possible reconciliation with the Organization should this be dictated by a superior political consideration. It was this same double-standard behaviour that dominated initial Soviet attitude towards the International Labour Organization with either hostility or a spirit of détente dominating the scene at any one given time. However, the period under review (1919-1934) was marked by one general trend in Soviet policy—an attitude of revolutionary antagonism towards the League and a hostile boycott of the ILO. This sort of attitude on the part of the Soviet government, however, did not discourage ILO officials from seeking ways and means of improving the relations between the Organization and Moscow.

We shall try to examine Soviet attitude towards the ILO during this period by drawing upon two independent sources: Soviet government policy statements directed either at the Organization itself or at the League of Nations, and quasi-government sources—commentaries by Soviet scholars and some leading articles in the government-controlled Soviet press.

A leading Soviet scholar on the history of the ILO, V. G. Shkunaev, writing in 1968,[42] had this to say: "It is interesting to note that (western sources) regard as some of the founders of the ILO the great English socialist-utopist Robert Owen; one of the leaders of the Chartist movement Charles Hindley; the French industrialist of the mid-nineteenth century Daniel Legran, and even . . . the German Emperor Wilhelm II. Not one of these (persons) had anything to do with the idea of an international labour legislation. . ."[43] To him the entire concept of an international labour legislation as a possible panacea to the deteriorating situation in the international labour front is nothing but a farce, a calculated attempt to obscure the true social roots of the International Labour Organization. V. G. Shkunaev sets outs what he calls the historical causes of the formation of the ILO in the following passage: "The first world war gave an impetus to the development of a revolutionary movement of the working class which attained an unprecedented height at this time. The victory of the Great October Socialist Revolution in Russia dented the world dominance of the capitalist system of economy, having established over one-sixth of the earth the power of the working masses. The socialist revolution in Russia meant not only the collapse of Russian capitalism, but it also dealt a serious blow at the capitalist system as a whole. The socialist revolution in Russia rocked to its very foundations the entire structure of capitalism, the world was now divided into two antagonistic systems. This sparked off the first stage of the general crisis of capitalism. . . It was this fear of a revolutionary struggle of the working class (of the world) that served as the root cause of the formation of the ILO and it was intended to serve as a response by the ruling circles of the capitalist world.[44]

Lenin himself as far back as 1910 set the stage for such sceptical commentaries by all subsequent Soviet writers on the subject. Dwelling then on what he termed "bourgeois tactics" in its struggle against the working class, Lenin wrote that "in actual fact the bourgeoisie in all countries unavoidably work out two systems of rule, two methods of struggle for the preservation of its interests and its dominance and these two methods are intended to alternate with each other or with any other combinations. The first one is the method of force, a method which calls for a flat rejection of any form of compromise with the workers' movement . . . the method of incompatible rejection of all demands for reform . . . the second method is one of liberalism, steps taken in the direction of the development of political rights, on the path to reforms and compromises, etc."[45]

All Soviet commentators have come to look upon the ILO as representing one of those pseudo-liberal moves calculated by the international bourgeoisie to halt the wave of workers' revolution throughout the capitalist world. "The formation of the ILO represents a link in the whole chain of measures adopted by the ruling classes in the capitalist countries in an attempt to halt the revolutionary struggle of the working class and direct it to the path acceptable to the bourgeoisie itself—the path of social reforms, the path of reformism. The ILO was founded on the basis of an agreement with certain reformist leaders[46] of the workers' movement. Just like all reforms, the formation of the ILO represents the product of a revolutionary struggle of the working class."[47]

The Soviet Union being faithful to its policy of peaceful coexistence—a policy which advocates peaceful cooperation with the imperialist West in the political and economic fields while at the same time flatly rejecting any such cooperation in the sphere of ideology—bluntly refused to see eye-to-eye with the ILO. Cooperation with the ILO was viewed as an unpardonable crime against the international communist movement. It should be noted, however, that Soviet interest in international communism, particularly during Stalin's era stemmed from its interest not only for its self-preservation, but in the desire to extend the Soviet sphere of influence. It is nothing but this megalomania which accounted for the fact that the Soviet Union always held the door open to its "ideological enemies" whenever it thought this desirable and if it thought this would further its foreign policy ideal of "Russia first, international communism later".

During this hectic period the ILO wooed the Soviet Union and the Soviet Union responded—sometimes positively, at other times, not so positively but at least in such a manner as not to slam the door at the ILO because the Soviet Union itself was deeply interested in such courtship on the part of the ILO.

In 1920[48] the ILO suggested to the Soviet government to grant access to an Investigating Committee which was set up by the ILO to study labour relations inside Russia. The request was flatly rejected by Russia and the official reason for the rejection was that Russia feared that the Committee might supply military information to Poland with which Russia was at war at this time.

Lenin himself expressed his antagonism towards such a mission in the following words: ". . . the gentlemen of the Allied Powers wish to send to Russia a co-mission which belongs to the Commission of Labour in Washington. The stage-directors of the Conference, these social traitors alongside with Albert Thomas [the then Director-General of the ILO—CO] have reached an agreement on certain social reforms and wish that this public, which represents a part of the League of Nations, should send to Russia, in order to investigate, to what extent the conditions in Russia correspond to the traditional demands of "civilised" states. This declaration about yesterday's decision by the Allied Powers clearly demonstrates to what extent these gentlemen are confused. . ."[49]

Similarly, prior to the admission of the Soviet Union into the League of Nations there were attempts at establishing bilateral relations between the International Labour Office in Geneva and the Soviet Commissariat of Labour. At this time also there were some forces inside the ILO that were genuinely interested in opening up contacts with Soviet Russia. For example, at the very first ILO Conference a Draft Resolution was tabled calling for the opening of peace talks with Russia. However, this draft resolution was practically buried at that point. At the sixth conference of the ILO in 1924 a representative of the Trade Union Group once again tabled a Draft Resolution which called on the Administrative Council to enter into direct contact with the Soviet government with the hope of getting the Soviet Union to participate in the work of the ILO.[50]

The maintenance of such "cold dialogue" between Moscow and Geneva did not stop the former from continuing its slanderous warfare against the ILO. The Soviets saw the ILO, right from its inception, as a British creation which it actually was.[51] The French were readily available to provide the support needed to keep the Organization going. Being a British-French oriented institution[52] it was bound to fight for the final victory of the British trade union principles in the International Labour Movement—the principle which calls for the separation of political and economic demands by trade unions, i.e. non-participation of trade unions in the political life of the society, the principle of economic activism and political neutrality.[53] This, to the Bolsheviks, was nothing but a dangerous reformist tactic which was bound to take the heat out of the revolutionary international labour movement.

Summing up ILO activities for the first fifty years of its existence 1919-1968) a leading Soviet commentator on the subject, V. G. Shkunaev, writes that: "During a period of half a century of its existence the ILO went through a very complicated and sufficiently contradictory process of development. Not minding all the zig-zags of this process, for more than thirty years it consistently remained a reliable bastion for the ruling circles of large capitalist countries—first of west-European and later of American capitalist groupings. Beginning from 1919 right up to the middle of the fifties representatives of the closed circles of capitalist states dominated almost absolutely (within the Organization) and came nearer to considering it their domain. The past history of the ILO, so to say, its 'yesterday' furnishes us with very many examples of its actions, directed not so much at alleviating the situation of the working masses in the capitalist countries but more so at the obstruction of their class struggles."[54]

In the view of the author of the above lines this gloomy picture changed radically after 1954 when the Soviet Union and two other Soviet Socialist Republics—Ukraine and Belorussia—finally joined the Organization. "Judging by a widely-accepted point of view, this marked the beginning of a new era in the development of the ILO . . . the admission of the Soviet Union into the ILO, the active participation of some socialist states which had long before been members of the ILO, radically altered the face of the Organization."[55]

If the period from 1919 to 1934 marked the period of hostile boycott of the ILO by the Soviet Union, the subsequent period from 1934 to 1954 marked the period of gradual drift away from the "deaf dialogue" which had hitherto existed between the ILO and Moscow into an age of active membership of the Soviet Union in the Organization in 1954. During this period of gradual transition (1934-1954) we notice two important trends: the first (1934-1939) represented a period of constructive dialogue between the ILO and the Soviet Union. Soviet admission into the League of Nations in September 1934 carried with it the automatic membership of the sister-institution—the ILO.[56] Thus, in July 1935 the Soviets, without making known their attitude towards Art. 387 of the Treaty of Versailles, for the first time were represented at the ILO 19th Conference. The Soviet delegation to the Conference, however, was not complete—it had on it only the government representatives. In June 1936 the ILO Conference was attended this time also by Russian Workers' delegates and advisers. This was definitely an improvement upon its attendance of the 19th Session a year earlier. It was not until June 1937[57]—two years after its first appearance at the ILO—that the Soviet Union sent a full team to the ILO Conference. At least this time the Soviet team to Geneva included not only government and workers' delegates, but also what it chose to call employers' representatives.

At the 23rd Session the credentials of the Russian workers' and employers' delegates were unsuccessfully challenged. The marriage of convenience[58] between the Soviet Union and the ILO, with all its uncertainties and attendant hazards, continued right until 1939 when the Soviet Union was expelled from the League of Nations for its attack against Finland in flagrant violation of her League obligations.

Anti-Soviet forces inside the ILO rejoiced at such a decision by the League Council and immediately invoked Art. 387 of the Treaty of Versailles against the continued membership of the Soviet Union inside the ILO.

It is interesting to note that the Administrative Council of the ILO approached the question of Soviet expulsion from the Organization in a much more delicate manner than the Council of the League did vis-à-vis Soviet expulsion from the League of Nations. The Administrative Council of the ILO, as a matter of fact, did not pose the question of Soviet membership of the ILO in its February Session of 1940. All it did was "just" to discuss the list of the eight most important industrial nations and in this list the Soviet Union "accidentally" found itself. The Administrative Council then went on to ask its President and Vice-President to re-examine the situation. After due appraisal the two-man Committee reported back that as a result of the decision of the League of Nations to expel the former from the Organization, "the Soviet Union no longer has the right to automatic membership in the Organization" and that its permanent place in the Council "had become de facto vacant and needs to be filled."[59]

The expulsion of the Soviet Union from the League of Nations on December 14, 1939 was held to have terminated its automatic membership of the ILO according to a decision of the Governing Body of the ILO in February 1940. (See ILO Yearbook, 1939-1940). However, the Director-General of the ILO in a letter to the "Economist" on August 11, 1945 stated: "It would have been possible for the Soviet Union, if it had so desired, to retain its membership of the ILO after leaving the League, as other states have done, but in fact it took no active part in the work of the ILO two years before it ceased to be a member of the League."[60]

However, this decision by the Administrative Council of the ILO to expel the Soviet Union from the Organization "as a result of the decision of the Council of the League of Nations" to expel the Soviets from the League raises a very serious interpretative problem. A Soviet commentator had long maintained that "the ILO Constitution does not provide for the expulsion of any of its members. This power [of expulsion] is not granted to any of its organs not even to the General Conference let alone the Administrative Council."[61]

As a matter of fact there had been instances in the past which tend to justify this Soviet stand. For example, when Japan pulled out of the League of Nations nobody thought of expelling her from the ILO the membership of which she continued to retain. The same thing happened when Germany decided to leave the League of Nations. In the latter case the ILO officially expressed regret at such a move by the German government and went on to express the hope that she might return soon to the Organization.[62] Similarly, when Brazil left the League of Nations in 1927 she was not expelled from the ILO. Under these circumstances V. G. Shkunaev comes to the conclusion that "it is hard to interpret the provisions of the ILO Constitution which confers automatic membership of the ILO on League members as meaning that withdrawal from the League carries with it automatic withdrawal from the ILO."[63]

One would rather tend to agree with the interpretation as given by V. G. Shkunaev. The relevant provision of the ILO Constitution which was Art. 387 of the Treaty of Versailles stipulates that "membership of the League of Nations shall carry with it membership of the ILO" without ever leading us to believe that the termination of such membership shall lead to an automatic termination of the membership of the ILO. The partial justification for this expulsion order given by the Director-General of the ILO in his letter to the "Economist" of London to the effect that "the Soviet Union took no active part in the work of the ILO two years before it ceased to be a member of the League"[64] is hardly convincing. For one thing there is nothing in the ILO Constitution which says that members of the Organization shall stand the risk of being expelled for inactive participation in the work of the Organization. In any event, these arguments not withstanding, the Administrative Council went ahead and expelled the Soviet Union from the ILO and this is the fact that is of interest to us at this point. There is no doubting the fact that the motivation behind the decision to expel the Soviet Union from the ILO was purely extra-legal. It was surely a political action.

Even then Soviet participation in the ILO from 1935-1939 was not a very fruitful one. A perusal of ILO Yearbooks for 1937-38 and 1938-39 shows that at this time the Soviet Union did not ratify even one Convention, let alone considering any of its recommendations. Soviet participation in the ILO between 1935-1939 left more questions unresolved than it ever resolved: the Soviet government refused to pronounce on the question of its automatic admission into the ILO by virtue of Art. 387 of the Treaty of Versailles. The actual fact was that whereas the Soviet Union was fully prepared to use the newly provided platform of the ILO for the furtherance of its foreign policy, it did not at any time consider itself a member of the International Labour Organization as such. Whereas most Western commentators[65] are apt to interpret the provisions of Art. 387 of the Treaty of Versailles in a most strict manner, i.e. as conferring, willy-nilly, automatic membership of the ILO on the Soviet Union, most Soviet commentators refuse to accept such "formalistic" interpretation.[66]

In our humble opinion, the fault is not in those Western scholars who insist on a strictly legalistic interpretation of the provisions of Art. 387 of the Treaty of Versailles, nor is the fault that of Soviet commentators who insist on a realistic rendering of the provision in question. One cannot confer membership of an Organization on any state against its wishes. For such a membership to be a reality and not a legal farce, the express consent of the member-state to be so admitted ought to be sought and received. The fault, in our opinion, is in the drafting of the treaty provision itself which, perhaps, is the result of over-zealousness on the part of its drafters.[67]

Other questions left unresolved by the participation of the Soviet Union in the ILO between 1934 and 1939 were those regarding the validity of the credentials of the Soviet workers' and employers' representatives. The fact that these credentials were un-successfully challenged at this time did not mean that the questions had been finally resolved.

However, what is interesting to note is that no sooner was the Soviet Union expelled from the International Labour Organization, than she resumed her invectives against the Organization. The anti-ILO campaign continued again throughout Russia between 1939 and 1953.[68] It is equally interesting to note that the turning point in this campaign was the death of Joseph Stalin. Had Stalin's personality, therefore, anything to do with this post-1953 Soviet change of attitude towards this "imperialist, reformist, anti-revolutionary" organization? Did the ILO loose all these attributes in 1954 as to attract the Soviet Union back into it, or was it probably the Soviet Union which retracted its invectives against the Organizations in 1954? What are the possible reasons for this counter-revolutionary comeback in 1954 and in what form did it actually manifest itself, what have been the activities of the Soviet Union inside the ILO since its return in 1954? These and other related problems will occupy us in the next paragraph.

Par. 2B. *Soviet activities inside the ILO since 1954*

In the name of peaceful coexistence the Soviet Union thought it a betrayal to the International Labour Movement to have anything to do with the ILO between 1919 and 1934. In the name of peaceful coexistence the Soviet Union found it tolerable to enter into some form of constructive dialogue with the ILO between 1934 and 1939. In the name of peaceful coexistence the Soviet Union opened up yet a new wave of battle of words against the ILO between 1939 and 1953. Finally, in the name of peaceful coexistence the Soviet Union considered full membership of the ILO in 1954 not bad afterall. "The participation of the Soviet Union, just like that of other socialist countries, in such international organizations (like the ILO) is a component element of its struggle for peace, for peaceful coexistence of countries with different social structure, against imperialist plans aimed at unleashing total nuclear war, (such participation) represents a practical application of the principle of peaceful coexistence as promulgated by V. I. Lenin and as developed and expounded upon in the decisions of the 20-23rd congresses of the Communist Party of the Soviet Union, in the declarations and statements of the consultative meetings of representatives of the communist and workers' parties, in the peace manifesto and declaratory statement addressed to all nations of the world, signed by the participants of these consultative meetings and in the documents of other communist and workers' parties."[69]

In an effort to justify Soviet return to the ILO in 1954[70] V. G. Shkunaev[71] explains that "a most important factor in taking this decision was the fact that the ILO broke off its relationship with the League of Nations and had become a Specialised Agency of the United Nations... (Thus) after the approval of the Relationship Agreement between the ILO and the United Nations Organizations by the competent organs of both organizations, i.e. after December 14, 1946 a favourable condition was created for the Soviet Union to participate in the work of the International Labour Organization."[72]

One thing is clear—the Soviet Union had not modified the original contents of its policy of peaceful coexistence. It still remains a fighting ideology aimed at the victory of socialism and eventually of communism in the entire world. The Soviet decision to join or re-join the ILO in 1954, depending on the point of view one holds on the issue, was nothing but a tactical move which represented a part of the global strategy laid out in its policy of peaceful coexistence.

Even then the Soviet Union had not fully made up its mind as to whether or not it was prepared to accept full responsibility for its membership within the Organization. On November 4, 1953[73] the Soviet Union in a letter sent through the Soviet Mission in Switzerland to Mr. Morse, the then Director-General of the ILO informed the latter of its willingness to accept the obligations of ILO membership with a reservation on the question of the jurisdiction of the ICJ as spelled out in Art. 37, paras. 1 and 2 of the ILO Constitution, and on the legal effects on the USSR of the past decisions of the ILO. The Soviet Union refused to accept the "optional clause" in the ICJ Statute of 1945 and she was only repeating this original position when she declared her reservation to the provision of Art. 31 of the Constitution of the ILO a provision which seeks to grant finality and binding force to ICJ decisions on matters concerning complaints arising from non-observance of ILO conventions.[74]

However, Mr. Morse refused to accept these reservations and finally in April 1954 the Soviet Union accepted the obligations of the ILO Constitution without reservations. Once again the reaction to Soviet admission or re-admission into the ILO was mixed both inside and outside the Organization itself. Some states welcomed the return of the Soviet Union into the ILO,[75] others expressed doubts as to the sagacity of such a move on the part of the Organization, while some others were openly hostile to such re-admission. Now that the Soviet Union was back into the Organization one would like to know how she comported herself inside it. Our appraisal of Soviet activities inside the ILO shall be based on three tests—its attitude towards ILO Conventions, its reactions towards the recommendations of the Organization, and its stand, whether positive or negative, on the concept of tripartism inside the Organization. How far has Soviet participation in the ILO gone to modify the concept of workers' and employers' representatives within the framework of the ILO Constitution? We shall begin with the last question.

Soviet participation and ILO tripartism

The ILO is probably unique, among other things, for its tripartism.[76] Unlike any other organizations which existed both before and after 1919, the ILO chose to grant to non-government delegates a strong voice in the decision-making process affecting the welfare of all parties concerned. Art. 3 par. 1 of the ILO Constitution stipulates that "The meetings of the General Conference of the representatives of the members (of the Organization) shall be held from time to time as occasion may require. It shall be composed of four representatives of each of the members of whom two shall be government delegates and the two others shall be delegates representing respectively the employers and the workpeople of each of the members." There is no doubt at all in anybody's mind that this arrangement was intended to serve as an international recognition of the bargaining power of both workers' and employers' unions within any traditional Western society. Consequently, between 1919 and 1934 there was virtually no dispute within the framework of the ILO as to what constituted a workers' union or an employers' association.

The Soviet Union's quasi-formal participation in the ILO between 1934 and 1939 raised certain questions along these lines,[77] but unfortunately they were not fully resolved by the time Soviet membership was terminated in 1939 as a result of her expulsion from the League of Nations.[78]

The Soviet Union's re-entry into the International Labour Organization raised afresh the question of tripartism in the Organization—could a communist country legitimately be fitted into this system as it was then understood, or must the concept of trade unions be widened in order to embrace the Soviet 'profsoyuz' (trade unions)? Thus, the right of communist workers' and employers' delegates to participate in the ILO was immediately challenged. When the Conference Delegation on Constitutional Questions in 1946 specifically considered the question of Soviet Union's re-entry, it concluded, and this was later confirmed by the Conference, that "appropriate provision for the representation of socialised management and of different sections of labour movements of Member-States can be within the framework of the present system of representation. . ."[79]

On the other hand, in the 30's the credentials of the Soviet workers' and employers' delegates had been challenged and in the much more hostile atmosphere of the early 50's it was inevitable that these challenges would be issued again. These questions were raised on and off until they were finally settled at the 43rd Conference of the ILO. It became almost natural to expect that Soviet activities inside the ILO at this time were principally directed at securing full membership rights within the Organization.

The real issues involved in the tripartite question were:
a) a challenge to communist employer and worker delegates' credentials;
b) the proposal to amend the Constitution of the ILO so that communist states could not appoint employer and worker delegates to the Conference;
c) the refusal to appoint communist worker and employer delegates to the Conference Committees.

The first challenges, none of which had succeeded, were based on the fact that such delegates cannot be free of government control. At the 37th Conference the majority of the Credentials Committee held that communist states could, within the framework of the ILO Constitution, appoint employer or worker delegates and implicitly ruled that freedom from government control was not a requirement. All later challenges were declared irreceivable on the grounds that no new issues were raised.

These unsuccessful challenges to the validity of Soviet credentials led to attempts to amend the Constitution of the ILO. At the November 1954 meeting of the Governing Body of the ILO, Sir Alfred Roberts on behalf of the Workers' Group proposed amendments to Art. 3 par. 5 which sought to make representatives so nominated to be free and independent of their governments. This was opposed by the government representatives and a committee which was later drawn up to report on the proposals came up with the conclusion that such an amendment was "politically impossible". This committee was headed by Lord McNair (1956).

After efforts to amend the Constitution failed, attention was directed towards other techniques. At all Conferences since the USSR resumed membership, the Employers' Group had refused to nominate communist employers for seats on the committee. These efforts continued for some time but they were soon discarded. Between 1954 and 1958 the communist delegates were sitted on the Committee but without a right to vote until the 42nd Conference in 1958 when the Soviet delegate argued that it could no longer tolerate the "discriminatory treatment". The Governing Body set up a Committee under the chairmanship of Professor Ago of the University of Rome (the Italian delegate to the ILO) to work out an equitable formula for sitting communist delegates in the Committees. The compromise arrived at was that the communist delegates should not only be seated in the Committee, but should also be granted the right to vote therein. It is perhaps fair to say that after the decisions taken at the 43rd Conference the Soviet Union had won the tripartite battle. If, therefore, between 1919 and 1958 Art. 3 of the ILO Constitution came to be interpreted, through a necessary assumption, to mean that the workers' and employers' delegates were to be nominated free of government control in view of the trade union-government relationship in traditional Western societies which dominated ILO membership at this time, the 1958 Ago Report, if nothing else, at least had modified this interpretation to mean that freedom from governmental control is not a prerequisite to be observed in the nomination of such delegates.

It would be fair to say that the talk about absolute freedom from government control in the choice of workers' and employers' delegates in itself was not even very palatable to the government delegates of many Western member-states. For one thing most trade union laws in most traditional Western societies would fall under the axe of this "absolute freedom" requirement.[80] In fact, if the Robert's recommendation had been adopted[81] by the Governing Body of the ILO it would have boomeranged against the Western member states to a considerable extent. So that the Ago Report, besides satisfying the needs of the communist member states of the ILO, at the same time served as a face-saving formula for most Western societies where there is a declared governmental interest in keeping the labour unions away from communist infiltration. Such a paternalistic policy certainly would have given way to the demands of the Robert recommendation.

In our opinion, the decision to admit the Soviet Union into the Organization and to sit its delegates in the various organs of the ILO is a highly commendable move on the part of the Organization. This notwithstanding, however, we find it extremely difficult to assert with any certainty whether the impact of Soviet return to the ILO on tripartism within the framework of the Organization was a positive or a negative one. Such a decision surely would be highly subjective and would therefore be incapable of any objective verification.

Even so, without necessarily passing any value judgments on these questions, by accommodating communist workers' and employers' delegates inside the Organization, the ILO has demonstrated its capacity for adaptation and change in the face of a crippling danger—a danger that threatened the entire efficacy of the ILO as an instrument for the regulation of international labour standards. There is every reason to believe that if this agreement had not been reached at this time, the Soviet Union would have given a second thought to the advisability of its continued participation in the Organization.

Now that the Soviet Union has fought and won the battle to sit its delegates on the decision-making organs of the ILO the question remains to be seen to what use the Soviet Union has put this newly acquired opportunity. What has been Soviet Union's attitude towards ILO conventions and recommendations?

Soviet attitude towards ILO conventions and recommendations

Art. 19 of the ILO Constitution states that "1. When the Conference (of the ILO) has decided on the adoption of proposals with regard to an item on the agenda, it will rest with the Conference to determine whether those proposals will take the form of: a) an international convention, or b) a recommendation to meet circumstances where the subject or aspect of it dealt with is not considered suitable or appropriate at that time for a convention." Paragraphs 5 and 6 of the same article stipulate the obligations of the member-states vis-à-vis these conventions and recommendations respectively. These obligations, inter alia, include: in the case of conventions—an obligation to bring the convention before the authority or authorities within whose competence the matter lies, for enactment of legislation or other action not later than eighteen months from the time of the closing of the session of the Conference; an obligation to inform the Director-General of the ILO of any measures taken to bring his convention before the competent authorities, to communicate any ratification of the convention by the competent authority (if at all it is ratified) to the

Director-General and in the case of non-ratification no further obligation shall rest upon the member-state except that it shall report to the Director-General of the ILO at appropriate intervals as requested by the Governing Body the position of its laws and practice in regard to the matters dealt with in the convention, showing the extent to which effect has been given, or is proposed to be given, to any of the provisions of the convention by legislation, administrative action, collective agreement or otherwise and stating the difficulties which prevent or delay the ratification of such convention." Thus, we find that there is no legal obligation upon the member-states to ratify any conventions so adopted by the General Conference of the ILO even after such a member state had voted for the convention at its adoption stage. It is probably safe to assume that the members, as a reasonable expectation flowing from their membership of the Organization and particularly so if they voted for the convention at the stage of adoption, are expected to ratify these conventions without necessarily infering any obligation upon them to do so. Ratification or non-ratification of any convention so adopted by the ILO is not obligatory upon the member-states.

The same situation applies to the recommendations of the ILO with the sole exception that member-states are not expected to ratify them but only to take note of them in their internal legislation on matters covered by such recommendations.

ILO conventions and recommendations are adopted on all matters which come within the general competence of the Organization[82] and these include hours of work, un-employment, minimum age of employment in industry, right of association of workers of all professions, women's compensation, emigrant labour, publication of statistics on wages and hours of work, social security, forced labour, and discrimination in employment and occupation, etc. Ever since the Soviet Union joined the ILO in 1954 she has ratified only 40 of the 130 conventions so far adopted by the Organization.[83]

This figure does not tell us very much, taken as it stands, about the Soviet attitude towards these conventions unless we try to compare it with other available data for other countries: as of the same date Great Britain ratified 65 conventions, France—80, and the United States—only 7. The conventions ratified by the Soviet Union include the followings: convention No. 10—minimum age (agriculture); No. 11—right of association (agriculture); No. 14—weekly rest (industry); No. 15—minimum age (trimmers and stokers); No. 16—medical examination of young persons (sea); No. 23—repatriation of seamen; No. 27—marking of weights (packages transported by vessels); No. 29—forced labour; No. 32—protection against accidents (dockers); No. 45—underground work (women); No. 47—forty hour week; No. 52—holidays with pay; No. 58—minimum age (sea); No. 59—minimum age (industry); No. 60—minimum age (non-

76

industrial employment); No. 69—certification of ships' cooks; No. 73—medical examination (seafarers); No. 77—medical examination of young persons (industry); No. 78—medical examination of young persons (non-industrial occupations); No. 79—night work of young persons (non-industrial occupations); No. 87—freedom of association and protection of the right to organise; No. 90—night work of young persons (industry) as revised in 1948; No. 92—accommodation of crews; No. 95—protection of wages; No. 98—right to organise and collective bargaining; No. 100—equal remuneration; No. 103—maternity protection; No. 106—weekly rest (commerce and offices); No. 108—seafarers' identity documents; No. 111—discrimination (employment and occupation); No. 112—minimum age (fishermen); No. 113—medical examination (fishermen); No. 115—radiation protection; No. 116—final articles revision; No. 119—guarding of machinery; No. 120—hygiene (commerce and offices); No. 122—employment policy; No. 123—minimum age (underground work); No. 124—medical examination of young persons (underground work) and No. 126—accommodation of crews (fishermen).

It is equally important to point out that of the ten most popular[84] ILO conventions the Soviet Union has ratified six. This is not too bad a record for a "late comer" into the ILO which the Soviet Union certainly is. However, it is one thing to ratify a convention and quite another thing to implement the provisions of the conventions so ratified by the ratifying state. Charter obligations require member-states which have ratified any particular conventions of the ILO to bring into line their respective legislations on the relevant matter to meet the demands contained in the provisions of the conventions so ratified. This obligation flows out of Art. 19 par. 5 of the ILO Constitution. In view of the expected differences in the legislative history, labour standards, and other socio-economic factors within the various member-states of the ILO, the ILO Constitution does take notice of the fact that the provisions of any particular conventions may have long been in practice in some member-states ever before their adoption by the ILO and, in fact, in some cases the provision of an ILO Convention on a particular subject matter might impose less favourable standards than those already in existence within any particular member-states. This accounts for the retention of par. 8 of Art. 19 of the ILO Constitution which stipulates that "in no case shall the adoption of any convention of recommendation by the Conference, or the ratification of any convention by any member, be deemed to affect any law, award, custom or agreement which ensures more favourable conditions to the workers concerned than those provided for in the convention or recommendation." Thus, whereas an ILO convention might serve as a catalyst for improvement in labour legislations in certain countries with regard to certain issues, it might still fall short of the labour standards in other countries. Let us now try to analyse in which aspects ILO conventions as ratified by the USSR have acted as catalyst for improvement of existing Soviet labour standards and in which fields these conventions have imposed less favourable conditions than those already provided for in existing Soviet labour legislations.

The most recent Soviet legislative regulation of labour relations is the new Fundamental Principles on Labour Legislation of the USSR which was promulgated by the edict of the Presidium of the Supreme Soviet of the USSR on July 15, 1970.[85] These new Fundamental Principles are divided into 15 chapters: general provisions, collective bargaining, labour contracts, working hours and period of rest, salaries, guarantees and compensation, labour discipline, protection of labour, women labour, child labour, privileges for workers and employees who combine work with studies, labour disputes, trade unions and the participation of workers in the administration of production, state social insurance policy, control over the implementation of labour legislations and concluding provisions, plus a preamble which deals in very general terms with the history and social functions of Soviet labour legislation.

ILO Convention No. 98—right to organise and collective bargaining—which the Soviet Union ratified seeks to guarantee all workers and employees against any anti-union discrimination in respect of their employment. Specifically it seeks to protect the workers and employees against acts calculated to make the employment of a worker subject to the condition that he shall not join a union or shall relinquish trade union membership or to cause the dismissal of or otherwise prejudice a worker by reason of union membership or because of participation in union activities outside working hours or, with the consent of the employer, within working hours. In other words, the Convention makes it purely voluntary for the worker to join or not to join a trade union for which choice he shall not be subjected to any discriminatory treatment by the employer. Similarly, the right of collective bargaining (collective contract) is regulated by Arts. 6 and 7 of the Soviet Fundamental Principles.[86] Art. 6 of the Fundamental Principles stipulates that collective bargaining shall be entered into by the local factory committee[87] of the trade union on behalf of all workers and employees of the production unit and what is more important the provisions of such collective bargaining shall apply equally to all workers and employees of the production unit irrespective of their membership or not of the local chapter of the trade union. This provision, in our opinion, seems to fulfil the basic requirement in the ILO convention mentioned above, viz. employment of a worker or employee shall not be based on his membership of any trade union organization.

However, on the right of individual workers or employees to join or not to join the trade union Art. 95 of the Fundamental Principles only stipulates that "in accordance with the constitution of the USSR workers and employees are granted the right to unite into trade unions." This provision does not seem to tell us whether or not a Soviet employee or worker can conveniently refuse to join the trade union. The only indirect reference to the worker's choice as to membership or not of such trade union is to be found in Art. 6 of the Fundamental Principles,[88] which reads: "The collective contract applies to all workers and employees of the enterprise or organization, regardless of whether they are members of the trade union."

The Soviet Union has also ratified ILO Convention No. 47[89]—forty hour week—by which she took upon herself the obligation to apply the principle of forty-hour week "in such a manner that the standard of living is not reduced in consequence." But Art. 21 of the Fundamental Principles stipulate that "the normal working hours of workers and employees in factories, enterprises and organizations shall not exceed 41 hours a week." As if recognising that the standard hereby imposed are in excess of the ceiling set by Art. 1 of the 47th ILO Convention the article (Art. 21 of the Fundamental Principles) quickly adds that with the progressive improvement of the economic and other necessary conditions the society shall switch over to a shorter working week.

Art. 22 of the Fundamental Principles does render an interpretation of the phrase "normal" as employed in Art. 21 above to mean that for workers and employees between the ages of 16 and 18 the working hours per week shall not exceed 36, and for those between 15 and 16 years of age, not in excess of 24 hours a week.

Convention No. 14—weekly rest in industry—requires that "the whole of the staff employed in any industrial undertaking, public or private, or in any branch thereof shall, except as otherwise provided for by the following articles, enjoy in every period of seven days a period of rest comprising at least 24 consecutive hours. Art. 30 of the Fundamental Principles stipulates both the 5-day and the 6-day week but in both cases the length of the weekly rest shall not be less than forty-two consecutive hours. This is certainly in excess of ILO Convention (No. 47) requirement.

Convention No. 52—annual holidays with pay—requires that all persons employed in business or commerce or in government employment, except those persons whose conditions of service entitle them to an annual holiday with pay at least equal in duration to that prescribed by this Convention, shall be entitled after one year of continuous service to an annual holiday with pay of at least six working days, whereas persons, including apprentices, under sixteen years of age shall be entitled after one year of continuous service to an annual holiday with pay of at least 12 working days—these days not including public or customary holidays or interruptions of attendance at work due to sickness.

But Arts. 32 and 33 of the Fundamental Principles stipulate that all workers and employees are granted an annual holiday "with the retention of their posts and average salaries" for a period not less than 15 days and for workers and employees less than 18 years of age—for a period not less than one calendar month. Art. 34 talks of other categories of additional holidays, for example, to persons engaged in production processes where the working conditions are particularly hazardous to health, persons with longer length of service, persons who work in the extreme northern sections of the country, etc. We, thus, find that whereas the Convention calls for a minimum of 6 and 12 working days respectively the Soviet legislation unilaterally imposes the 15-day and 30-day minimum standards.

The favourable conditions of Soviet annual holiday law vis-à-vis the ILO Convention requirement is not in any way rendered less favourable by the fact that whereas the ILO Convention calls for the retention of full pay with such annual holidays, the Soviet law only calls for the retention of the "average pay".

Art. 2 of the 1953 Convention No. 100 on equal remuneration clearly calls on ratifying states, by means appropriate to the methods of operation for determining rates of remuneration, "to promote and, in so far as is consistent with such methods, ensure the application to all workers of the principle of equal remuneration for men and women workers for work of equal value."

However, the Soviet legislation toed the line promulgated in the Convention above. Art. 36 of the Fundamental Principles states that "In accordance with the Constitution of the USSR the labour of all workers and employees is paid according to its quality and quantity. Any reduction whatever in the amount of pay because of sex, age, race or nationality is forbidden." This Soviet provision has certainly outdone the ILO standard and personal observations inside Russia and reports coming out of that country point to the fact that the Soviets are keeping strictly to the letters of this law.

The provision of ILO Convention No. 95—protection of wages—is adequately taken care of in Arts. 36-50 of the Fundamental Principles. As if to outstrip the ILO requirement Art. 36, par. 2 of the Fundamental Principles stipulates that "monthly remuneration of employers and workers shall not be less than the minimum amount set by the state." It is quite true that this Soviet "basic minimum salary" is much lower than the current standard in most Western countries but the idea of setting a "floor" for salary scales is probably the best guarantee a worker or an employee can ever have as to the size of his salary.

ILO Convention No. 103[90] in a most comprehensive manner seeks to protect the maternity privileges of any female worker and employee. The Convention applies to women employed in industrial and non-industrial undertakings, as well as in agricultural occupations and also to women wage earners working at home (Art. 1. parag. 1). Art. 3 states that "a

80

woman to whom this Convention applies shall, on the production of a medical certificate stating the presumed date of her confinement, be entitled to a period of maternity leave; the period of maternity leave shall be at least twelve weeks and shall include a period of compulsory leave after confinement." The period of compulsory leave after confinement shall be prescribed by national laws or regulations, but shall in no case be less than six weeks. Art. 4 requires that "while absent from work on maternity leave in accordance with the provisions of Art. 3 the woman shall be entitled to receive cash and medical benefits" the rate of which shall be fixed by national laws or regulations so as to ensure benefits sufficient for the full and healthy maintainance of herself and her child in accordance with a suitable standard of living. And, finally, Art. 6 requires that "while a woman is absent from work on maternity leave in accordance with the provisions of Art. 3 of this Convention, it shall not be lawful for her employer to give her notice of dismissal during such absence, or to give her notice of dismissal during such a time that the notice would expire during such absence."

Let us now turn our attention to what Soviet labour legislation has to offer on the protection of maternity privileges for the Soviet woman worker or employee. This protection is provided in Arts. 70-73 of the Fundamental Principles.

Art. 70 of these Fundamental Principles stipulates that "expectant mothers on the production of a medical certificate to that effect[91] shall be transferred during the time of her pregnancy to a lighter job with the retention of the average remuneration for her previous job." Similarly, all nursing mothers and women with children under one year of age, if they are unable to carry out their previous jobs, shall be transferred to another job with the retention of the average remuneration for their former job for the entire period of such baby-nursing or until the child attains the age of one." (Art. 70, par. 2)

Art. 71 on the other hand regulates maternity leave by providing that women shall be granted maternity leave for a length of 56 calendar days prior to birth and 56 days after birth and for this period she shall be paid the state social insurance allowance. In the case of an abnormal birth or in the case of two or more children the post-natal leave shall be fixed at 70 calendar days. Alongside the (compulsory) maternity leave the woman, if she so requests, shall be granted extra time off without pay until the child attains the age of one.

Art. 72 states that "nursing mothers and women with children who have not attained the age of one shall be granted, alongside the general break for rest and food, extra time to feed the child. Such break shall be granted her not less than after every three hours and for a time not extending for less than thirty minutes each time. The time so granted her for breast-feeding her child shall be considered as part of her work time and shall be remunerated with an average pay.

Art. 73 concludes this section by stipulating that "it is forbidden to refuse to employ a woman or to cut down her salary for reasons connected with her pregnancy or with the fact that she is breast-feeding a child." Similarly, the expulsion of women, nursing mothers, and women with children who have not attained the age of one on the initiative of the administration shall be prohibited, except under such circumstances when the enterprise, plant or organization is completely liquidated (wound up)." Under such extreme circumstances expulsion but with the provision of an alternative job shall be allowed.

These four articles, along with two other previous provisions, Arts. 68 and 69, which regulate the use of female labour in extremely difficult jobs or in night or overtime jobs combine to present a highly venerable Soviet edifice to female labour and maternity leave for a woman. Art. 68, for example, stipulates that the use of female labour in jobs with extremely difficult conditions or in jobs that pose special health hazards or in underground jobs—except when such underground jobs do not require physical exertions—is prohibited. These provisions seem to tally with those contained in ILO Convention No. 45—underground work for women—which the USSR did ratify. Art. 1 of this Convention says that "no female, whatever her age, shall be employed on underground work in any mine" but Art. 2 goes on to stipulate a possible derogation from the general rule of Art. 1 to the effect that "national laws or regulations may exempt from the above prohibition (a) females holding positions of management who do not perform manual work; (b) females who are employed in health and welfare services; (c) females who, in the course of their studies, spend a period of training in underground parts of a mine; and (d) any other females who may occasionally have to enter the underground parts of a mine for the purpose of a non-manual occupation.

The following ILO Conventions—No. 10 (minimum age in agriculture), No. 15 (minimum age for trimmers and stokers), No. 58 (minimum age at sea), No. 59 (minimum age in industry), No. 60 (minimum age for engagement in non-industrial employment), No. 112 (minimum age for fishermen), and No. 123 (minimum age for employment in underground work)—all of which the USSR has ratified stipulate the minimum age for employment in the various spheres concerned. For example, Convention No. 10 requires that "children under the age of 14 years may not be employed or work in any public or private agricultural undertaking or in any branch thereof, save outside the hours fixed for school attendance. If they are employed outside the hours of school attendance, the employment shall not be such as to prejudice their attendance at school." Similarly, Art. 1 of ILO Convention No. 15 stipulates that "young persons under the age of 18 years shall not be employed or work on vessels as trimmers or stokers" without prejudice to those exceptions as provided for in Art. 2 of the same Convention. ILO Conventions Nos. 58, 59, and 60 respectively fix the minimum age for employment at sea, in industry, and in non-industrial undertakings at 15 years of age. Similarly, ILO Conventions Nos. 79 and 90 regulate the use of child labour in night jobs in both non-industrial and industrial undertakings.

Soviet legislative principles on the employment of child labour are articulated in the various articles of chapter 9 of the Fundamental Principles. Art. 74 begins by stating the general rule that "the employment of persons under 16 years of age is prohibited" but in a subsequent "lex specialis" it provides that "in exclusive circumstances, with the consent of the local factory committee of the trade union organization, persons who have attained the age of 15 may be employed." (Art. 74, parag. 2) But then Art. 75 categorically affirms that "the employment of the labour of persons under 18 years of age in jobs with extremely difficult conditions or in jobs that pose health hazards and also in underground jobs is prohibited." In a similar fashion Art. 78 extends such prohibition to the employment of child labour in night or overtime shifts or on public holidays.

Since the provisions of ILO Convention No. 10 were specifically worded to protect the right of children to complete their basic education it is important to draw attention to the provisions of chapter 10 of the Soviet Fundamental Principles which is entitled "Privileges for workers and employees who combine work with studies". The articles under this section extend the protection articulated in ILO Convention No. 10 to both children and adults. The Soviet Union can rightly be described as a nation of professional students—a country where almost everybody is engaged either in a full-time formal education or in some form of part-time studies designed to "improve ones professional qualifications". The inevitable result of such a phenomenon is that almost all Soviet workers and employees no matter how old or young he or she may be and irrespective of how long he or she has been on the job inevitably lays claims to some sort of "study time off."

On the medical examination of young persons requirements in ILO Convention No. 77—medical examination in industry, or in Convention No. 78—medical examination in non-industrial occupations, Convention No. 124—medical examination of young persons engaged in underground work, and No. 16—medical examination of young persons at sea, Art. 76 of the Soviet Fundamental Principles specifically require that "all persons under the age of 18 years shall be employed only after a preliminary medical examination and thereafter until he or she attains the age of 18 shall be subjected to an annual medical examination".

So far we have seen that the Soviet Union has implemented in its legislations all the requirements of those ILO conventions which she ratified. And, in fact, the relevant Soviet legislative regulations of such matters continue to set better standards than the minimal requirements often provided for in these ILO Conventions. As far as these conventions are concerned the Soviet record is almost without blemish.

But great doubts continue to hang over any effective implementation by the USSR of ILO Convention No. 87—freedom of association and protection of the right to organise. This Convention was adopted at the 31st session of the International Labour Conference in San-Francisco (17 June-10 July 1948) and it came into force on July 4, 1950. The Soviet Union has since ratified this Convention. The International Labour Conference, "considering that the Preamble to the Constitution of the ILO declares 'recognition of the principle of freedom of association' to be a means of improving conditions of labour and of establishing peace", and "considering that the Declaration of Philadelphia reaffirms that 'freedom of expression and of association are essential to sustained progress' ", went on to affirm in Art. 2 of this Convention that "workers and employees, without distinction whatsoever, shall have the right to establish and, subject only to the rules of the organization concerned, to join organizations of their own choosing without previous authorization."

Art. 3 of the same Convention goes on to state that "1. workers' and employees' organizations shall have the right to draw up their own constitutions and rules, to elect their representatives in full freedom, to organise their administrative activities and to formulate their performances. 2. The public authority shall refrain from any interference which would restrict this right or impede the lawful exercise thereof." Art. 4 goes on to strengthen the principle of autonomous existence of such trade unions as stipulated in Art. 3 above by providing that "workers' and employees' organizations shall not be liable to be dissolved or suspended by administrative authority." As if to provide the much-needed guarantee to the above articles, Art. 11 imposes on all ratifying states this obligation: "Each member of the ILO for which the Convention is in force undertakes to take all appropriate and necessary measures to ensure that workers and employees may exercise freely the right to organise." In short the fundamental principles promulgated by this Convention are: the inalienable right of workers and employees to organise into professional unions, the autonomous existence of such unions, and the obligation by any ratifying states to provide the requisite guarantees for the exercise of this right. The big question here is—to what extent has the Soviet Union lived up to expectations under the obligations she assumed under this Convention?

Art. 95 of the Fundamental Principles states: "In accordance with the Constitution of the USSR workers and employees are guaranteed the right to organise into trade unions. The trade unions shall operate on the basis of a constitution which they shall adopt for themselves and such constitutions shall not be subject to any registration with a state organ.

State organs, plants, enterprises, or organizations are obligated to grant fullest support to trade unions in all their activities."

On the face value such provisions appear to fulfil the requirements of Art. 2 of the ILO Convention No. 87 according to which membership of any trade union organization by any worker or employee shall be purely voluntary. It is not enough that the Soviet Constitution legally guarantees to all Soviet workers and employees the right to organise into trade unions, but is this "right to organise" to be construed to mean an "obligation to organise"? A close observation of Soviet trade union practices[92] shows that any worker or employee who refuses to join the trade union organization is not only socially ostracised, but is denied all the privileges which trade union membership carries with the inevitable result that membership of trade unions in the USSR is at best non-voluntary and at worst, quasi-obligatory. This, however, is not the same thing as saying that the Soviet legislative principle of "the right to organise" fails to meet the ILO standard. Certainly no strictly legal construction of these principles will lead us to such a conclusion. But if we move into the twilight region where law runs into politics then we will certainly find that Soviet application of the provisions of Art. 95 of the Fundamental Principles certainly falls short of the original expectations of the parties to the ILO Convention in question.

Arts. 96-99 of these Fundamental Principles go on to expound upon the rights of trade union organizations in the Soviet Union. These are surely very wide powers if compared to the powers wielded by their Western counterparts, but the realistic fact is that this "gross advantage" of Soviet trade unions over their Western opposite numbers is nullified by the fact these trade unions are de facto state economic agencies planted in these various production units to oversee the entire production process.

The fact that the Soviet Union most carefully handpicked these 40 most convenient conventions out of a total of 130 while quietly leaving out such controversial conventions like No. 21—inspection of immigrants, No. 48—maintenance of migrants' pension rights, No. 63—supply of statistics of wages and hours of work, No. 66—migration for employment, to mention just a few, portrays the traditional Soviet politics of treaty ratification—never sign away your sovereign rights to any international observer teams.

Having surveyed very briefly Soviet ratification attitudes towards ILO Conventions, let us now move into another aspect of Soviet activities inside the ILO—the sponsorship of, and participation in debates over, resolutions inside the various organs of the International Labour Organization.

A general perusal of Soviet activities inside the ILO since 1954 shows that she has been most active in the consideration of three items—freedom of association, forced labour, and discrimination in employment and occupation.[93] It is hardly suprising to find that the Soviets show maximum enthusiasm in these enumerated areas of ILO activities. The Soviets would be prepared to lend support to any convention which in any way would strengthen the hands of the working classes in "capitalist" countries and therefore would constitute an embarrassment for the governments of Western member-states. After all, the fundamental aim of Soviet participation in the ILO is to get at the heart of the proletarian class in the Western democracies. This aim the Soviets are prepared to achieve through any possible methods—either by making pseudo-revolutionary proposals within the various organs of the Organization, or through its careful selection of the Conventions which it would be prepared to ratify. In making any of these decisions the Soviet Union perpetually has in mind its attempt to woo to its side the international proletariat. When the Soviet Union ratified the freedom of association and protection-of-rights-to-organise convention—No. 87, or the right-to-organise and collective-bargaining convention—No. 98, it obviously relied on the psychological impact this would have on the workers' movements in the Western countries.

Current ILO statistics shows that the Soviet Union is a member of nine of 10 ILO industrial committees. The Soviet Union is currently participating in such industrial committees as the committees on inland transport, coal mines, iron and steel, metal trades, textiles, petroleum, building, civil engineering and works, chemical industries, and the Advisory Committee on Salaried Employees and Professional Workers. Like the United States, Great Britain, Italy, and Japan, who are also members of the above mentioned nine committees, the USSR is not a member of the Committee on Work in Plantations. Thus, only India, with a record membership of all the ten industrial committees, tops the Soviet Union in membership activism in these ILO functionary organs.[94]

The real test of Soviet sincerity and dedication to the ideals of the ILO comes when we discuss questions dealing with finance and the necessity to waive certain sovereign rights. These two issues to the USSR are taboo, and unless there is a higher interest to be served, the Soviet Union is hardly ready to compromise on either of these issues. Thus, for example, whereas the Soviets profess their adherence to the Marxist slogan "Proletariat of all countries, unite", they would never append their signature to any convention which is intended to grant to the very same "proletariat of all countries" the right to migrate, if need be, to the Soviet Union in the quest for job opportunities.

The Soviets, of course, might as well argue that by allowing emigrant workers to move out of such countries where the unemployment situation is utterly bad one is practically slowing down a progressive development of an otherwise revolutionary situation. In other words, if you do not allow these un-employed "armies of workers" to migrate, they would invariably remain inside these countries to foment a social revolution. There is no doubt, of course, in our minds that the Soviet Union's reasons for closing the gates of its factories and enterprises to aliens are limited to these factors. The Soviet attitude towards ILO Convention No. 66—migration for employment,[95] is uncompromisingly negative. The same attitude is adopted by the Soviet Union towards the following ILO Recommendations: No.19—migration statistics, No. 61—migration for employment, and No. 62—migration for employment (cooperation between states), and a host of other recommendations.

The situation was the same ten years ago when H. K. Jacobson observed that "financial questions and matters involving sovereignty provide nearly the only exceptions to the USSR's general attitude concerning issues before the ILO. On both questions Soviet delegates exhibit conservatism. The USSR has staunchly resisted attempts to increase its budgetary contributions above the ten per cent figure[96] set when it resumed membership and it generally opposes suggestions for increased spending. It always jealously guards its sovereignty."[97]

Despite this politically-motivated selective approach to the activities of the ILO, the Soviet Union has, no doubt, had a great impact on the ILO itself from the time it re-entered the Organization in 1954. At least on this point most commentators on the Soviet-ILO relationship tend to agree. Dwelling on the same question of Soviet impact on the ILO, H. K. Jacobson wrote that "To say that the USSR's influence in the ILO is limited, however, is not to argue that its re-entry has been futile from its point of view... Even though the Soviet Union has not been able to still the Organization's criticism concerning forced labour and violations of freedom of association, it probably suffered less being in the ILO than it would have otherwise. And Soviet delegates have utilised to the fullest extent the opportunities that the Organization provides for contacts with non-communists and for propaganda... Nor does the generalization imply that the Soviet Union's re-entry has not effected the ILO. To the contrary the impact has been profound. For one thing, the USSR's move touched off a long and often acrimonious debate on ILO's structure. Although many have received this with distaste and alarm, it is impossible to substantiate their claim that the debate has had damaging effects on the Organization's work."[98]

It is probably true that in terms of political strength, the USSR's position in the ILO remains weak and disproportionately low in most organs. It is equally probably true that some of the original hostility inside the Organization towards the Soviet Union has lessened. But it is highly doubtful if the Soviet Union can rightly be regarded as an "outsider"[99] in the Organization today. Soviet participation in the ILO is so active today and its impact on the Organization so great that a more realistic evaluation of the Soviet role in the present development of the ILO will be to regard her as an "active insider".[100] Soviet membership in the ILO today, if nothing else, throws open two serious challenges—the first challenge is to the ILO itself to re-examine some of its traditional approaches to certain problems that confront the Organization, e.g. a call on the Organization to abandon or, at least, to modify, part of its inherently British approach to the contents of trade union rights and, ipso facto, its approach to the functions of the ILO in protecting these rights, and finally, a Soviet call to the Organization to spread out the composition of its personnel to cover a wider geographical distribution.[101]

"When the Soviet Union resumed membership in 1954, an almost universal reaction within the Organization was to express the fear that this would introduce 'politics' into what had hitherto been considered technical considerations . . . the ILO of 1960 is much more political than it was a decade earlier. . . It is dealing with more basic questions.[102]

It is most probably true that the ILO became more "political" than it ever was before the Soviets came into it. As a matter of fact the Soviets have never considered the possibility of an Organization like this remaining apolitical to international problems.[103] Consequently, the Soviet delegation often introduced highly political and sometimes very embarrassing and often out-of-place topics into the delibrations of the Organizations. Examples of such political topics include: the Soviet draft resolution on the question of bringing a stop to the arms race, reduction of military budgets of member-states of the Organization and the re-direction of such extra funds towards meeting the needs of peaceful industrial projects and the improvement of the conditions of living of the world population,[104] the draft resolutions calling for a halt to the testing of nuclear and atomic weapons in the light of the tasks of the ILO,[105] the draft resolution presented to the so-called special Maritime Session of the International Labour Conference calling for a stop to all nuclear and hydrogen weapons which violate the safety of navigation in the high seas and threaten the lives of sailors,[106] a draft resolution on the activities of the ILO aimed at the liquidation of the relics of colonialism in the sphere of labour conditions and the life of the working masses.[107] There is no doubt at all in anybody's mind that the contents of these draft resolutions go far beyond the powers of the ILO and it would have been ultra vires for the Organization to have engaged itself in discussing such issues. Nevertheless, the Soviets were less bothered with legal niceties and they went ahead to introduce such draft resolutions which obviously were intended for propaganda purposes.

The second challenge thrown open by Soviet participation in the ILO is probably directed at the hitherto unchallenged US leadership within this Organization. It is highly ironical to note that the ILO was most probably a bastard child of the United States but because the Americans refused to accept paternity of this Organization by virtue of the refusal of the US Senate to ratify the Covenant of the League of Nations, the right of fatherhood of the Organization went over to the British. But when the US defector finally decided to return in 1934, it naturally arrogated to itself the role of leader of the Organization. For more than three decades this leadership went on un-challenged. But today things are no longer as smooth for the US in the ILO as they were before. Soviet re-entry into the ILO is threatening US influence not only inside the Organization, but also in the eyes of the working class of the world.

In the words of a Soviet commentator "the entry of the Soviet Union into, and the active participation of socialist countries in, the ILO which meant the end of the monopoly of countries of the capitalist system in the representation inside the ILO and of the largest capitalist countries in the direction of the affairs of the ILO created, ipso facto, legal possibilities for the development within the framework of the ILO of actual international cooperation in questions coming within the competence of the Organization, i.e. in questions pertaining to the improvement of the conditions of labour, the life and the protection of the rights of the working masses".[108]

While we welcome the entry of the Soviet Union into the ILO, it must be stated, however, that we do not share the unrealistically optimistic view expressed by Shkunaev in the above passage. Soviet admission into the Organization certainly does not in itself remove the obstacles to international cooperation which existed in the ILO prior to this time. In fact, one would say that such entry even would tend to inflame an already bad enough situation—the Soviet delegation was expected to come in with its ideological baggage and this was bound to meet with very strong opposition from the Western delegations thus creating a most unfavourable atmosphere for international cooperation in matters that come within the competence of the ILO.

Expectedly, the US sought to resist this unpleasant phenomenon by marshalling the anti-communist forces both inside and outside the Organization to undercut the Soviets. In some US circles the idea was even being voiced that the US should pull out of the ILO. This challenge to US leadership and the resultant US fear of growing communist influence inside the ILO was heightened when a Soviet Assistant Director-General of the ILO was appointed by the newly installed British-born Director-General of the Organization.[109] The situation is a very awkward one. After twenty-two years of very distinguished service as Director-General of the ILO David A. Morse, a US citizen, was succeeded in May 1970 by C. Wilfred Jenks who immediately went ahead and appointed a Soviet citizen to this 8th most important post in the Organization. As an Assistant Director-General of the ILO Mr. Pavel Astapenko was to head the Department concerned with social security and maritime and other affairs. This latter appointment immediately sparked off an anti-Soviet reaction in the

US Congress. On July 31, 1970 Congressman John E. Rooney of New York, asserting that "this bird Jenks thinks that he has inherited the ILO lock, stock and barrel...",[110] concluded that "Mr. Jenks needs to be rocked. I know of only one way to rock him, cut off his water."[111]

Certainly not willing to keep this a secret from Mr. Jenks, Mr. Rooney suggested that the Assistant Secretary of State for International Affairs telephone the Chief of US Mission in Geneva, "Ambassador Rimestad and tell him to hootfoot it over to Mr. Jenks and tell him before nightfall that there will be no money for the ILO..."[112] The appointment of a Soviet representative was, in Mr. Rooney's view "the last straw".[113] Not only was it the contention of Mr. George Meaney, the President of the AFL-CIO, that the Soviet Union was becoming disproportionately influential in the Organization, but, as he put it, "it is quite obvious that the (International Labour) Office is, and has been for some time, in the Russians' corner."[114]

After a heated debate in both chambers of the US Congress, the Senate-House Conference Committee and the House of Representatives finally voted to "cut off the water" from the ILO by suspending any further US contributions to the Organization.[115] As if not satisfied with this move, the Senate Appropriations Committee, led by Senator John L. McClellan, decided to recommend that "the proper legislative Committee review the continued participation of the United States in this Organization."[116]

Stephen M. Schwebel was voicing the concern of many observers of the ILO scene when he wrote: "What is clear in this assault by the US Congress on the ILO [the US Congress through its resolution had decided to cut off further funds for the Organization] is that a sense of proportion, of intelligent and practical purpose, of legality, has been lamentably lacking. It is to be hoped that this gross display of international insensitivity and illegality would have been reversed by the time these comments appear in the print; the longer it is prolonged, the greater will be the damage to the ILO; to international law and organization, and to the interests of the United States".[117]

In conclusion we might attempt a summary of what we consider the principal Soviet aims and objectives inside the International Labour Organization:

First, the Soviet Union sees the ILO as an international platform from which to present its policy of peaceful coexistence with the West, and, in fact, looks upon its participation in this Organization as a practical demonstration of the "successes" of this policy;

Second, the Soviet Union intends to utilize to the maximum the organs of the ILO in its struggle against what it calls "bourgeois-reformist methods of resolving social problems" and for staging its battle against what it calls Western "bourgeois reformist ideology" as a whole;

Third, the Soviet Union sees the ILO as an effective platform from which to reach the heart of the international proletariat and from which to demonstrate to the working classes of the world "the great achievements of socialism" in order to point out to this international proletarian movement as represented here at the ILO by its proletarian aristocracy "the gross superiority of socialist economy over its decadent capitalist counterpart";

Finally, with the considerable increase in the representation of the third world in the ILO,[118] particularly after 1960, the Soviet Union constantly has its eyes on winning over these young nations through its professed solidarity with the aims and aspirations of these countries. Soviet activism[119] while the ILO is discussing issues involving labour conditions in colonial territories is a practical demonstration of this policy.

It is a combination of these political factors which finally made the Soviet Union join the ILO "with the aim of cooperating with other countries in the resolution of those problems which are posed before the (Organization)."[120]

Reviewing the history of the ILO from a dialectical point of view, a leading Soviet expert on the ILO sees the "yesterday" of the ILO as being essentially anti-communist, the "today" of it as representing a practical demonstration of the policy of peaceful coexistence between the relatively balanced forces of the capitalist West and the communist East and, on the basis of such observations, he tends to forecast an inevitable pro-communist or, at least, anti-imperialist "tomorrow" for the Organization.[121]

Whether such a forecast will be vindicated by history is yet to be seen. But at this stage at least one fact is clear to any observer of the ILO scene —this Organization which was conceived by, and born to, anti-communist feelings in the West is developing today under the partial tutelage of those forces which it originally sought to destroy. If the West is to halt this un healthy situation it must fight to win back its lost leadership of the Organization. The West must present the international proletariat with a new menu—not the present one which is filled up with anti-communism, but an entirely new menu calling for a fresh approach to the East-West dilemma. The West must think of opening up some constructive dialogue with the communists. Only under such circumstances can we guarantee to the International Labour Organization any continued existence.

1. Separate invitations to send missions also came from the governments of the Ukrainian and the Belorussian Soviet Socialist Republics which are members of the ILO. The same Mission visited both these Republics and other parts of the Russian Federation.

2. The Mission was made up of members of the Freedom of Association Survey Division. Like the previous Mission to the United States this was headed by Mr. John Price, Chief of the Division and Special Assistant to the Director-General of the ILO. Other members of the Mission included: Mr. Jean Renaud who also was in the earlier Mission to the United States, Miss Anna Fidler and Mr. Victor Ratnavale. Miss Maisie Cross acted as the Mission's Secretary. The Mission was accompanied by Mr. Y. I. Gouk, Counsellor in the International Labour Office. The Mission was immediately followed by a two-week visit to the Soviet Union by the Head of the Mission in August 1960.

3. See "The Trade Union Situation in the United States", ILO, Geneva 1960, pp. 1-6.

4. In particular: The Right of Association (Agriculture) Convention of 1921, No. 11; the Collective Agreements Recommendation of 1951, No. 91; and the Voluntary Conciliation and Arbitration Recommendation of 1951, No. 92.

5. See ILO Official Bulletin, vol. XXXIX, 1956, No. 9.

6. "The Trade Union Situation in the United States", at p. 4.

7. See parag. 2 for a discussion of the controversy over the use of the term "rejoined" to describe Soviet participation in the ILO after 1954.

8. See ILO, "Trade Union Rights in the USSR", Studies and Reports, New Series, No. 49, Geneva, 1959.

9. The Constitution of the USSR in Arts. 4-12 underlines these fundamental departures of the Soviet society from any traditional Western society.

10. See Ustav Profsoiuzov SSSR (Rules of the Trade Unions of the USSR) adopted at the 12th Congress of the AUCCTU, March 27, 1959, Moskva (Profizdat) 1959.

11. See 'Profsoiuzy v SSSR', Bolshaia Sovetskaia Entsiklopediia, Moskva, (2nd. Edition), vol. 35.

12. The theory was probably first put forward by V. I. Lenin in his Draft Party Program drawn up in 1895-1896 and subsequently reiterated in his pamphlet entitled 'Chto Delat'?' (What is to be done?") which was published in 1902. On this question the Bolsheviks fell out with the Mensheviks who were agitating for a British-type politically neutral trade union organization.

13. 'Novyi Shag v Razvitii Sovetskoi Sotsialisticheskoi Demokratii', Peredovaia Stat'ia, 3 SGP 1958.

14. For a historical analysis of the evolution and development of trade union organizations in both tsarist and Soviet Russia see Joseph Freeman, The Soviet Worker, N.Y. 1932, at pp. 103-136.

15. See Postanovlenie TsIK, SNK SSSR i VTsSPS of June 23, 1933: "Ob Ob'edinenii Narodnogo Kommissariata Truda Soiuza SSR so VTsSPS" (On the Unification of the People's Commissariat of Labour with the AUCCTU), Sbornik Zakonov SSSR 1933, No. 40.

16. The right and guarantees granted under the Constitution of the USSR are accorded only to citizens of the USSR with only very few exceptions.

17. The use of the word "nationality" in this context refers only to the various nationalities (there are more than 100 of them) that make up the Soviet Union. This fact is very clearly demonstrated in that section of the Preamble to the Fundamental Principles which says: "In accordance with the Constitution of the USSR citi-

zens (of the USSR) are guaranteed equality in the sphere of labour irrespective of nationality or race. . ." Obviously in this context the law means specifically Soviet nationalities only.

18. It is practically impossible for foreign nationals who may be resident in the Soviet Union to obtain a work permit to be able to work in any Soviet enterprise. This in effect means that the extension of Soviet trade union membership rights to aliens is merely an act of window decoration. Sometimes, it is true, foreign students who are studying in the Soviet Union are invited to become members of the various local chapters of the trade union organization just to demonstrate "the right of foreigners in the Soviet Union".

In view of such observations one really does not know what Boguslavskii and Rubanov meant when they asserted that "foreigners resident within the USSR, just like Soviet citizens, have a right to work . . . all foreigners who are willing to work (in the Soviet Union) can always find adequate application of their knowledge and know-how in a job of their specific qualification and special training". See I. M. Boguslavskii and A. A. Rubanov, Pravovoe Polozhenie Innostrantsev v SSSR (The Legal Status of Foreigners in the USSR), Moskva 1962 at p. 95.

The authors, however, do not hesitate to add that there are certain jobs in the USSR that are specifically reserved for Soviet citizens, e.g. under the provision of Art. 19 of the Soviet (Federal) Air Code only citizens of the USSR can be employed as crew members of all airlines registered in the Soviet Union. Similarly, the Soviet Commercial Maritime Navigation Code specifically reserves the jobs of ship captain, his assistants, chief engineer, radio man on any Soviet ships to Soviet citizens only, whereas under the provision of Art. 41 of this Code (Navigation) "only citizens of the USSR may be members of the ship's crew" but "exceptions to this rule may be made in accordance with the procedure to be established by the USSR Council of Ministers".

For restrictions on the fishing rights of foreigners in Soviet waters see Federal Decree of October 15, 1958—Law on the Preservation of the fish resources and the regulation of fishing in Soviet waters", Sbornik Postanovlenii SSSR, 1958 No. 16.

Furthermore, a strict interpretation of Art. 3 of the Model Collective Farm Charter ("any citizen [of the USSR] who has reached the age of 16 and expresses the desire to participate through his labour in the communal sector of the collective farm may be a member of the collective farm") would suggest that only Soviet citizens may join these collective farms. Only Art. 12 of the Principles of Legislation of the USSR and the Union Republics on Public Health (PRAVDA, Dec. 20, 1969) comes nearest to a formal equation of the rights of foreigners and Soviet citizens inside the USSR to seek employment in the medical profession. Parag. 2, Art. 12 of the Health Principles stipulates that "Foreign citizens or stateless persons permanently residing in the USSR who have received special training at and a degree from an appropriate higher or specialised secondary educational institution in the USSR may engage in the practice of medicine or pharmacy on the territory of the USSR in accordance with their specialty and the degree received".

But since the right to practice medicine in the USSR cannot be realised unless one seeks and receives a job with a medical institution (and all such institutions are state-owned), there will be nothing left of this "right" if such employment is denied to the holder of such certificates.

Other professions in the Soviet Union have similar reservation clauses. All such restrictive practices as imposed by the various "professional codes" would lead one to the conclusion that whereas the few foreigners that are permitted to take up residence in the USSR possess the right to seek employment and practice their professions as was rightly pointed out by Boguslavskii and Rubanov, this "right" in actual practice becomes so truncated and castrated by these various professional reservation clauses that any similarity between this "right" and that of a Soviet citizen is only apparent. In fact, the caveat entered above by Boguslavskii and Rubanov to the effect that certain jobs are reserved strictly for Soviet citizens constitutes not the exception as the authors would rather have us believe, but the rule in contemporary Soviet Union. Thus, megalomaniac and xenophobic attitudes still remain the chief determinant factors of the extremely paternalistic policy of the Soviet government in this highly sensitive area of Soviet domestic policy.

19. Art. 153 of the Kodeks Zakonov o Trude (The Federal Labour Code) specifically states that "all other unions not registered, in accordance with Art. 152. with an inter-union organ cannot be called trade unions nor can they claim any of the rights reserved for such trade unions".

20. See The Fundamental Principles of Labour Legislation of the USSR, Vedomosti Verkhovnogo Soveta SSSR, No. 29 (1531), July 22, 1970. For a fuller analysis of the provisions of these Fundamental Principles, vide infra.

21. For a discussion of what comes nearest to being an express legal prohibition of the right of Soviet workers to strike, vide supra.

22. See Sobranie Zakonov i Rasporozhenii SSSR, January 23, 1929.

23. This information is contained in the ILO Report on "The Trade Union Situation in the USSR", Geneva 1960 at pp. 63 etc.

24. See Vestnik Truda (Labour Bulletin), 1922, Nos. 11, 12, cited in ILO: "The Trade Union Movement in Soviet Russia", Studies and Reports, Series A, No. 26, Geneva 1927 at p. 170.

25. For example, in December 1938 a Decree of the Council of People's Commissars was published whereby "with a view to the regular supervision of workers and salaried employees in undertakings and institutions" work books (trudovye knishki) were to be issued to all workers and employees. These books contained employment information concerning the worker and were kept by the management and handed to the worker on his leaving the employment. See Sobranie Postanovlenii i Rasporozhenii Pravitel'stva SSSR, No. 58, Dec. 1938.

Similarly, on June 26, 1940 the termination of a contract of employment and change of jobs without the consent of the management were specifically prohibited. Any breach of this Regulation rendered the offender liable to imprisonment, as did unjustified absence from, and late arrival at, work. However, on April 25, 1956 the Presidium of the Supreme Soviet issued a Decree abrogating these instructions. See Vedomosti Verkhovnogo Soveta SSSR, 1956, No. 10.

26. See Vedomosti Verkhovnogo Soveta SSSR, December 25, 1958.

27. See Vedomosti Verkhovnogo Soveta of the Russian Federation, No. 38 (416), Sept. 22, 1966, at p. 819.

28. See ILO Reports: The Trade Union Situation in the USSR, Geneva 1960, at p. 65.

29. A course in Labour Law in a Soviet Law School is broken up into two illustrative divisions—part 1 deals with Soviet Labour Law and Practices, and part 2—with the Labour Law of Bourgeois Countries. The study of the Labour Law of the other socialist countries of Eastern Europe and of the developing countries respectively are tailored into parts 1 and 2 as above.

30. See Sovetskoe Trudovoe Pravo, Izdatel'stvo 'Vysshaia Shkola', Moskva 1965.

31. Ibid. at pp. 426-429.

32. Similarly, all Soviet commentators on the social origins of labour (industrial) disputes attribute this phenomenon to the inherently capitalistic dichotomy between the interests of the capitalist employer and the exploited proletariat. Nevertheless, these commentators concede the undeniable fact that even Soviet industries have not been rid of labour disputes but, of course, in this case the possible causes of such industrial disputes are seen as "the hang-over from capitalism" which the present "Soviet man" has not fully abandoned even though the fact that the private ownership of the means of production and distribution has been liquidated in the

Soviet Union makes these labour disputes "non-antagonistic". See N. G. Aleksandrov et alt., Zakonodatel'stvo o Trude—Kommentarii (A Commentary to the Labour Legislation), Moskva 1953, at pp. 311-312.

33. See ILO: The Trade Union Situation in the USSR, at p. 72.

34. The Soviet trade union organization is practically responsible for operating all the Rest Homes and Sanatoriums throughout the Soviet Unions with the exception of the very top-class Health Resorts which are under the direct control of the Party Secretariat. This, in fact, means that if a Soviet citizen wishes to obtain a trade union subsidised 'putiovka' to any of these Rest Homes, he must be a member of the trade union organization or else he will be left with the unpleasant option of paying a prohibitive price for such a ticket.

Other fringe benefits accrueing from Soviet trade union membership include: union backing for a member's application for an exit visa, trade union subsidised social security payments to members, easy loan rasing in case of extreme emergency, etc.

35. The present Soviet trade union boss, Mr. Shelepin is a former Director of the Committee on State Security (KGB) whereas his immediate predecessor in office, Mr. V. V. Grishin is currently the First Secretary of the Moscow City Committee of the CPSU—a very powerful chapter within the entire Communist Party organization. Both Mr. Shelepin and Mr. Grishin are members of the recently enlarged 15-man Politbureau of the CPSU as elected at the 24th Party Congress in April 1971.

36. The First All-Russian Trade Union Congress which met in Petrograd in January 1918 demanded, among other things, obligatory participation in trade union organizations for all persons engaged in any given industry, but beginning in Feb. 1922 a campaign was inaugurated for placing trade union membership entirely on a voluntary basis. Trade unionists were given the freedom to decide whether or not they wished to remain members of the trade unions and to pay individual contribution. About 95 per cent of the members voted in favour of rejoining the trade unions on this new basis. The principle of optional membership of the trade unions eventually found its way into the second Labour Code of 1922. Vide supra.

37. It is no secret, for example, that when a Soviet citizen applies for an exit visa even to a neighbouring socialist country his standing in the trade union organization of his regular place of employment or study is taken into consideration in reaching any decision as to his or her eligibility for such visa and since the Otdel' Viz i Registratsii (OVIR)—the Visa Division of the Soviet People's Militia—generally does not give reasons for refusing to grant such visas the case remains closed once refused.

38. See Slogans for the 51st Anniversary of the Great October Revolution, adopted by the Central Committee of the CPSU, Item 14, PRAVDA, Oct. 13, 1968.

39. See LNTS vol. 4, No. 34.

40. For fuller details vide infra.

41. For a historical survey of League-Soviet relationship, vide supra.

42. V. G. Shkunaev: Mezhdunarodnaia Organizatsiia Truda—Vchera i Segodnia, (The International Labour Organization—Yesterday and Today) Moskva 1968.

43. Ibid. at p. 8.

44. V. G. Shkunaev: Ibid. at pp. 14-15.

45. V. I. Lenin: Polnoe Sobranie Sochenenii (Complete Works) vol. 20 (4th Russian Edition) at p. 67.

46. The reformist leaders singled out by the author include the following: E. Banderveld whom he describes as "one of the leaders of the second International and a leading social-opportunist"; S. Hompers, "a dedicated enemy of the international solidarity of workers who until his death was even opposed to such re-

formist union like the Amsterdam International of Trade Unions"; L. Juo, "an active supporter of the reactionary principle of independent trade unions, i.e. non-participation of trade unions in political struggles"; G. Barnes, "a former trade union activist and later became a member of the British war cabinet". All these individuals, in the opinion of the author, were traitors to the International Workers' Movement and, therefore, their association with the formation of the ILO was in itself enough to alienate the Soviet Union from such an Organization. See V. G. Shkunaev, M.O.T.—Vchera i Segodnia, at pp. 18-19.

47. V. G. Shkunaev: Ibid. at p. 16.

48. See Official Bulletin of the International Labour Office, vol. 1, 1923 at pp. 490, 502.

49. V. I. Lenin: Polnoe Sobranie Sochenenii, vol. 40 (4th Russian Edition), p. 160.

50. See ILO Conference, 6th Session, 1924 at pp. 47, 48, and 640.

51. Right from 1919 until 1934 when the United States finally decided to join the ILO the Organization was dominated by the British—most of the top executive posts went to British subjects and the guiding philosophy of the Organization was fundamentally British in orientation. Between 1919 and this day the ILO has had more British Directors-General than all other countries put together have ever had.

52. The gradual drift away from this Eurocentrism by the Organization to embrace other non-European countries was noted by the Director-General of the ILO in his Report in 1938. See Report of the Director, International Labour Office, 1938, at pp. 22, 71, etc.

53. It should be pointed out, however, that this original concept of British trade unionism has long been abandoned even in Britain itself where the trade unions continue to act as the power base for the British Labour Party.

54. V. G. Shkunaev: M.O.T.-Vchera i Segodnia, Moskva 1968 at pp. 3-4.

55. V. G. Shkunaev: Ibid. at p. 4.

56. It should be pointed out, however, that Soviet commentators reject this idea of automatic membership of the Soviet Union in the ILO. For example, commenting on the issue, V. G. Shkunaev writes that "in this connection it should be mentioned that the Soviet Union specifically joined the League of Nations and not the ILO. While joining the LN there was no official statement by the Soviet government with regard to its relationship with the ILO. Besides, in June 1935 when the government delegate of the USSR participated in the working of the 19th Session of the ILO General Conference he declared that the Soviet government is presently studying the activities of the ILO without participating in any active form in its function". See V. G. Shkunaev: Op. cit. at p. 129.

Most other Soviet authors, while referring to Soviet admission into the ILO in 1954, use terms which suggest initial admission rather than a re-admission.

57. Soviet participation in the ILO at this time was limited and sporadic. She attended but five of the seven conferences during its membership and she sent full delegations to only three of these. The Soviet Union sent a representative to the Governing Body of the ILO though his attendance was highly irregular. During this time not only did the Soviet Union not ratify even one convention of the ILO, it just did not make any impact whatsoever on the Organization.

58. Max Beloff, commenting on Soviet participation in the ILO between 1934 and 1939 had this to say: "In contradistinction to its work in the League, however, Soviet participation in ILO activities was minimal and there seems no evidence that the Soviet Union at any time contemplated making their membership of the ILO an avenue toward greater cooperation with the western democracies, as was hoped by some British labour circles. And it does not appear to have ratified a single convention". Max Beloff: The Foreign Policy of Soviet Russia, (2 vols.) vol. 1, N.Y. 1947 at p. 198.

96

59. See Strictment Confidentiel, B.I.T. Procès-verbaux de la Sixième Seance (Privée) de la 98me Session du Conseil d'Administration, L., 3-5 Fevr. 1940, p. 46.

60. Quoted by Max Beloff: Op. cit at p. 198.

61. V. G. Shkunaev: M.O.T., Moskva 1968 at p. 136.

62. See C.I.T. Dix-neuvième Session, Rapport du Directeur, 1935, p. 75.

63. V. G. Shkunaev: Op. cit. at p. 136.

64. Vide supra.

65. See Max Beloff: The Foreign Policy of Soviet Russia (2 vols), vol. 1, N.Y. 1947; Charles P. Prince: The USSR and International Organizations, 36 AJIL 1942; H. K. Jacobson: The USSR and the ILO, International Organization 1960, No. 3; etc.

66. See V. G. Shkunaev: (The ILO—Yesterday and Today) M.O.T.-Vchera i Segodnia, Moskva 1968; E. A. Shibaeva: Spetsializirovannye Uchrezhdeniia OON, Moskva 1967; V. Vladimirov, M.O.T., Moskva 1959; etc.

67. The unpleasant experience with the interpretation of Art. 387 of the Treaty of Versailles vis-à-vis Soviet membership of the Organization probably played a leading role in the subsequent rejection of the concept of automatic membership in the amended version of the ILO Constitution.
Parag. 3, Art. 1 of the new ILO Constitution states: "any original member of the UN and any state admitted to membership of the UN by a decision of the General Assembly in accordance with the provisions of the Charter may become a member of the ILO by communicating to the Director-General of the International Labour Office its formal acceptance of the obligations of the Constitution of the ILO". There is no doubt that this is a better admission policy than the one that was contained in Art. 387 of the Treaty of Versailles.

68. Original Soviet hostility towards the ILO re-appeared during the UNCIO in San-Francisco in 1945. The British suggestion that the ILO be specifically mentioned in the UN Charter drew heavy attack from the Soviet Union. The Soviets even refused to include in the Rapporteur's Report a statement recognising the ILO as a Specialised Agency of the United Nations. The Soviet Union vehemently objected to the suggestion that the ILO should participate in the ECOSOC, the Trusteeship Council, to present its views before the General Assembly, or even to request the Advisory Opinion of the ICJ. See UNCIO Docs. vols. 1-15, San-Francisco, 1945.

69. V. G. Shkunaev: M.O.T. at p. 144. Most Soviet authors often quote that section of Lenin's statement in which he exhorted communists to partipate actively even in "reactionary trade unions and in bourgeois parliaments" if this will in any way serve their ultimate purpose. See V. I. Lenin. "Left Wing Communism, An Infantile Disorder", Moscow, Foreign Languages Publishing House 1950. For further details on Lenin's strategy of communist participation in bourgeois parliaments. See our "Conclusion" below.

70. On April 26, 1954 the Soviet Union, having accepted the obligations flowing from the Constitution of the Organization, became a member of the ILO. This step was followed by the Ukraine and Belorussia who also became members of the Organization on May 12, 1954. In a government statement released on the occasion of Soviet Union joining the ILO it was stated that such a move was taken "with the aim of widening cooperation with other countries in the solution of these questions posed before the ILO". See 'PRAVDA' Nov. 6, 1953.

71. V. G. Shkunaev is not just a leading Soviet authority on the ILO but, perhaps, the only contemporary Soviet jurist to devote an entire monograph to the legal problems of ILO. Vide infra.

72. V. G. Shkunaev, Op. cit. at p. 140.

73. We may at this point recall that Joseph Stalin died of a stroke on March 5, 1953 at 9.30 p.m. at the age of 73.

74. In the same letter the Soviet Union stated that, as she had always stressed in the past, she considered it necessary to alter the present structure of representation in the ILO in order to grant more votes to representatives of Trade Unions in ILO organs.

75. Commenting on the desirability of Soviet entry into the Organization, G. de Lusignan wrote that such Soviet presence in the ILO is not only desirable but also would be necessary if the Organization is to attain the universality proclaimed in its Constitution. See G. de. Lusignan, L'Organisation Internationale du Travail (1919-1959), Paris 1959, p. 37.

76. Tripartism and universality are the two fundamental principles of the ILO but whereas universality was a principle also applicable to other international organizations, tripartism remains a special peculiarity of the ILO. Soviet commentators have often viewed the concept of tripartism as being founded on an anti-Marxist and reformist idea of cooperation between labour and capital and aimed at diverting the attention of the working class from its primary interest—class struggle. Thus, we find that whereas most Western scholars looked upon ILO tripartism as a plausible innovation. (See P. Walline, 'La Crise de l'Organisation Internationale du Travail'. Revue des deux Mondes, Paris 1. VIII, 1959, p. 479; see also B. Béguin: Le tripartisme dans l'O.I.T., Genève 1959, p. 5; G. Fischer, La Caractère Tripartite de l'Organisation, AFDI 1955, p. 377), Soviet commentators look upon this institution with an evil eye. See S. A. Ivanov, Voprosy Predstavitel'stva v Mezhdunarodnoi Organizatsii Truda, SEMP 1961 at pp. 266-267.

77. Vide supra.

78. Vide supra.

79. In fact, the Employers' Representative noted that the existing ILO Constitution had permitted the appointment of a representative "of socialised management when the USSR was a member of the Organization... If the USSR resumed membership of the Organization and the Employers' representatives shared the general desire that it should do so, it would naturally appoint as Employers' delegate a representative of the socialised management of the USSR". See ILO Conference Report 11 (I) 1946, 29th Session, Constitutional Questions, pp. 358-359.

80. Most Western societies, under the fear of a possible communist infiltration into the trade union movements, pass laws which proscribe such communist-front labour unions.

81. Vide supra.

82. As of January 1, 1970 the ILO had adopted 130 conventions whereas the number of recommendations as of 1967 (51st Session) stood at 131.

83. See: "ILO Conventions—Table of Ratifications, Jan. 1, 1970", ILO Geneva 1970. The Ukraine and Belorussia have each ratified 27 and 26 respectively as of January 1, 1970.

84. Our criterion for determining the popularity of a convention is the number of ratifications it has received so far. The ten most popular conventions as of Jan. 1, 1970 are: convention No. 29—Forced Labour, 105 ratifications; No. 98—Right to Organise and Collective Bargaining, 90 ratifications; No. 105–Abolition of Forced Labour, 88 ratifications; No. 11—Right of Association (Agriculture), 87 ratifications; No. 19—Equality of Treatment (Accident Compensation), 85 ratifications; No. 14—Weekly Rest (Industry) and No. 26—Minimum Wage-Fixing Machinery, as well as No. 87—Freedom of Association and Protection of the Right to Organise, each with 77 ratifications; and No. 111—Discrimination (Employment and Occupation), 71 ratifications.

85. See Vedomosti Verkhovnogo Soveta SSSR, No. 29 (1531) of July 22, 1970, Zakon No. 265 at pp. 349-350. The new Fundamental Principles of Labour Legislation of the USSR came into effect on Jan. 1, 1971. See Art. 1 of the Federal Edict. Ibidem. For a full English translation of the Fundamental Principles, see

The Current Digest of the Soviet Press, vol. XXII, No. 34, Sept. 22, 1970.

86. In the analysis that follows we shall use the term "Fundamental Principles" to refer to the new Soviet Fundamental Principles on Labour Legislation of the USSR.

87. The FZMK—Fabrichnoi Zavodskoi Mestnyi Komitet Profsoiuza (The Factory-Plant Local Committee of the Trade Union).

88. Vide supra.

89. Date of coming into force: June 23, 1951.

90. The Convention was revised in 1952 and came into force on Sept. 7, 1955.

91. The Russian formulation of the law itself is not very clear as to what the phrase "to that effect" refers—either to the fact of her pregnancy or to the necessity for a transfer to a lighter job. We, however, would interprete the provision to mean "to the effect of her pregnancy" as this would lead us to the conclusion that any medically certified pregnancy automatically imposes the necessity for a transfer of the pregnant worker to a lighter job.

92. For fuller analysis vide supra.

93. In 1957 the Soviet government delegation introduced a draft resolution on the lifting of all anti-trade union legislations in all member-states. See International Labour Conference, 140th Session, 1957 at p. 622; and in 1956 the Ukrainian delegate introduced a draft resolution calling for a removal of all discriminatory practices in wages based on sex. See I.L. Conference, 39th Session. 1956 at pp. 463, 593-600.

94. The Ukrainian Republic participates in five such committees: Inland Transport, Coal Mines, Iron and Steel, Metal Trades, and Building, Civil Engineering and Public Works; whereas the Belorussian Republic is a member of only one—the Committee on Metal Trades.

95. This was replaced by a new Convention (No. 97)—Migration for Employment adopted at the 32nd Session of the International Labour Conference.

96. The Soviet Union contributes 10% of the ILO budget; Ukraine Republic—1%; and the Belorussian Republic—0.45%, thus giving the USSR a gross total of 11.45% of ILO annual budget.

97. H. K. Jacobson: "The USSR and the ILO", International Organization 1960, No. 3 at p. 425.

98. H. K. Jacobson: Ibid. at p. 426.

99. Vide H. K. Jacobson, Op. cit. at p. 426.

100. Between 1934 and 1939 the Soviet Union participated in the deliberations of five ILO Conferences and she was very active in the adoption of 13 draft conventions which yielded the following results: convention No. 47—Forty Hour Week, No. 52—Holidays with Pay, No. 58-60—Minimum Age at Sea, Minimum Age in Industry, and Minimum Age in Non-Industrial Employment.

101. The Soviets had consistently charged that the ILO Office is dominated by citizens of Western nations particularly of British, French and US origins and they always point to the fact that since 1919 only citizens of this rulling triumvirate have alternatively held the office of Director-General of the Organization. The present Director-General of the ILO, Mr. C. Wilfred Jenks is a British subject.

102. See H. K. Jacobson: "The USSR and the ILO", International Organization, 1960 No. 3, at p. 427. A similar negative attitude to the admission of the Soviet Union into the ILO was adopted by P. Walline who expressed the fear that Soviet entry into the Organization would destroy the tripartite nature of the Organization. See P. Walline, 'La Crise de l'Organisation Internationale du Travail', Revue des deux Mondes, Paris 1. VIII, 1959 at p. 479.

103. As a matter of fact Soviet commentators have always argued that no international organization can afford to steer clear of international politics. Politics is introduced into these organizations either in the form of state representatives par-

ticipating in the organs of these organizations (if they represent states, which they do, they must act as the executors of state policies inside such organizations). See G. I. Tunkin: 119 Hague Recueil 1966-III; or in the form of questions which are constantly being resolved by these international bodies. See E. A. Shibaeva, Spetsializirovannye Uchrezhdeniia OON, Moskva 1966.

104. See International Labour Conference, 39th Session 1956 at p. 594.

105. See International Labour Conference, 40th Session 1957, at p. 626.

106. See International Labour Conference, 41st Session 1958, at p. 215.

107. See International Labour Conference, 45th Session, 1961 at pp. 720-721; also the 64th Session, 1962, at pp. 674-675.

108. V. G. Shkunaev: M.O.T.—Vchera i Segodia, Moskva 1968 at p. 122. The author mentions that in the early post-war years only the delegates of Poland and Czechoslovakia participated regularly in the work of the ILO. Ibid. at p. 122.

109. One of the five Assistant Directors-General of the ILO is Mr. Pavel E. Astapenko of the Belorussian Soviet Socialist Republic.

110. Hearings before a Sub-Committee of the Committee on Appropriations, House of Representatives. 91st Congress, 2nd Session, "Additional Testimony on the ILO", p. 79.

111. Ibid. at p. 69.

112. Ibid. at p. 76.

113. Ibid. at pp. 59, 66.

114. Ibid. at p. 75.

115. The United States is responsible for 25% of the Organization's annual budget. The Senate Appropriations Committee voted by 49 to 22 with 29 abstentions to delete funds for the ILO. The Senate-House Conference Committee and the House of Representatives respectively upheld the deletion some three weeks after the Soviet Assistant Director-General took office in Sept. 1970. See Congressional Record, House Oct. 6, 1970 at H 9622-9633. Thus an ILO assault which began in the Sub-Committee of the Committee on Appropriations (House of Representatives, 91st Congress, 2nd Session) culminated in the adoption of this openly anti-ILO resolution by the Congress of the United States.

116. See Congressional Record, Senate August 24, 1970 at S 14103. For an analysis of the legal and political implications of such US action see Stephen M. Schwebel, "The United States assaults the ILO", 65 AJIL Jan. 1971, No. 1 at pp. 136-142.

117. Stephen M. Schwebel, Ibid. at p. 142. By the time the article appeared in print (January 1971) there was yet no change in the US position on the question as presented above.

118. By the end of the second world war there were only four African members in the ILO, but by 1966 there were already 35 of them whereas Asian membership of the Organization for the same period rose from 7 to 22. Similarly, by 1966 all independent Latin-American states were members of the ILO.

119. It may be recalled that the Soviet Union was highly instrumental in mobilising forces within the Organization to strike down the so-called "colonial clause" (Art. 35) of the ILO Constitution. This article granted to the metropolitan powers the option of not applying any conventions ratified by them to their colonial territories. The article was eventually amended in 1964. By such scattered actions the Soviet Union gradually built up for itself the image of a "protector of the interests of the colonial and oppressed peoples". For a detailed analysis of the practical application of this clause to the advantage of the metropolitan powers, see S. A. Ivanov, Primenenie Mezhdunarodnykh Konventsii o Trude, SEMP 1958 at pp. 446-451.

120. See PRAVDA, Nov. 6, 1953.

121. See V. G. Shkunaev, M.O.T.–Vchera i Segodnia, Moskva 1968, pp. 241-242.

Chapter Three

THE SOVIET UNION AND THE WORLD HEALTH ORGANIZA-
TION (WHO)

Introductory Remarks

"Law is not merely a fact of social life; it is also a body of ideas. Implic-
it in legal concepts and often explicit in them as well, are theories of human personality. Moreover, both through de facto operation and through
its concepts and theories, law—like psychiatry—seeks to influence human
personality. In helping to maintain social order, law at the same time and
by the same token helps to maintain the mental health of the individual
members of the society."[1] If national laws, viewed through their therapeu-
tic and psychological functions, are effective instruments for influencing
the health of any given nation, so also are international health conventions which in their operation, unlike national laws however, are intended
to cover a wide cross section of the international community of nations.

Just as the creation of the ILO in 1919 was the first bold step towards
the institution of a mechanism for international labour legislation, so the
establishment of the WHO represented also the boldest transnational attempt to "legislate" on the health of the world community at large. The
founding fathers of the WHO sought through the instrumentality of this
new organization to try to standardise health services throughout the
world.

But as we shall notice later on in this chapter the establishment of the
WHO in 1948 was not the first successful attempt by the concerned international society of nations to internationalise health regulations. Before
this time there had been at least two relatively successful attempts to do
exactly this. That the creation of the WHO drew heavily upon the scanty
experiences of these forerunners cannot be gainsaid. But while the drafters
of the Constitution of 1946 transplanted into the new instruments certain
institutions of the predecessor organizations, they refused to inherit any of
the 'hereditas damnosa' of these earlier organizations. In this context the
WHO represents some marked improvement upon the weak mechanisms
of the predecessor organizations even though she directly inherited the
aims and objectives which these other organizations sought to achieve,
viz, the improvement of world public health.

In the succeeding paragraph we shall try to analyse from a historical perspective the evolution and gradual development of international cooperation in health matters—a process which began in the second half of the 19th century and culminated in the adoption of the Constitution of the WHO in the mid-20th century. In all of these efforts law has proved to be an effective instrument. Either in the form of international health conventions, international health regulations or national health statutes, law has consistently served mankind in its efforts to promote a healthier world. It is this marriage between international law and international public health as performed on the altar of international politics that will constitute our main concern throughout this chapter.

Par. 1. *The evolution of the World Health Organization*

For the first time in the history of mankind the question of international cooperation in the field of public health was raised over a hundred years ago in connection with the then widespread epidemics of plague (black death), cholera and yellow fever. The untold misery which these diseases brought upon many countries and sometimes upon whole continents forced various governments and local authorities to take measures aimed at protecting their local populations from these infections—these included the establishment of sanitary posts along the frontiers, the setting up of quarantine stations and the isolation of a whole population area. Floating vessels that were suspected of carrying infected persons were not allowed to come to the harbour and the penalty for violation of any of these prophylactic measures sometimes included death sentences. But, unfortunately, not in all cases were these measures successful.

The danger of contacting these infectious diseases particularly hung over those European traders who had to sail out to far countries in Asia. Thus, the original aim of an international cooperation in the field of international public health was to protect these European traders from contacting deadly diseases. For this end it was decided to convene an international conference. The conference opened in Paris on 23rd July, 1851 with 12 countries represented.[2] After many months of hot discussions the Conference adopted the draft of the First International Sanitary Convention which was signed, ad referendum, by all the 24 delegates on Jan. 16, 1852. But after 5 months from the time of the signature ad referendum, only 5 countries had finally signed the Convention while only France and Sardinia ever ratified it. However, despite the fact that the Convention did not receive enough positive reactions from the various states, it should be noted that the Paris Convention of 1851 represented a landmark in the field of international cooperation in health matters.

In 1859 a second International Health Conference gathered in Paris at which a second International Convention was drawn up. But this Convention, like the first, did not get off the ground. However, at this Conference only diplomats represented their various governments—a fact which made the decisions of the Conference medically unsound.

The third International Conference took place in Constantinople and it lasted for seven months but the technical agreements reached at the Conference, like all previous agreements in this line, atrophied.

The crucial point was the fourth International Health Conference which met in Vienna on July 1, 1874. At the suggestion of the French delegate the Conference adopted a Resolution to set up a Permanent International Commission on Epidemy with a seat in Vienna. The Commission was to be made up of highly qualified physicians duly appointed by their respective governments and its decisions were to be strictly limited to technical questions to the complete exclusion of political issues.

At the fifth International Sanitary Conference in Washington (1881) a decision was taken to set up yet a new permanent Organization—a Permanent International Sanitary Information Agency (PISIA) with centers both in Vienna and in Havana. The agencies were charged with the dissemination of sanitary and epidemiological information received from countries of Europe, Asia and Africa. A center was to be set up in Asia at a later date.[3]

It should be noted that all the international efforts in this field up till this time, i.e. up till the end of the 19th cent., were limited to the particular problem of combating the spread of plague or cholera into Europe. In view of the limited knowledge of the medical nature of these diseases, it can only be said that the results of these international efforts were minimal. However, by the beginning of the 20th century medical science had acquired enormous knowledge in the field of epidemiology and microbiology to make the 11th International Sanitary Conference of 1903 a revolutionary success in this aspect.

The Conference which convened in Paris not only reviewed all the existing international sanitary conventions, but also drew up a new convention of its own—the International Sanitary Convention of 1903. The most important decision of this Paris Conference was the setting up of the first international health organization—The International Bureau of Public Hygiene (IBPH). The principal function of this new Bureau was to grant moral, i.e. non-material, help to member states without attempting to interfere in their respective domestic affairs. The new Bureau was to advise member states on methods of combatting epidemic diseases and to coordinate their efforts in this respect.

The constituent instrument of the new Organization was adopted at the 12th International Sanitary Conference in Rome in 1907 and was signed by 12 states (out of which 9 were European). In the final analysis, about 60 other states acceded to this instrument thus bringing the membership of the Organization to over 70 at this time. The primary functions of the IBPH as provided in Arts. 4 and 5 of its Statute were: to gather and make available to member states facts and documents concerning public health, especially information on such epidemic diseases as plague, cholera and yellow fever; to advise on methods of combatting these diseases, to propose amendments to the existing international sanitary conventions as well as to draw up new drafts for future international conventions. Thus, we find that its functions were essentially promotional.

For the first 40 years of its existence (1907-1947) it served principally as an information center for the coordination of health information and achieved only very little success in the sphere of international health legislation. The Soviet Union joined the IBPH in 1926 after which time she agreed to send delegations to subsequent IBPH Conferences.

However, the monopoly of the IBPH in the coordination of information on public health was broken when a new international health organization was set up after the first world war—the Health Organization of the League of Nations (HOLN). The legal basis for the foundation of the new Organization was Art. XXIII(f) of the Covenant of the League of Nations in which the members of the League pledged their determination "to take steps in matters of international concern for the prevention and control of disease."[4]

The original intention of trying to bring the IBPH under the aegis of the League of Nations and thus converting it into the central organ of a new international organization as was envisaged in Art. XXIII(f) of the Covenant of the League of Nations was thwarted by US opposition—the US was not prepared to cooperate with any international organization that was to be placed under the direction of the League of Nations bearing in mind, of course, the fact that the US itself was not a member of the League of Nations. This friction between the US, the LN and the IBPH led to the formation of an independent organization by the LN for the purpose of carrying out the ideas set out in the Covenant of the League of Nations. Thus, we now had two rival international health organizations.

The rivalry, however, between these two organizations was minimised when in 1923 a Joint Commission comprising representatives of both the LN and the IBPH agreed to work out some cooperation arrangements 'inter se'—the Standing Committee of the IBPH was to act as the General Consultative Council on Health Questions to the LN, other Health Committees of the LN were to seat representatives of the IBPH. As time progressed closer cooperation was established between the LN and the IBPH but all the same the two organizations—the International Bureau of Public Hygiene (IBPH) and the Health Organization of the League of Nations (HOLN) continued to exist independently along parallel lines.

As was expected the HOLN inherited all the inherent Soviet antipathy towards the League of Nations as, in the view of many Soviet commentators, this "Health Organization of the League of Nations incorporated in itself all the deficiencies which characterised the League of Nations as a whole. This Organization to a great extent was a political instrument of the large imperalist powers. . ."[5]

However, it is equally important to note that the HOLN had more ambitious aims than the IBPH ever had—the aim was not just to disseminate information on certain epidemic diseases, but to combat these diseases at their place of origin. It sought to carry its activities into those disease-infected regions of Asia—much effort was to be devoted to the training of more qualified medical personnel for these areas, a Far-Eastern Bureau was opened in Singapore for the conduct of the fight against epidemic diseases and the Organization published periodic reports on the epidemic situation throughout the world. The HOLN not only had a more ambitious program than the IBPH, but also it had more funds to meet these grandiose ends.

During the grim days of the second world war the activities of these two organizations ground to a virtual standstill. They both proved helpless in the face of the great challenges of the war. They subsequently atrophied—a fact which immediately led to the quest for a more effective and immediate replacement. The state of the world's health had been aggravated by the horrors of the second world war—there was hunger, malnutrition and disease in addition to the high demand for mass evacuation operations of populations from one place to another. These and a host of other related factors called for the creation of an immediate international health organization. The battle for a new organization at this stage automatically shifted to the United Nations Conference in San Francisco.

We may attempt a summary of the foregoing survey of pre-1945 international efforts to promote world health by saying that all such attempts had certain peculiarities common to them all—the first obvious peculiarity of them all was the avid Eurocentrism that lay at the bottom of all the efforts. The driving force behind all such moves was the high priority interest in keeping these diseases out of Europe. The Europeans were not really interested, or at least did not show any such interest, in helping these unfortunate Asians to overcome these diseases. It was this Eurocentic consideration that forced the trading nations of Europe to think of some joint efforts to combat the "Asian disease" from infesting Europe.

The second characteristic feature of these efforts was that there was no intention to impose any form of superior authority on the various European states in these health matters. Since the aim was not to combat these diseases in Europe (obviously these diseases had not been introduced into Europe at this time), but rather to try to keep them out of Europe, these joint international efforts were strictly limited to making such recommendations that member states felt could be effective in achieving the declared goals. There was no attempt whatsoever to resort to any form of international legislation at this stage.

Therefore, with the outbreak and the conclusion of the second world war new health hazards arose both in Europe and in other parts of the world. This time the guiding principles of pre-1945 international cooperation in health matters no longer could serve the interest of mankind. There was an urgent need to replace pre-war Eurocentrism with some form of extra-European philosophy to guide any new organization. At this stage there was a genuine concern for the state of world health—there was a determination to stamp out diseases in all the corners of the world and not just an attempt to restrain these diseases to those areas where they already existed. In the face of this urgent task some form of quasi-international legislation was not only desirable but also necessary. The creation of the WHO was a genuine attempt to embody these two new principles in one Organization.[6]

The great breakthrough: the creation of the WHO

When in the summer of 1946 (July 22) representatives[7] of 61 nations (including observers from Germany, Japan and Korea) signed into being the Constitution of a World Health Organization in the City of New York, they were not only putting into effect the great ideas which were first hatched at the San Francisco Conference (UNCIO) of 1945,[8] but they were also establishing a landmark in the history of international cooperation in the sphere of public health and medicine. The new 'Magna Carta Sanitatis' was certainly a revolutionary breakthrough in the field of international cooperation as far as public health was concerned.

It is interesting to note that among the signatories to all the four instruments adopted at this International Health Conference—the Final Act, the WHO Constitution, the Arrangement for the immediate establishment of an Interim Commission and a Protocol providing for the gradual liquidation of the Office International d'Hygiène Publique—were the USSR, the Belorussian and the Ukrainian Soviet Socialist Republics.[9]

Under the provisions of Art. 5 of the WHO Constitution "the states whose governments have been invited to send observers to the International Health Conference held in New York, 1946 may become members by signing or otherwise accepting this Constitution in accordance with the provisions of Chpt. XIX and in accordance with their constitutional processes provided that such signature or acceptance shall be completed before the first session of the Health Assembly". Accordingly, the Soviet Union became a member of the Organization, having signed the Constitution on March 24, 1948.[10]

Under the provisions of Art. 62, par. 1 of the UN Charter the ECOSOC of the UN "may make or initiate studies and reports with respect to international economic, social, cultural, educational, health and related matters and may make recommendations with respect to any such matters to the General Assembly, to the members of the UN and to the specialised agencies concerned." The first practical materialisation of the powers granted to the UN under this provision is the creation of the WHO—an organization of which the UN can rightly be regarded as the "constitutional father".[11] The fact that the Soviet Union was an active participant in the creation of the UN itself probably explains the initial enthusiasm which the Soviets showed towards this new off-spring of the UN—the WHO.[12]

If, however, the UN may be referred to as the "constitutional father" of the WHO, the League of Nations has been, in our opinion, correctly regarded as the "organic grandfather" of the WHO[13] in the sense that the Report of the Technical Preparatory Committee of Experts which served as the "travaux preparatoires" for the deliberations of the International Health Conference relied heavily on the experiences of the League in health matters.[14]

However, since the link between the WHO and the LN was only remote and indirect, the new Organization did not inherit the traditional hatred which the Soviet Union had towards the League of Nations and towards all subsequent organizations that drew heavily upon the legacy of the League of Nations.[15]

It is equally interesting to note that the new Organization did not content itself merely with the task of carrying forward the accomplishments of all previous international undertakings in the field of public health. On the contrary the new Charter decided to plough new grounds in this field. In the Preamble to the Constitution of the WHO "health" is defined not just as the absence of disease or infirmity, which was all too familiar in those days, but rather as "a state of complete physical, mental and social well-being", the enjoyment of which is "one of the fundamental rights of every human being without distinction of race, religion, political belief, economic or social condition". The attainment by all peoples of the highest possible level of health is set out as the over-all objective of the Organization which based on the philosophy that "germs know no frontiers", that "health is indivisible", and that "germs carry no passports", was intended to work for a universal membership.

The Constitution of the WHO[16] conferred on the Organization a wide range of functions among which are the followings: administrative coordinational, technical and research services, informational, assistance and promotion, and quasi-legislative. Under the provisions of its Constitution the WHO was to direct and coordinate all international health operations. Specifically it was to administer the previous functions of the

Office International d'Hygiène Publique and the UNRRA as assigned to these Institutions under the existing international sanitary conventions. As parts of its functions under this general authorization the WHO was to formulate draft proposals for unifying, strengthening and extending such conventions. The WHO was also to enter into cooperative agreements with other organizations—international or national, inter-governmental or non-governmental—with similar functions.

By far the most important function of the WHO is its quasi-legislative activity under Arts. 19-23 of the Organization's Constitution.[17]

Arts. 19-20 of the Constitution spell out in fuller detail the obligations of member states vis-à-vis any such convention after it has been adopted by the Health Assembly. The obligation here is not like the one we have already noticed above with regard to ILO Conventions.[18] Whereas the ILO sought to provide the framework for an international labour legislation, the WHO made very bold strides towards the formulation of an International Health Code.

Of equal importance are probably the provisions of the WHO Constitution which govern the adoption by the Organization of technical regulations (Art. 21). By simple majority vote the Health Assembly is authorised to formulate regulations on five classes of subjects: sanitary and quarantine requirements; nomenclatures as to diseases, causes of death, and of public health practices; standards as to diagnostic procedures for international use; standards affecting the safety, purity and potency of biological, pharmaceutical and similar products moving in international commerce; and the advertising and labelling of such products.[19]

Under the provisions of Art. 22 of the Constitution "Regulations adopted pursuant to Art. 21 shall come into force for *all* members after due notice has been given of their adoption by the Health Assembly except for such members as may notify the Director-General of rejection or reservations within the period stated in the notice". This is certainly an innovation in international treaty practice and has been aptly described as the principle of "contracting out",[20] i.e. a state is considered to have consented to be bound by the regulation through its tacit acquiescence if it refuses or fails to notify the Director-General of the WHO to the contrary.[21] The innovative significance of this principle of "contracting out" as against the hitherto dominant concept of "contracting in" is almost revolutionary from the point of view of international treaty making.

The regulations adopted by the Assembly apply not only to those member states who have not "contracted out", but also, under certain circumstances, to non-member states of the Organization. The competence of the World Health Assembly to provide for the extension of such norms to non-member states, on their acceptance by the latter, is not expressly stated in the WHO Constitution but may be inferred from the provision of Art. 18 (m) which permits the Assembly "to take any other appropriate action to further the objective of the Organization." The fact that these regulations which were adopted by the WHO on the basis of Arts. 21 and 22 of the WHO Constitution not only are unilateral in nature, but also have full legal force for non-rejecting member states and are intended for general application has led some commentators on the powers of the Organization to conclude that the Assembly of the WHO is endowed with legislative powers in regard to the five subjects enumerated in Art. 21 of the Constitution.[22]

Another important aspect of the WHO that is worth examining is its mechanism for withdrawal from membership of the Organization.

Whereas chapter three of WHO Constitution (Arts. 3-8) regulates the qualifications for becoming a member of the Organization, the Constitution as a whole remains silent on the question of the right of member states to withdraw from the Organization. When the World Health Assembly convened for the first time in 1948 (Palais des Nations, Geneva, June 24, 1948) it was called upon to decide whether a state that had accepted the Constitution subject to an express reservation of the right to terminate its membership on one year's notice might be admitted as a member.[23] The Assembly chose not to debate the legal issues of this question but rather decided to admit the state as a member after receiving a declaration from its Chief delegate as to its intention to grant full support to the aims and objectives of the Organization. Thus, while accepting the US reservation, the Health Assembly in effect permitted the possibility of withdrawal from the Organization without necessarily spelling this out in any greater details. At least this was the implication of the Assembly's decision to accept US reservation.[24]

The question of the right of members to withdraw from an international organization the membership of which they had voluntarily taken upon themselves is far from settled in general international jurisprudence. A school of thought on the issue would argue that membership, once voluntarily accepted, cannot be unilaterally revoked because the act of voluntary acceptance on the part of such a state creates an obligation before the Organization to remain therein except if otherwise provided by the constituent instrument of the Organization. This theory definitely suggests some form of supranationality which is hardly characteristic of contemporary general international law. It will be dangerous to borrow an example from municipal law where certain acts of voluntary acceptance of a general offer, with good consideration, can create an obligation from which the offeree cannot unilaterally absolve himself. Such an analogy is certainly unacceptable in general international law.

The second school of thought contends that once a state voluntarily enters an international organization that is not in any way supranational, it reserves to itself the right to withdraw from such an organization unilaterally as it pleases subject, of course, to any such regulations that might be established within the organization, e.g., the requirement that such a member should clear up all its financial obligations before the organization. Except for such procedural regulation, there is no other obligation before the organization that might prevent the member state from withdrawing therefrom. This argument is, as expected, based on the sovereign rights of such states to determine where and when continued membership of any particular international organization is conducive to its foreign policies.

This was the attitude adopted by the US when it decided to accept membership of the WHO. The 80th Congress which convened in January 1947 failed to take any actions on US membership until June 1948 when it adopted a resolution (P.L. 643, 80th Congress) imposing strict statutory restrictions on US membership in the WHO—this joint resolution of the 80th Congress reserved the US right to withdraw from the Organization on one year's notice. The instrument stated: "In adopting this joint resolution the Congress does so with the understanding that in the absence of any provisions in the WHO Constitution for withdrawal from the Organization, the US reserves its right to withdraw from the Organization on a one year notice; provided, however, that the financial obligations of the United States to the Organization shall be met in full for the Organization's current fiscal year."[25]

However, in an attempt to bridge the gap between these two theories the WHO adopted a middle-of-the-road doctrine of considering any such states as merely "inactive members". This was the case in 1949 when the Soviet Union decided to withdraw from the Organization and the Official Records of the WHO insisted on considering her (between 1949 and 1957) as an "inactive member".[26]

It is equally important to note that even though the Soviet Union, the Ukraine and Belorussia were the first to tender their respective "resignations" or "withdrawals" from the WHO, the year 1949 actually saw a flood of resignations from active membership of the Organization.[27] The Soviets were followed by Nationalist China, Albania, Bulgaria, Rumania, Czechoslovakia, Hungary and Poland. The adoption of the "non-active membership" formula was intended to serve as a face-saving device for the WHO which remained highly embarassed as one state after another pulled out of the "active membership roster" of the Organization.

Another specific characteristic of the WHO as compared with any other international organizations is the constitutional provision for regionalization[28] with a degree of autonomy for the various regional offices. Under this provision the regional organizations were to be set up in such geographical areas as shall be designated by the Health Assembly. These areas were delineated by the first World Health Assembly in 1948 as Africa, the Americas, South-East Asia, Europe, Eastern Mediterranean, Western Pacific. These areas were variously defined by enumeration of

110

countries and by geographical description and it was later found necessary to expand and amend, in effect, the original designations as to take
into account the wishes of the individual states and to include territories
omitted at the outset.

We may like to end our brief survey of the juridical nature of the
WHO by stating that whereas the WHO possesses wider powers and
more comprehensive functions than its predecessors, it certainly is not a
supra-national organization. Like the ILO and many other specialised
agencies of the UN, the WHO remains without any direct authority over
its member entities. Its powers are essentially advisory, recommendatory,
promotional and coordinational and are not in any way legislative or
executive. This direct reliance of the WHO on the consent of and authorization from its member states is more a source of strength than of weak-
ness.

In paragraph 3 we shall try to examine what role the Soviet Union
has played inside the WHO since its return in 1957. We are still not very
sure of the real reasons which led to Soviet decision in 1949 to defect
from the Organization she had helped to set up, nor are we sure of the
forces that drove her back into it after such a long absence. All these
searching questions shall constitute the subject matter for our speculative
discussion under the appropriate section below.

Par. 2. *The State of public health inside the Soviet Union today*

Since one of the primary functions of the WHO is to coordinate international efforts in the promotion of public health in the various member
states, it might be necessary for us at this point to take a quick glance
at the state of public health inside the Soviet Union today.

There is no doubt that the level of public health and medical services
inside the Soviet Union today has definitely come a long way from what
it was in the grim days of the tsarist régime. At the 4th session of the 7th
USSR Supreme Soviet (June 25-27, 1968) a Report on "The Status of
Medical Aid to the Population and Measures to improve the Public
Health System in the USSR" was presented to both Houses of the Su-
preme Soviet by Deputy B. V. Petrovskii, the USSR Minister of Public
Health.[29]

In this Report Deputy Petrovskii traced the development of Soviet medical services from pre-1917 days until 1968. He stated, for example, "We
received a grim heritage from tsarism: devastation, famine, epidemics
and a high rate of disease and mortality. Before the Revolution state protection for the working peoples' health was not even mentioned. The average life span among workers and peasants was a little more than 30
years and children suffered especially from the lack of medical aid. Great

efforts were required of the Party and the people to overcome the backwardness and lack of culture that impeded the normal development of public health and education. After October 1917 our Soviet state became the first in the history of mankind to take upon itself the extremely humane task of concern for protecting the peoples' health and provided skilled medical aid free of charge to every member of the society. . ."[30]

As if to prove what the Soviet government had done to date in the field of public health the Deputy went on to give the following statistical data on the current status of public health in Russia: "By the beginning of 1968 our country had 2,400,000 hospital beds, an average of 101 beds per 10,000 persons[31]—a very high index among developed countries. At present we have 600,000 doctors keeping their responsible vigil, i.e. more than 25 doctors per 10,000 persons. The Soviet Union outstrips the developed capitalist countries by a large margin in the proportion of physicians to population."[32] Furthermore, "the overall death rate has decreased by almost 75% since the pre-revolutionary period. The USSR has become the country with the lowest death rate; infant mortality has dropped more than 90%. The average life span has increased 150%-to 70 years."[33]

The third impressive point in his Report was that "the offensive against infectious and other diseases is being waged successfully in our country. In a brief period such dangerous infections as smallpox, plague, cholera and parasitic typhuses have been liquidated. Malaria and trachoma have, for all practical purposes, become things of the past, and polio has been eradicated. The rate of brucellosis and whooping cough has dropped sharply and rheumatism, tuberculosis and other diseases are declining. Not one capitalist country has known or knows such striking and cardinal changes in the improvement of the population's health."[34]

However, the achievements of Soviet medicine today are not strictly confined to curative measures only. There is an extensive network of prophylactic operations inside the Soviet Union today, there is a genuine attempt to maintain good sanitary and hygienic conditions in populated areas and to improve the working and living conditions of the people. The enormous task of educating the people in the basic principles of hygiene is carried out concurrently by the various federal and republican ministries, departments and public organizations, the Union of Red Cross and Red Crescent Societies, the All-Union Knowledge Society and by the peoples' universities (narodnye universiteti) which in the Soviet Union today number over 2000.

The Report went on to discuss what measures have been taken so far to combat air pollution and to preserve the environment in Russia. Soviet anti-pollution measures are directed not only at keeping the air and water clean, but also at minimizing noise in industry and in everyday life.

On the annual expenditures on public health in contemporary Russia as compared to the situation under the tsar, Deputy Petrovskii had very impressive statistics to offer—in tsarist Russia this amounted to only 91 kopecks (less than one ruble) per capita whereas under the 1968 appropriations for public health this stood at 34 rubles. In order to administer the health facilities to the people the Soviet government has set up an incredibly extensive network of sanatoriums, resort polyclinics, health centers, rest homes and guest homes. In 1967 more than 9,000,000 persons obtained treatment and rested in such institutions throughout the Soviet Union. Great emphasis is also placed on medical research in the Soviet Union. In addition to the regular medical institutes which specialise in offering medical education to future medical personnel, there are other specialised medical research centers throughout the Soviet Union—these include 21 oncology, 21 traumatology, 18 anti-tuberculosis and 87 epidemiology institutes.

However, despite these glowing remarks about the grandiose achievements of Soviet medicine, the Minister had a few words to say about the flaws in contemporary Soviet medical services: "Comrades, I must also note that there are still serious shortcomings in the organization of medical aid. At a number of medical institutions the standard of work is low, polyclinics are overcrowded and hospitalization is not always provided in good time, especially for patients suffering from chronic diseases. Not all medical institutions are equipped with the necessary inventory, linens, dishes, etc. In some hospitals the quality of the service is such as to evoke criticism among the patients, and in many areas the number of pharmacies is still inadequate, which has impeded the timely provision of medicines for the population. There have been instances of inconsiderate treatment of patients by medical personnel."[35]

In conclusion, the Minister recommended the adoption of new laws to regulate public health in the USSR particularly as most of the then current laws were passed in the 1920's and 1930's and were naturally outdated. There was call for an urgent adoption of new Federal Principles on Public Health Legislation that would fully "reflect the humane principles of Soviet medicine and our state's enormous concern for the people's health".[36] After a thorough consideration of this Report the Central Committee of the CPSU, acting in conjunction with the Council of Ministers of the USSR, adopted a Resolution accepting the recommendations contained in Comrade Petrovskii's Report.[37]

As noted above, one of the recommendations of the Petrovskii Report was the urgent need to adopt a new Federal legislation on Public Health. Accordingly, the Public Health and Social Security Committees of the Council of the Union and Council of Nationalities of the Supreme Soviet of the USSR, acting jointly with the Legislative Proposals Committee of the two chambers and with the participation of the All-Union Central Council of Trade Unions, the USSR Ministry of Public Health and the USSR Council of Ministers' Juridical Commission, drew up Draft Principles of Legislation of the USSR and the Union Republics on Public Health and submitted it to the Presidium of the Supreme Soviet of the USSR.[38] The Draft was discussed at large, as is the practice with all Soviet federal legislations,[39] after which it was finally adopted in December 1969.[40]

The highlights of this Statute include: Art. 4 under which "citizens of the USSR are provided with free professional medical assistance, accessible to all; this assistance is furnished by state public health institutions"; the practice of medicine and pharmacy in the USSR is restricted to such persons who received special training at and a degree from an appropriate higher or specialised secondary educational institution in the USSR, but persons trained outside the USSR may engage in such practices only in accordance with the procedure established by the USSR legislation (Art. 12); "foreign citizens and stateless persons permanently residing in the USSR are entitled to medical assistance on equal basis with citizens of the USSR. Medical assistance to foreign citizens and stateless persons temporarily sojourning in the USSR is provided under a procedure established by the USSR Ministry of Public Health" (Art. 32). Under the provision of Art. 55 "if an international treaty or international agreement to which the USSR is a party has established rules other than those contained in the public health legislation of the USSR and the Union Republics, the rules of the international treaty or international agreement are applied".

Looking through all these health measures so far taken by the Soviet government since 1917, one cannot help reaching the conclusion that the Soviet Union is fully committed to the attainment by all Soviet peoples of the highest possible level of health. The Soviet Union certainly has a very impressive record measured by the efforts put into its health services and not necessarily by the positive results received from these measures. On the domestic front such a record still has to be equalled by many other modern states, but the bitter fact is that Soviet participation in the activities of the WHO aimed at the promotion of international public health remain far behind her efforts at home.

While conceding the fact that Soviet health standards have improved a lot since 1917, we must enter a caveat with regard to the statistical figures supplied by Comrade Petrovskii in the above passage—these figures are not to be taken at their face value particularly in any attempt to evaluate Soviet medicine or medical services. Whereas we are told above that the Soviet Union today has about 25 doctors to every 10,000 persons—a figure which is phenomenally high by any standards—we find it extremely difficult to understand why Soviet hospitals are overcrowded and its polyclinics overcongested. The partial explanation for this is that Soviet hospitals, just like all Soviet institutions, are plagued with burocracy; attendance by hospital personnel is highly inefficient and the quality of the doctors leaves much to be desired. Our conclusion, therefore, would be that these impressive figures on Soviet medical care today have not led to the expected high quality results in the administration of medicine in the Soviet Union. Besides, the Soviet concept of a 'vrach' (doctor) includes what would normally be termed medical aides just as the idea of an engineer in the Soviet Union is invariably expanded to cover such things like mechanics and electricians.

Par. 3. *The offensive return—Soviet Union "rejoins" the WHO in 1957*

Under normal circumstances one would assume that statesmen on both sides of the iron curtain would pledge themselves to the humanitarian task of keeping politics out of the sphere of public health since germs know no ideological frontiers. Cholera is an epidemic disease which could start in a remote region of Asia and move across the frontiers into Soviet Russia and if not halted by some joint international efforts it could spread not only into Eastern Europe, but also into Western Europe, Africa and even into the Americas. One does not have to be a capitalist or a communist to contact cholera or plague or yellow fever. These diseases pose a common threat to the whole of mankind. This is all the more reason why some measure of transnational effort and trans-ideological commitment is needed to combat these "common enemies".

But, unfortunately, in an era of cold war politics, i.e. an era in which cold war considerations play a considerable part in all transnational dealings, public health has come to be subjected to cold war rhetorics and this politics of public health has come to be centered on the international organization which was specifically created to promote international cooperation in the field of public health and mental services.

The US attitude towards the WHO continues to be determined by the policy goals as set by President Eisenhower in a 1955 speech in which he was reported to have said, "For more than half of mankind disease and invalidity remain the common phenomena and these [constitute] soil for the spread of communism." It stands to reason, therefore, as the US government's argument goes, that if the US is to combat the spread of communism in the world she must fight these "breeding grounds of communism" by contributing money to the WHO.[41] Another leading US commentator on the subject of public health and international politics, D. Logan calls on the US government not to hesitate to spend more money in getting to the heart of the underdeveloped countries of the world through the grant of more medical aid to these countries.[42]

At the 78th Annual Meeting of the American Public Health Association in October 1950 the Honourable Willard Thorp, Assistant Secretary of State for Economic Affairs, told the Assembly that "world health improvement has become a major concern of American foreign policy. Health has become recognised as a major factor in economic and social progress throughout the world—and thus in the preservation of peace."[43] It is this close connection between public health and foreign policy that has long determined the growth and development of all international efforts aimed at the eradication of disease.

For the Soviet Union the goal is a generally fixed one, and all Soviet government activities are necessarily geared towards this target—the victory of communism over the entire world. Be it through its policy of socialist internationalism, by which the Soviets seek to consolidate their stronghold in Eastern Europe and thus perpetuate the 'status quo' in this area, or through its policy of proletarian internationalism, by which she seeks to subvert legally constituted governments in that 'res nullius' known as the third world and thus seek to implant pro-Soviet left-wing "democratic republics", or yet through its unilaterally declared policy of peaceful coexistence with the "imperialist West", the Soviet Union makes no secret of the fact that the goal of its foreign policy is the attainment of a final victory for World Communism.

In this paragraph we shall try to see what political considerations motivated a Soviet return to an Organization she unilaterally decided to quit and from which she persistently kept away for almost eight years (1949-1957). We shall also try to analyse Soviet political moves, strategies and tactics within the various organs of the Organization since its return in 1957.[44]

The first positive move by the Soviet delegation inside the WHO was its sponsoring of a proposal at the 1958 11th Health Assembly calling for an international effort aimed at the complete liquidation of small pox throughout the world and for the peaceful use of atomic energy in the field of medicine. These Soviet proposals received unanimous support in the Assembly. This was, perhaps, one of the few apolitical proposals that was ever tabled by the Soviet delegation at any WHO Assembly and hence the general support which it received.

In addition to being the author of the proposal for such international anti-small pox program, the Soviet Union offered the services of its medical doctors in helping to implement the program coupled with a promise to donate up to 25 million doses of vaccine. These Soviet offers were viewed by most Western member states of the Organization as calculated for propaganda purposes and an unsuccessful attempt was made to convince the Soviet Union to keep these offers to itself. No doubt, of course, both the Soviet offers and their rejection by Western member states were dictated by political considerations.[45]

But at the 14th Health Assembly in 1961 the Soviet delegation embarrassed the Conference by proposing the adoption by the Assembly of a "Declaration on the Granting of Independence to Colonial Nations and

116

Peoples and the Immediate Task of the WHO". In the official Soviet reasoning such a Declaration was calculated to grant support to a similar Declaration which had just been adopted by the General Assembly of the United Nations and would subsequently serve as a means of "decolonizing" public health. One does not need to be skilled in international politics to understand that this move was calculated to gain the support of the newly emergent states of Africa who constituted the main target of such political manoeuvres by the Soviet delegation.

The Soviet delegate tried to impress this upon the Assembly by focussing the debate on the pathetic situation of medical care in the colonial countries of Africa. For example, attention was drawn to the fact that in most countries of Africa for every 30-40,000 persons there was just one medical doctor whereas in a country like the Congo there was not a single native medical doctor. As a result of this, the Soviet delegate pointed out, it was not surprising that the population of a place like the Congo declined from 20m. to its present level of 14m.[46] The Soviet delegate blamed all this on colonialism and thus, in its opinion, the only sure panacea to all the medical ills in the countries of Africa was immediate decolonization of these territories. This Soviet formula of "improved public health for Africa through immediate de-colonization" is not entirely strange to any student of Soviet foreign policy.

It is interesting, however, that this draft resolution slipped through the Assembly and at Soviet insistence the Assembly "welcomed the granting of independence" to new states and their subsequent admission into the WHO. The Assembly went on to request the Director-General of the WHO to take all necessary measures to grant help to these young nations including help in the preparation of local medical personnel sufficiently qualified to undertake the responsibility for the struggle against infectious and parasitic diseases and for the purposes of improving the various national health services. There is no doubt at all that the adoption of such a resolution enhanced the image of the Soviet delegation in the eyes of these highly gullible young African states. The timing of the resolution itself is crucial. Very many African countries attained statehood in the early 50's and the early 60's and the Soviet Union went all the way to woo them by posing to be the champion of the African cause in such world assemblies where the colonial masters of yesterday sat side by side with their ex-colonies.

The grounds for such a Soviet position at the Assembly debates were laid in a message to the 14th World Health Assembly from the Soviet Premier Nikita S. Khrushchev when he said: "The Soviet government and the entire Soviet people are doing and will continue to do all that lies within their powers for the strengthening of peace and the development of an all-sided cooperation among nations, including international cooperation in the fields of medicine and public health. I hope that the participants of the present Assembly ... do appreciate their responsibility and the critical situation as not to remain passive to the progressive historical struggle of nations for peace, for the granting of independence to all colonial peoples and shall make their full contributions to this just cause."[47]

On reading through this message emanating from a head of government and addressed to a World Health Assembly, and on going through all the various arguments advanced by the Soviet delegation at this Conference, one would immediately pause to ask—what exactly is the immediate connection between public health and medical services on the one hand, and de-colonization on the other hand as to warrant such comments? The answer, of course, lies in the inherent nature of the politics of public health as a by-product of the cold war. The Soviet government as well as Soviet legal experts have never sought to make any secret of their basic position on the inherently political nature of any such international organizations like the WHO, the ILO, the UNESCO or, in fact, any of the specialised agencies of the United Nations no matter what the constituent instruments of these Organizations hold their respective principal aims to be—be they world labour relations, international public health or international cultural, scientific or educational cooperation.[48]

At this same 14th World Health Assembly which was held in 1961 at Delhi, the Soviet delegation showed particular enthusiasm when the time came to discuss the draft resolution which called for a ban on the testing of nuclear weapons.

Another issue that led to a heated debate at the 14th World Health Assembly was the question of universal membership for the Organization. The Soviet delegation granted active support to the draft resolution which sought to open up the gates of the WHO to all states. This resolution drew heavy barrage from the delegations of the United States, Great Britain and France. When the Soviets supported such a draft resolution they certainly had at the back of their minds the possible admission of such satellite states as East Germany, North Korea and North Vietnam whose applications for membership had hitherto been consistently opposed by most Western governments.

Once again the Soviet position scored a partial victory in the sense that the Assembly resolved that all countries that could become members of the WHO or which shall have this right (of membership) by virtue of chapter 3 of the WHO Constitution, but which are not represented at the WHO, should give consideration to the question of taking up membership in the Organization. Art. 3 of the WHO Constitution, of course, says that "membership of the Organization shall be open to *all states*". One would assume that this resolution would pave the way for a subsequent admission of North Vietnam, North Korea and East Germany into the Organization, but so far not one of them has been admitted into the WO.[49]

The question of the admission of the communist halves of these divided countries into most of the specialised agencies of the UN poses a special problem and the Soviet Union has never failed to avail itself of the opportunity to raise this thorny issue whenever it suited its purpose to do so.

It will be recalled, however, that at the International Health Conference of 1946 the question of universal membership proved to be a difficult problem. Despite the proposal that membership should be made open to *all* states on the ground that a counter position would impair the effectiveness of the Organization, the ECOSOC of the UN took another view of membership. In the Report of the Council's Drafting Committee, approved by the Council and adopted by Resolution of June 11, 1946, the desirability of universal participation "in the struggle against disease and particularly epidemic disease is recognised, but the competent authority of the UN should regulate admission to membership".[50] This latter line of thinking has since provided the basis for WHO admission policy.

The preoccupation of the Soviet Union with problems of the third world inside the WHO becomes understandable if we recall an appraisal of the WHO as given by a leading Soviet commentator. Professor L. L. Rozanov, writing in 1967 said: "If prior to the second world war the primary function of the international health organizations boiled down to attempts to create a system that would protect the economically developed states from any possible infiltration of infections from without the chief function which confronts the WHO today is the granting of medical aid to the developing countries in the creation and development of their national health services, in declaring an all-out attack on disease, in the destruction of diseases right in their place of origin."[51] Thus the center of gravity of WHO's preventive and curative measures lies today in the remote areas of Africa, Asia and Latin America—the areas of the world that most need the services of the World Health Organization.

As if to underline the contribution of the Soviet government to these ideals which today confront the WHO, L. L. Rozanov tells us in the same paragraph of two positive measures taken by the Soviet government:
1. The Soviet government grants great help, often without strings attached, to the peoples of the developing countries in the preparation of national medical cadre. This fact is borne out by the large number of medical students (on Soviet government scholarship) who are offered places in Soviet medical schools;
2. The Soviet government offers maximum help to the developing countries in the construction and maintenance of hospitals and health centers e.g. in Burma, Cambodia, Ethiopia, Pakistan, India, Iraq, etc.

At the 15th Session of the World Health Assembly in May 1962 under strong pressure from the Soviet Union, the Assembly adopted a Resolution

"On the role of doctors in the maintenance and strengthening of peace" in which it was stressed that the attainment of the highest level of health is impossible without first maintaining international peace. The Soviet delegate in his speech before the Assembly emphasised what he called the close relationship between peace and total disarmament on the one hand and the successful accomplishment of the main objectives of the WHO.[52]

In 1964 the Executive Committee of the WHO went completely out of its way, at Soviet insistence, to adopt a Resolution commending the Moscow Partial Test Ban Treaty. In the course of the 18th Session of the World Health Assembly (Geneva, May-June 1965) the Soviet delegation, falling back on the support of the delegations of some African, Asian and European members, succeeded in making the World Health Assembly adopt a resolution strongly condemning US "aggressive actions in Vietnam" as being "incompatible with the spirit of the WHO Constitution."[53] The Soviet delegation also succeeded in drumming up support from the African and Asian countries to make it possible for the Health Assembly to adopt an amendment to the WHO Constitution, thus making it possible to suspend any member that carries out the policy of racial discrimination at home. Under certain circumstances the amendment would make it possible to expel such a member from the Organization.

At the same 18th World Health Assembly the Soviet delegation tabled a draft resolution which called on the Organization to grant more attention to the question of training national cadres to man the medical services in the developing countries and, as if to demonstrate its preparedness to set an example, the Soviet delegate expressed his government's readiness to increase the number of places offered to students from the developing nations in Soviet medical schools.[54] These and other similar resolutions certainly did curry great favour for the Soviet Union in the eyes of these recipient nations.

Besides cooperation with other countries within the world-wide framework of the WHO, the Soviet Union persistently pursues its regional cooperation with other socialist countries of Eastern Europe in the same fields of public health and medical care. Such parochial regionalism is not by any means precluded by the Constitution of the WHO. On the other hand, it is not granted any express support either. As has been pointed out above, WHO's answer to the UN's regional arrangement technique was to create a number of de-centralised regional organizations which, however, were to remain as integral parts of the parent body in Geneva.

The Soviet Union, seizing full opportunity of this Charter "silence", has developed a very intricate network of bilateral agreements with most of its East European allies. For example, on Dec. 4, 1957 (in Prague) the Soviet Union entered into a bilateral cooperation agreement on health matters with Czechoslovakia. Similar agreements have also been entered into between USSR and the German Democratic Republic (Oct. 21, 1958) and between USSR and Hungary (April 17, 1959).

The principal goal of such health agreements, as proclaimed in their Preambles, is "to work together for the promotion of better health standards among the peoples of the socialist camp."[55] These cooperation agreements cover much wider grounds than any of the sort that the Soviet Union will ever be willing to enter into with non-socialist countries. For example, some of the agreements cover the possibility of the transfer of patients from the hospitals of one country to those of another contracting party, free medical treatment for the citizens of the contracting parties within the territory of the other party, exchange of draft legislation on health regulations, exchange of statistical data on public health, a wide range of administrative cooperation in hospital management, joint medical research projects, etc. The socialist countries also hold regular conferences to discuss important aspects of public health and medicine. So far there have been six such regional conferences—the first was held in Poland in 1956 and it was devoted to a discussion of matters concerning public health in general, then in Bucharest (1956) on the question of the unification of hospital facilities, in Prague (1958) on the provision of medical service to industrial workers, in Sofia (1959) on the question of medical service in rural areas and coordination in such matters, in Moscow (1960) on the questions of heart diseases, and in Budapest (1961) on the question of health plans.

In addition to these bilateral agreements the socialist countries have entered into a multilateral Veterinary Convention (Dec. 14, 1959, Sofia). This Convention calls for a joint international effort on the part of the contracting parties to combat veterinary diseases through exchange of veterinary information, joint programs to combat such diseases on their various border zones, etc.

In fact, the general impression one gets when observing the growth and development of this regional (socialist) health cooperation is that there is a strong tendency toward unified medical services within these socialist countries. There is no doubt, of course, that the Soviet Union is more committed to this intra-socialist commonwealth health cooperation than she is or ever will be to the question of cooperation within the framework of a universal international organization like the WHO. One is not exactly sure of the degree of significance the Soviet Union grants to its participation in the WHO at this stage in view of its deep committments to the principle of regional cooperation on the East European plane. It should be pointed out, however, that cooperation on the regional level does not in any way conflict with the general principles of WHO operation as both organizations are not intended to be mutually exclusive.

The apparent impression that the Soviet Union is determined to substitute East European cooperation for WHO membership is granted some support when one recalls that the idea of this socialist regional cooperation in health matters sprang up during the short time that most of the socialist countries of Eastern Europe, either by design or through mere coincidence, tactically withdrew from membership of the WHO. During this period of "medical hibernation" the socialist countries decided to close their ranks by entering into all forms of bilateral and multilateral cooperation arrangements.

They, nevertheless, voted to return to this world body if only to dismiss any possible speculations of any anti-WHO plot by members of the socialist commonwealth. But ever since their return to the WHO they have never made any secret of their preference for this regional health alliance or of the fact that their continued presence inside the WHO shall to a great extent depend on what the WHO has to offer them in terms of political considerations.

Forms of Soviet Participation in the WHO

Turning to the question of direct Soviet involvement in WHO activities one can very easily find many such instances. Under Art. 2 par. (j) of the WHO Constitution one of the principal methods for achieving the ideal goals set out by the Organization is the promotion of cooperation among professional and scientific groups which contribute to the advancement of health. Under this rubric the WHO encourages the conduct of itinerant seminars and training courses in the field of public health bij member states. Between 1958 and January 1970 the Soviet Union had organised 44 such itinerant seminars and training courses at which representatives of all regional organizations of the WHO as well as delegates from various member states of the WHO participated.

The first of such itinerant seminars was held from October 16-November 21, 1958 on the question of public health administration in the USSR. The Seminar visited Moscow, Leningrad, Kiev, Tbilisi, Sukhumi, and Tashkent and attracted delegates from 21 countries including representatives of all the 6 regional organizations of the WHO.

This was followed by other travelling seminars in the Soviet Union (the seminars often visited up to 5-6 Soviet cities in the course of the deliberations) and the topics of discussion ranged from maternal and child health services in the USSR (27th Augustust-12 Oct. 1960), venereal diseases in the USSR (Sept. 8-Oct. 7, 1961), undergraduate medical education in the USSR (April 9-28, 1962), the organization of epidemiological services and its role in the control of communicable diseases in the USSR (Oct. 7-22, 1963), obstetrics and gynocology in the USSR (June 29-July 17, 1964), public health components in the training of medical personnel in the USSR (Oct. 5-24, 1964), public health and sanitation aspects of city planning (May 24-June 15, 1968), disinfection of drinking water (Sept. 2-24, 1968), etc. The last of such travelling seminars and training courses was held from Sept. 14, 1969 to Jan. 8, 1970 in Moscow on the epidemiology and Control of Communicable Diseases in the USSR.[56]

The other aspect of active Soviet participation in WHO activities is in the operation of a network of reference centers in the USSR. Reference centers, one of the main pillars of the WHO research program, play important roles in providing services to research. These centers, both international and regional, are selected on the basis of the high sientific standards of their output, their workers and their scientific equipment. They are responsible for the standardization of technique, reagents, etc. and are available for consultation to other research workers in their regions or in other parts of the world. The contributions of these national institutions in the various countries throughout the world have made possible much excellent service at little cost to the Organization.

As of 1969 there were 11 WHO Research Centers in the Soviet Union and these included:

1. Division of Immunology and Oncology, Gemaleia Institute of Epidemology and Microbiology, Moscow. (International Reference Center for Tumour-Specific Antigens).

2. N. N. Petrov Research Institute of Oncology, Leningrad (International Reference Center for Evaluation of Methods of Diagnosis and Treatment of Female Genital Tract—Ovarian Center and International Reference Center for the Histopathology of Ovarian Tumours).

3. Department of Community Hygiene, Central Institute for Advanced Medical Training, Ministry of Health of the USSR, Moscow (Regional Reference Center on Air Pollution).

4. Department of Aboviruses, Institute of Poliomyelitis and Viral Encephalitides, Moscow (Regional Reference Center for Aboviruses).

5. Institute of Poliomyelitis and Viral Encephalitides, Moscow (Regional Reference Center for Enteroviruses).

6. Ivanovskii Institute of Virology, Moscow (Regional Reference Center for Respiratory Viruses other than Influenza).

7. Research Institute of Virus Preparations, Moscow (Regional Reference Center for Smallpox).

8. Department of Public Health Statistics, Semasko Institute of Social Hygiene and Public Health Administration, Moscow (International Reference Center for the Classification of Diseases).

9. Gemaleia Institute of Epidemiology and Microbiology, Moscow (WHO Brucellosis Center).

10. Gemaleia Institute of Epidemiology and Microbiology, Moscow (WHO Leptospirosis Reference Laboratory).

11. Institute of Poliomyelitis and Viral Encephalitides, Moscow (International Reference Center for Rabies).

The mere fact that the Soviet Union was prepared to open the gates of its top medical research centers to the WHO is in itself to be highly commended. It cannot be ruled out, of course, that the Soviet Union probably has some set political goals it hopes to achieve by such acts of generous cooperation with the Organization. But in the long run, an analysis of whatever these political objectives are definitely shows that the technical benefits to be derived by international health cooperation outweigh this "political price" which the WHO may have to pay in terms of the advancement of Soviet foreign policy goals.

The Soviet Union has, at least in the open, demonstrated its dedication to the great ideals of the WHO by its generous donation of vaccine to the Organization's vaccine bank. During the three years between 1968 and 1970 donations of up to 75 million doses of vaccine were received by the WHO from the USSR as the latter's contribution to the "special account of smallpox eradication". In addition to these the USSR has provided over 100 million doses of vaccine for the eradication program on the basis of bilateral assistance.

Available statistics on Soviet participation in the various organs of the WHO speak very glowingly of its activism in these bodies—there are at the moment 147 Soviet experts on the various WHO Expert Panels from which members of Expert Committees are periodically chosen to meet and discuss newest knowledge in a given subject and to prepare a report for the Director-General of the WHO.

The USSR, like all the other member states of the WHO, participates in the World Health Assemblies and usually sends important delegations to the sessions of such Assemblies. Under the provision of Art. 11 of the WHO Constitution each member is allowed up to 3 delegates, and under Art. 12—as many advisers and alternates as it sees fit. Many Soviet citizens have served on the 24-member Executive Board.

The other crucial issue is the question of Soviet representation on the staff of the Organization. Under Art. 30 of the WHO Constitution the Secretariat of the Organization shall comprise the Director-General and such technical and administrative staff as the Organization may require. Under Art. 41 of the Staff Regulations of the WHO,[57] "The Director-General shall appoint staff members as required" and Art. 42 stipulates that "the paramount consideration in the appointment, transfer or promotion of the staff shall be the necessity of securing the highest standards of efficiency, competence and integrity. Due regard shall be paid to the importance of recruiting and maintaining the staff on as wide and geographical basis as possible", "without regard to race, creed or sex" and so far as practicable, selection shall be made on a competitive basis". (art. 43)[58]

As of 1970 (Jan.) there were 44 citizens of the USSR on the staff of the WHO out of which 15 are serving at the headquarters in Geneva and the rest in various regional and country projects. The highest post held by a Soviet citizen is that of Assistant Director-General[59] and the incumbent since 1964 has been Dr. N. F. Izmerov. Other Soviet staff members include medical officers, translators, administrators and one public information officer. The figure of 44 taken on its own sounds quite big, but if fed back into the background of the large army of international civil servants which the WHO maintains today, it certainly is a very insignificant number. We, therefore, have no cause to fear any possible "sovietization" of the WHO Secretariat. There is no doubt that the Soviet Union would like to see more Soviet citizens as well as more citizens from countries of Eastern Europe appointed to executive posts in the WHO Secretariat. But fundamental principles (political and legal) which determine the WHO recruitment policy will make such hopes, at least for the moment, unrealizeable.

Turning to the question of Soviet financial cooperation with the WHO, we will certainly notice that this is one of the most sensitive aspects of Soviet participation in any international organization of such a universal nature. Arts. 55 and 56 of the WHO Constitution use the double terms of "budget" and "expenses" to refer most probably to its income and expenditure. The experience of the UN[60] has shown that a different interpretation can be and, in fact, has been read into such switching of terms. However, the WHO has not yet found itself in the awkward dilemma of being put in a position of being required to define what "expenses" means in these articles—whether they refer to the regular expenses of the Organization or to its extraordinary or emergency expenditures.[61]

Under Art. 56 of the WHO Constitution "the World Health Assembly shall review and approve the budget estimate and shall apportion the expenses among the members in accordance with a scale to be fixed by the Health Assembly". The Soviet Union has so far not taken any issues with such apportionment by the Health Assembly and as of 1970 she contributed $9,151,360 to the budget of the Organization thus accounting for 13.13 per cent of the total budget of the WHO.

As regards the possible reasons for Soviet return to the Organization in 1957, one cannot help but link it up with the great event of 1953—the death of Joseph Stalin. This single event seemed to have opened up the window to the West for Russia. Almost in quick succession she joined the ILO in 1954, the UNESCO in 1954, the IAEA in 1956, the WHO in 1957 and the IMCO in 1958. The 1950's really saw the storming of Western Europe by the Soviets.

The Soviet Union also saw in the WHO machinery a very convenient platform from which to demonstrate to the peoples of the West "the superiority of Soviet socialist medicine". Public health and social medicine are certainly granted a priority consideration in Soviet domestic policy with the result that the public health of the entire nation has improved markedly as compared with what it was in 1917.

Thirdly, whereas the Soviet Union would be prepared to render medical aid to her socialist neighbours of Eastern Europe on a bilateral basis, she would rather prefer to offer the same help to nations of the third world within the mechanism of multilateralism of the WHO. At least such a method of offering aid has its political advantages—it is very easy to let the world at large know what exactly you are doing to help these recipient nations. Thus, the WHO serves as a distribution center for Soviet medical aid to these needy countries in Asia, Africa and Latin America.

All these reasons which, in our opinion, led the Soviets to return to Geneva in 1957 can be summarised into one phrase—Soviet political interests. But whereas peaceful coexistence was equally responsible for the Soviet off-and-on attitude towards the ILO, as we have seen in chapter two above, it is essential to point out that the material contents of this same multi-edged principle of peaceful coexistence vary from one organization to another. In its dealings with the ILO the Soviet Union manipulated the principle of peaceful coexistence to achieve certain goals, while here, we have seen how she once again very dexterously manipulated the same weapon again to reach an entirely different goal.

In the next chapter when we come to look at Soviet-UNESCO relations we shall see how the same principle has successfully served yet another different purpose. In short, the particular practical application of this principle of peaceful coexistence by the Soviet Union vis-à-vis different organizations represents just individual tactics within the same general strategy—the promotion of Soviet foreign policy. As far as the Soviet Union is concerned the policy of peaceful coexistence is not a political catechism which must be followed to the strict letter. It is only ideological platform for political action.

NOTES

1. Harold J. Berman: "Law as an instrument of mental health in the US and Soviet Russia", 109 U. of Pa. Law Rev. 361, Jan. 1961. For a more complete elaboration on the question of the various functions of law, see also by the same author, The Nature and Function of Law, 1958.

2. The countries represented were France, Great Britain, Austria, Russia, Spain, Portugal, Sardinia, the two Sicilies, the Papacy, the Toskans, Greece and Turkey. Each delegation was made up of one physician and one diplomat. The Conference was convened by the French Minister of Agriculture and Foreign Trade and the aim was to devise measures for keeping out the infectious diseases of Asia from entering Europe without necessarily jeopardizing the profitable trade with these Asiatic countries. It is interesting to note that the Conference did not care to bother itself with the faith of those Asians who were suffering in the hands of these epidemic diseases, but was only interested in protecting European lives while preserving the vital trade links with the "disease-infested" Asian continent.

3. At the end of the 19th century series of international sanitary conferences were held—6th International Sanitary Conference was held in 1885 in Rome, 7th —in 1892 in Venice, 8th—in 1893 in Dresden, 9th—in 1894 in Paris, and 10th— in 1897 in Venice. All these conferences focussed their attention on the question of how to combat plague, cholera and their efforts resulted in the adoption of a series of international conventions and quarantine regulations.

4. See Arnold Toynbee and Fred L. Israel, Major Peace Treaties of Modern History 1648-1969, vol. II, N.Y. 1967, p. 1285.

5. V. S. Mikhailov: Vozniknovenie i Razvitie Mezhdunarodno—Pravovykh Form Sotrudnichestva Gosudarstv v Oblasti Zdravookhraneniia, SEMP 1961, p. 287.

6. It is of interest to note that not withstanding the fact that Russia participated at the Paris Conference of 1851 (July) which resulted in the adoption of the first International Health Convention, and irrespective of the fact that the Soviet Union joined the IBPH in 1926 while understandably keeping out of the HOLN, the Soviets never at any time showed any keen interest in the pre-1945 international efforts to promote public health. This practice changed radically with the creation of the WHO. The probable reason for such a change will constitute our immediate concern in this chapter.

7. There were also observer delegates from such international organizations as the IBPH, the League of Red Cross Societies, the ILO, the World Federation of Trade Unions, etc.

8. The idea of creating a new world-wide health agency had its origin at the UNCIO in 1945. At the insistence of the Brazilian and the Chinese delegations a resolution was unanimously adopted requesting the UN to convene, as soon as possible, a conference with this aim in view. The following February the ECOSOC initiated action to this effect by establishing a Technical Preparatory Committee for Experts to formulate draft constitutional proposals for the new organization and instructing the Secretary-General to convene an International Health Conference in New York not later than June 20th.

9. The signatures were appended 'ad referendum'.

10. Ukraine did not become a member of the WHO until April 3, 1948 and the Belorussian Republic—not until April 7, 1948. See WHO—Basic Documents, 31st Edition, Geneva, April 1970 at pp. 144-141.

11. In 1948 the WHO entered into a Relationship Agreement with the UN (adopted by the First World Health Assembly on July 10, 1948. See Official Records of the WHO, 13, 81, 321) under which it became a Specialised Agency of the UN— a fact which in effect meant that the WHO voluntarily converted itself into one

of the "planets" of the "UN solar system".

12. To demonstrate the close affinity of the WHO to the UN four different verbal combinations were considered for the name of the Organization—the United Kingdom and Australia suggested "United Nations Health Organization" or "Health Organization of the United Nations"; China stressed the universality conveyed by the term "World" in its preference for the name "World Health Organization"; in an attempt to satisfy both extremes the Netherlands suggested "United Nations World Health Organization". In the long run, however, the Conference chose the simplest name for the new Organization—WHO.

13. See W. R. Sharp: "The new WHO", 41 AJIL 1947, No. 3 at p. 511.

14. This Report is reproduced in the Journal of the Economic and Social Council, No. 13, May 22, 1946.

15. The case of the ILO has been discussed above. Another example of Soviet hatred towards an organization that relied heavily on the League of Nations experience is the present Soviet attitude of critical negativism towards the International Court of Justice—an Organization which drew heavily from the experiences of the Permanent Court of International Justice, the latter being a sister-institution of the League of Nations.

16. The Constitution of the WHO was signed on July 22, 1946 but did not go into force until April 7, 1948. Ever since then April 7 of each year has been designated as World Health Day. On the same day that the Constitution of the WHO was signed the 61 states signed a parallel Protocol on the abrogation of the Rome Convention of 1907, on the dissolution and transfer to the WHO of the functions and property of the IBPH, the HOLN, and the Health Division of the UNRRA. This final act granted a monopoly to the WHO in the field of coordination of international cooperation in health matters.

17. The WHO has since entered into Cooperation Agreements with the Pan-American Health Organization (1949); the United Nations (1948); the ILO (1948); the FAO (1948); the UNESCO (1948); and the IAEA (1959). The Organization has also worked out standard Working Principles Governing the Admission of Non-Governmental Organizations into official relations with itself. (First World Health Assembly). For a full text of these Relationship Agreements and Working Principles, see WHO—Basic Documents, 21st edition, Geneva, April 1970.

18. Vide supra, chpt. 2.

19. The range of this revolutionary action (Art. 21) was extended by the Conference beyond the Draft Proposals presented by the Technical Preparatory Committee so as to include not merely "drugs in official pharmacopoeia and biological products", but "similar products" as well. On the other hand the Conference yielded to the views of the Soviet and Latin American delegations in refusing to include in the regulatory powers of the WHO the prevention of the importation of products "not conforming to standards adopted by the Health Assembly".

20. See W. R. Sharp: 41 AJIL 1947, No. 3 at p. 525.

21. As was probably expected the Ukrainian Soviet Socialist Republic spearheaded an attack on this calculated "infringement on the sovereignty" of member states. Similar provisions with regard to tacit consent as a method of acceptance of international obligation are to be found in the 1933 Convention for Aerial Navigation and in the 1944 Chicago Convention on International Civil Aviation.

22. See Edward Yemin: Legislative Powers in the UN and Specialised Agencies, Leyden 1969 at pp. 203-205.

23. Incidentally the Constitution is silent on the question of reservation by states (not including those reservations mentioned in Arts. 78, 79 and 81) willing to become members of the Organization.

24. It should be borne in mind, however, that the Health Assembly at this time

was dominated by medical doctors who preferred practical solutions to any strictly legal consideration of the question of admission of new members. This is probably why the US got away with its reservation at this time.

25. The Instrument of acceptance by the US of the WHO Constitution was deposited with the Secretary-General of the UN acting as the designated Depository for the WHO Constitution. But the Secretary-General on June 30, 1948 informed the respective parties to the WHO Constitution that he regretted that he was not in a position to determine whether the US had become a party to the Constitution or not and that he was prepared to be guided by the action of the World Health Assembly in the exercise of the Assembly's interpretative powers under Art. 75 of the WHO Constitution.

On July 2, 1948 the World Health Assembly adopted a unanimous resolution recognising the validity of such US ratification. It was however, added in an explanatory note by the Secretary-General that this decision was based on the specific circumstances of the case and should, therefore, not be interpreted to cover any subsequent reservations that may accompany any future acts of ratifications of the WHO Constitution. See: Legal Note, The US reservation to the Constitution of the WHO, 44 AJIL 122 (1950).

26. See Official Records of the WHO, No. 17 Geneva 1949 at pp. 19, 52.

27. Early in 1949 the Ministries of Health of the USSR, the Ukraine and Belorussia informed the Director-General that their states no longer considered themselves members of the Organization. In May 1950 the government of the Republic of China followed suit but resumed membership in May 1953. Between 1948 and 1950 notifications of withdrawal were received from Bulgaria, Romania, Albania, Czechoslovakia, Hungary, and Poland. However, in January 1957 the governments of Bulgaria, Albania, and Poland resumed active membership only to be followed by the three Soviet members in April 1957 and by Czechoslovakia in January 1958.

28. On WHO regionalism, see R. Berkov: The WHO—A Study in Decentralised International Administration, Geneva 1957; see also Howard B. Calderwood: The WHO and Regional Organizations, 37 Temple Law Quarterly, No. 1, 1963-64, pp. 15-27; C. Wilfred Jenks, Coordination in International Organizations: An Introductory Survey, XXVII, BYIL 29 (1951).

29. For a full text of this 7,500-word Report see PRAVDA and IZVESTIIA, June 26, 1968. The salient points in the Report are reproduced in the Current Digest of the Soviet Press, vol. XX, No. 26 at pp. 15-20.

30. Current Digest of the Soviet Press, vol. XX, No. 26 at p. 15.

31. Ibid. at p. 15.

32. In accordance with the Directives of the 23rd CPSU Congress by the end of 1970 the hospital beds in the USSR will have increased to 2,680,000, i.e. 110 beds to every 10,000 persons.

33. Ibid.

34. Ibid. at p. 16.

35. The Current Digest of the Soviet Press, vol. XX, No. 26 at p. 17.

36. Ibid. at p. 27.

37. See The Current Digest of the Soviet Press, vol. XX, No. 31 at pp. 12, 15.

38. For a full text of the Draft Principles of Legislation of the USSR and the Union Republics, see IZVESTIIA, Nov. 5, 1969 at pp. 2-3. The English translation of this Draft is reproduced in The Current Digest of the Soviet Press, vol. 21, No. 48 at pp. 12-17, 41.

39. See The Current Digest of the Soviet Press, vol. 21, No. 50, 1969-70 at p. 16 et seq. for a vivid description of the discussion which preceded the adoption of this Federal Legislation. A documentation of this discussion is contained in the Current Digest of the Soviet Press, vol. 22, No. 1, 1970 at p. 6.

40. The full text of the Public Health Principles as adopted by the USSR Supreme Soviet is published in the IZVESTIIA, Dec. 20, 1969 at pp. 3-4.

41. See "Journal of the American Medical Association", 1955, vol. 157, No. 7 at pp. 13-14.

42. See D. Logan, 45 Public Health 1955, No. 8 at pp. 1017-1021.

43. Willard L. Thorp: "New International Progress in Public Health", 40 Amer. Journal of Public Health, Dec. 1950 at pp. 1479-1485.

44. The problem of the annual assessments, which had been unpaid during the inactive period of Soviet membership, was satisfactorily resolved under the formula according to which "states resuming active membership should pay in full their arrears of contributions for years in which they participated actively, that a token payment of five per cent should be accepted in full settlement of their financial obligations for the years in which they had been inactive and that such payments could be made in equal annual instalments over a period of ten years." See The First Ten Years of the WHO, Geneva, WHO 1958, p. 80.

45. See R. Pethebridge: The Influence of International Politics on the Activities of 'Non-Political' Specialised Agencies—A Case Study, Journal of Political Studies Association of the UK, 1965, vol. XIII, No. 2, at p. 251.

46. Unfortunately, the factual information supplied by the Soviet delegation about the state of public health in Africa is true but the subsequent political exploitation of this naked truth can hardly be considered apolitical. We do note, of course, that such political manipulation of statistical figures is not restricted to the Soviet Union alone.

47. PRAVDA, Feb. 8, 1961.

48. Vide supra, chpt. 1.

49. The Federal Republic of Germany was admitted into the Organization on May 29, 1951 and South Vietnam on May 17, 1950. The seat reserved for China continued to be occupied by a representative of the government of Nationalist China to the exclusion of the Peoples' Republic of China. The situation, however, changed with the admission of Peking to the UN—a factor which has led to a chain reaction in the various UN Specialised Agencies.

50. See International Health Conference, Final Act and Related Documents, Annex 2, Washington, Department of State Publication 2703, Conference Series 91, 1947.

51. L. L. Rozanov: 'Nekotorye Mezhdunarodnye Problemy Zdravookhraneniia i Deiatel'nost' VOZ'. Spetsializirovannye Uchrezdeniia OON v Sovremennom Mire (ed. by G. I. Morozov), Moskva 1967, at p. 184.

52. See 15 WHA, Official Records of the WHO, Geneva No. 119, 8-25, May 1962, Part II, Plenary Meetings, Geneva 1962, pp. 102-105.

53. See Documents of the WHO—World Health Assembly 18, 48, May 20, 1965, Annex A, p. 3; A/18 V.R./12, May 20, 1965.

54. It is an accepted practice of Soviet Universities not to offer medical courses as these are reserved for the various medical institutes, but the University of Friendship among Nations named after Patrice Lumumba (popularly known as the Friendship University), perhaps, is the only Soviet University that deviates from this general practice. The Friendship University has a medical faculty (department) with heavy leanings towards the teaching of tropical medicine as most of its students are from Asia and Africa and Latin America. The Soviet Students who go through this medical school are invariably sent out to practice medicine in the various tropical countries by the Soviet government.

55. In addition to legal cooperation in health matters socialist countries often resort to such other methods like exchange of medical doctors and scientific research personnel, exchange of medical literature, offer of places to students from other socialist countries in Soviet medical schools, etc.

130

56. We have data on these travelling seminars and training courses only up till January 1970.

57. Text adopted at the 4th World Health Assembly (Resolution WHA 4.51) and amended by the 12th World Health Assembly (Resolution WHA 12.33). See WHO, Basic Documents, 21st. Edition, Geneva 1970 at pp. 82-87.

58. For our discussion of basic Soviet grievances at the staffing of international secretariats, vide supra.

59. In the hierarchy of WHO executive appointments the rank of Assistant Director-General (there are usually several Assistant Directors-General) comes after the Director-General and the Deputy Director-General but before that of Regional Directors. See Staff Regulations of the WHO.

60. See Certain Expenses Case, ICJ Reports, 1962.

61. Any possible double interpretation of this clause is probably clarified under the provision of Art. 58 which states that "A special fund to be used at the discretion of the Board shall be established to meet emergencies and unforseen contingencies."

Chapter Four

SOVIET PARTICIPATION IN THE UNITED NATIONS EDU-
CATIONAL, SCIENTIFIC, AND CULTURAL ORGANIZATION
(UNESCO)

Introductory Remarks

Since wars begin in "the minds of men"[1] thus making it necessary that
the defense of peace must be constructed in the minds of men, and having
just gone through "the horrors of war which twice in our lifetime has
brought untold devastation upon mankind," the United Nations resolved
to supplement the United Nations Organization, qua an international instrument for the maintenance of international peace and security, by creating the UNESCO. Thus, the creation of the UNESCO was based on the
assumption that the resources of education, science and culture could use-
fully contribute to the international effort "to save the succeeding generations from the scourge of war".

The founding fathers of the UNESCO were convinced that "the wide
diffusion of culture and the education of humanity for justice and liberty
and peace are indispensable to the dignity of man and constitute a sacred
duty which all the nations must fulfil in a spirit of mutual assistance and
concern", that "a peace based exclusively upon the political and economic arrangements of governments would not be a peace which could secure
the unanimous, lasting and sincere support of the peoples of the world and
that that peace must therefore be founded, if it is not to fail, upon intellectual and moral solidarity of mankind."[2]

It is significant to recall that the representatives of 44 nations[3] decided
to meet in London—the war-marred British capital—in the Institute of
Civil Engineers on Great George Street not far from the Westminster
Abbey in the grim days of November 1945 to write the Constitution of the
UNESCO. At this time the guns of the second world war had hardly si-
lenced. All around there were reminders of the yesteryears—bombed out
buildings, delegates in uniform, fighters in the Allied Forces and the underground resistance movements, recent prisoners of war returned to freedom. They all wanted peace and hated war. The first step toward a lasting peace had already been taken in San-Francisco with the creation of
the UN—a body to which the UNESCO founders sought to give a soul
here in London.[4]

At the London Conference all delegates almost with one voice condemned Nazism, rather than the basically similar Italian fascism or Japanese militarism as the "chief enemy", as a "totalitarian practice" which drew "a curtain around the minds of the people" and there was a unanimous call for what the Belgian delegate aptly described as a "moral disintoxication".[5] It is, therefore, interesting to note that whereas the Soviet Union hated the Nazi regime, she refused to take part in this international crucifixion of Nazism. Was the Soviet Union afraid that such an action might boomerang against her? Was the Soviet Union suspicious of the real intentions of the London Conference in terms of the impact this might have on her domestic policy, in terms of the undesired inroad it might grant to the UNESCO into the jealously guarded Soviet society? Did the Soviets see the condemnation of Nazism as an indirect disapproval of the "fascism of the left" which she was practicing at home? These and other possible reasons are worthy of consideration when we come to analyse the motivations behind initial Soviet antagonism towards the new Organization.[6]

At the London Conference the French draft for the Constitution, one of the two drafts that were tabled before the Conference, proposed that the annual conference of the new Organization should be a tripartite body of representatives of governments, national commissions, and leading non-governmental "world associations". This attempt to introduce a modified version of ILO tripartism into the workings of the UNESCO was rejected by the Conference which instead resolved that only governments could be members of the Organization. It was envisaged that only representatives of governments should have the right to vote at such annual conferences.

Even though the tripartite battle was lost, it became increasingly clear that if the Organization was to implement what came to be accepted as its triple purpose—promotion of intellectual understanding and of human welfare and the advancement of knowledge—it must devise a channel of communication with the various national groups and individuals as well as other non-governmental organizations.

The possibility of an international organization having direct access to individuals in their various countries has always been a nightmare to communist regimes, and Soviet reaction to any such moves by the UNESCO to enter into direct contact with Soviet citizens will take little guess work to predict. In the Soviet society the role of the intellectual is very crucial to the existence of the 'status quo' and it is only an act of self-preservation for the Soviet government to try to protect these intellectual pillars of communism from outside corruption through over exposure to an organization which is dominated by an ideology antagonistic to the communist order.

When the London Conference condemned Nazism for its dicatatorial regimentation of public opinion the Soviets certainly understood its meaning. When the new UNESCO Constitution declared that wars were the product of "the minds of men", the Kremlin disciples of the policy of peaceful coexistence sighed. And when one delegate after another rose up at the London Conference to call for the strengthening of intellectual cooperation among the various national intellectual circles Moscow's only expected answer would be—keep those intellectual internationalists off our doorstep.

But on the other hand it would be incorrect to assume that the Soviets had no interest at all in the new possibilities which the UNESCO could offer her. From the point of view of possible infiltration of communist ideology into the intellectual power house of the West the UNESCO was to be an ideal organ. Just as the ILO provided the Soviets with an unprecedented opportunity to reach the minds of the proletarian aristocracy of the West, so the UNESCO was bound to serve as a vehicle for conveying communist ideology right into the center of western culture. But as in the case of the ILO also the Soviets feared a possible boomerang—the possibilities that these communist ideological missionaries that were to be sent out to convert the West might themselves defect to the West were always present and these tended to deter the Kremlin from any such cultural offensive against the West. The obvious result of all these political calculations, at least in terms of the situations of that time, was the decision of the USSR to stay out of the UNESCO.

The evolution of a UNESCO "philosophy" was yet another source of fear for the Soviet Union. Julian Huxley as Executive Secretary of the Preparatory Commission of the first session of the General Conference attempted to outline the basic ingredients of a UNESCO "philosophy" which he hoped might serve as a general frame for the Organization's program.[7]

Huxley's philosophy for the Organization was what he called "world scientific humanism"—"humanism" because UNESCO was concerned with peace and human welfare; "world" because it had to do with all the peoples of the world and with individuals on the basis of equality of all; "scientific" because science provided "most of the material basis for human culture" and because science needed to be integrated with intellectual and spiritual values. A more controversial aspect of this philosophy was the element of evolution which its author sought to inject into it. In the opinion of Julian Huxley this philosophy must be evolutionary because the theory of evolution had indicated man's place in nature and his ultimate relationship with the rest of the universe.

The Yugoslav delegate, Mr. Rubnikar was on hand to present the dominant communist doctrine.[8] In his view the adoption of an international official philosophy would "lead to the enslavement of thought and of the spirit of creation and would form an arbitrary obstacle to the spread of culture".[9] He branded such an approach as "a kind of philosophical esperanto".[10] An adoption of the Huxley approach would be tantamount to a rejection of the marxist dialectical materialism and the mere fact that an anti-dialectical materialist philosophy[11] was being strongly proposed for the UNESCO was enough to raise doubts in the minds of Kremlin foreign policy makers as to the desirability of Soviet participation in such an Organization. However, it was undoubtedly consoling to the Kremlin to note that the Huxley approach was not adopted as representing the official view of the UNESCO, but it was equally disquieting to Moscow to think that countries with liberal democratic views almost dominated the scene inside the Organization.

It is opportune at this moment to state that the authors of the UNESCO Constitution did not envisage a supranational organization of any sort. It was strictly to be an international organization deprived of any powers to interfere in the domestic affairs of member-states. UNESCO can best be described as being analogous to an international Ministry of Education even though to be sure it does not have those powers that are generally lodged with national education ministries. Her primary function is to try to coordinate educational policies in the various member-states while granting reasonable autonomy to the various "educational units"—the states.

Under the provisions of Art. 4, par. 4 of the UNESCO Constitution, "The General Conference shall, in adopting proposals for submission to the member states, distinguish between recommendations and international conventions submitted for their approval... Each of the member states shall submit recommendations or conventions to its competent authority within a period of one year from the close of the session of the General Conference at which they were adopted". And, furthermore, Art. 8 requires that "Each member state shall report periodically to the Organization in a manner determined by the General Conference, on its laws, regulations, and statistics relating to educational, scientific and cultural life and institutions, and on the action taken upon the recommendations and conventions referred to in Art. 4, par. 4".

It is equally important to draw attention to the controversy which has always surrounded the desirability of certain draft conventions which have been proposed by the UNESCO for adoption by member-states. Whereas the conventions adopted by the ILO have, as a general rule, met with wide acceptance by member states,[12] UNESCO conventions have always been suspect to the member states. Member states have not tended to view such conventions with favour, sometimes by reason of fear lest the national sovereignty be undermined, and sometimes because of the federal structure of the various governments, e.g. in the case of the US.

Perhaps the most important achievement of the UNESCO to date has been the adoption of the Universal Copyright Convention of Sept. 6, 1952.

At this time the Soviet Union saw the Convention as constituting an intolerable interference in its domestic affairs while at the same time tending to see in the Convention an act of Western propaganda. Poland is the only signatory among the Soviet satellite countries. The only conclusion one can draw from this fact is that the UNESCO has not been as successful as the ILO in the field of adoption of conventions and recommendations.[13]

Even though the UNESCO was envisaged as an intergovernmental organization, with due regard to the associate membership status which Art. 2, par. 3 grants to "territories or groups of territories which are not responsible for the conduct of their international relations", Art. XI provides a mechanism for establishing relations between the UNESCO and certain non-governmental organizations. For example, under the provision of Art. XI, par. 4 "The UNESCO may make suitable arrangements for consultation and cooperation with non-governmental international organizations concerned with matters within its competence and may invite them to undertake scientific tasks. Such cooperation may also include participation by representatives of such organizations on advisory committees set up by the General Conference".

Similarly, under the provisions of Art. VII a quasi legal recognition is granted to various national commissions or national cooperating bodies where such exist. Thus, the stage is set for the existence of a truly international organization devoid of any supranational powers and yet not totally cut off from the peoples which make up the member entities. Such legal checks and balances did not seem to suit the taste of the Soviet Union, as she decided to stay out of the Organization. The Soviets, probably, were more concerned with the political setting and the ideological undertone of the Organization. The founding fathers of the new Organization made all attempts to woo the Soviets into the Organization[14] but the Soviet Union persisted in her determination to stay out. Soviet resolution, however, was not just restricted to her staying outside the Organization, she was equally resolved to fight this "imperialist plot" with all the forces at her disposal. This she did between 1946 and 1954 as we shall be examining in the next paragraph.

Par. 1. *Official Soviet Attitude towards the UNESCO, 1946-1954*

The official constituent instrument of the UNESCO, designated as its Constitution, was adopted at the London Conference on Nov. 16, 1945 and it came into force on Nov. 4, 1946. As has been pointed out above the Soviet Union did not participate in the London Conference of 1945 nor did she signify any intention of becoming a member of the new Organization. The official reason given for Soviet refusal to attend the Preparatory Conference was that the British Government—host of the Conference—had failed to agree to the Soviet proposal that the Conference be postponed until the ECOSOC of the UN had been organized and could summon the founding conference of the UNESCO. The British and the US turned down this proposal because it would cause an unnecessary delay and so decided to go on with the Conference without the Russians. While, however, expressing their regret at Soviet absence at the London Conference, the general attitude of the Conference delegates was that the Soviets were only temporarily absent.

But ironically enough, as it would seem to us, the Constitution of the UNESCO repeated almost the same pitfall that was contained in the Treaty of Versailles vis-à-vis the setting up of the ILO.[15] Art. 2, par. I of the UNESCO Constitution provides that "Membership of the United Nations Organization shall carry with it the right to membership of the UNESCO". Par. 6 of the same article, however, provides member states with a machinery for contracting out of the Organization should they wish to do so. Since the Soviet Union was an original member of the UN, as well as the Ukraine and Belorussia, it would follow from a strict construction of this provision of the UNESCO Constitution that the Soviet Union, to the extent to which she did not declare a contrary intention, acquired automatic membership of the Organization prior to 1954. It is, therefore, remarkable that neither the Soviet Union nor the UNESCO itself raised any issues over the question of automatic membership right of the Soviet Union in the Organization.[16]

It would appear, however, that there is some difference between the English and the Russian texts of the UNESCO Constitution both of which are not equally authentic.[17] A literal translation of the Russian text would read: "admission to membership of the UNESCO shall be open to member states of the UN".[17a] This certainly presupposes some positive actions on the part of the UN member who wishes to become a member of the UNESCO. Such actions include positive acts of acceptance and signature of the Constitution (as provided in Art. XV) and the deposit of the instrument of acceptance with the Government of Great Britain which had been designated as the depositary for the constituent instrument of this Organization. If the Russian version of Art. II, par. 1 were to be accepted over its English counterpart then the dilemma of automatic membership for the USSR in UNESCO would have been eliminated. But since the Russian translation is "inferior" to the English text, at least in the official UNESCO hierarchy of choices, we shall abide by the English text for any interpretations of Art. II. Thus, at least in principle, the Soviet Union was a member of UNESCO through no positive acts of its own, right from 1946.[18]

In the meantime the Preparatory Conference drafted a Constitution for the new organization. In the interval between the ratification of this

Constitution and the assembling of the first session of the General Conference of UNESCO its new Director General, Mr. Julian Huxley, under the auspices of the UNESCO issued a short book in which he propounded the controversial philosophy[19] of "world scientific humanism" which, in his views, should rest on a "truly monistic, unitary philosophic basis."[20]

In Huxley's views the UNESCO was to be an instrument dedicated to "help the emergence of a single world culture, with its own philosophy and background of ideas and with its own broad principles". He believed that only such a synthesis could overcome the antithesis presented by the opposition of the conflicting philosophies of East and West.

Traditional Soviet interpretation of the principle of peaceful coexistence[21] presupposes not just peaceful cooperation with the West in political and economic matters, but also strict incompatibility in the area of ideology. In view of such a declared policy it was only to be expected that the concept of any monolithic ideology for the UNESCO based on any form of mechanical synthesis of opposing ideologies would meet with hostile attack from the Soviet camp. The fact that the UNESCO decided to regard this point of view as representing the individual position of Mr. Huxley did not go far enough to quiet Soviet fears for the new Organization. Whether or not this was the personal view of Julian Huxley the fact remained, as the Soviets would perhaps argue, that the man appointed to be the Chief Executive Officer of the new Organization nurtured such hostile ideological views. Thus, as far as we can see, the stage was set for the ideological confrontation between the Kremlin and UNESCO. One can say that it was the appointment of Mr. Julian Huxley as the Director General of the UNESCO—an act which in itself granted quasi-official recognition to the philosophical position of "world scientific humanism"—that, among other factors, prepared the ground for the war of attrition which was to ensue between the Soviet Union and the UNESCO.[22]

Soviet antagonism towards the UNESCO gradually manifested itself in various ways: for example, when a draft agreement between the UNESCO and the ECOSOC—an agreement by which the UNESCO was to become a specialised agency of the UN—came up for discussion at the ECOSOC, the Soviet Union fought to limit the powers of the UNESCO in a very wide range of activities. She insisted on restricting membership of the UNESCO to UN members only, while on the other hand she demanded that UNESCO transmit information to other UN agencies only through the ECOSOC. Obviously if these Soviet proposals had been adopted, they would have placed very heavy restrictions on the new Organization both in terms of its membership and from the point of view of operational flexibility.

Secondly, the Soviet Union vehemently opposed the idea of transferring to the UNESCO the property of the International Institute for Intellectual

Cooperation—an LN organization generally corresponding in purpose to the UNESCO—on the grounds that the property of the UN (the UN being the legal heir to the property of the Institute) should not be transferred to an agency of the UN.

The year 1948 marked a turning point in Soviet bloc's relations with the UNESCO. At the fourth session of the General Conference held at Beirut in June, none of the East European states was represented. The feeling was that Moscow had pressed the button on her Eastern satellites to support its boycott of the imperialist dominated Organization. This certainly was cause for much concern in UNESCO circles as it unavoidably would have dealt a great blow at the universal character of the Organization. After all what would remain of UNESCO's declared policy of encouraging "cultural diversity" if the communist half of Europe pulled out of the Organization.

At the 1949 General Conference the Poles and the Czechs were present thus dispelling the fear of any contemplated bloc action on the part of communist Eastern Europe. However, as it turned out, their participation took a different turn. Their sole reason for participating at all in the General Conference, as it would seem to any observer, was to launch a violent attack against "western imperialism" while at the same time glorifying Soviet communism. Thus, even though the Soviets were not present at this Conference, their position was certainly very adequately represented there.

In 1950 the Soviet attitude towards the UNESCO was contained in a highly critical article by a Soviet international law expert, Mr. N. Evgenev in a Soviet Foreign Affairs Journal "New Times" on March 29. He then wrote, no doubt with official sanction: "Under the flag of cosmopolitanism, UNESCO preaches and defends the policy of American aspirants to world domination. It serves to further the ideological expansion of dollar imperialism and shares actively in propaganda hostile to the Soviet Union and the Peoples' Democracies... In actual fact, this supposedly international agency is an auxillary of the US State Department..."[23]

UNESCO's intervention in Korea and Spain drew heavy barrage from the Soviet camp. In 1951-52 Poland and Czechoslovakia withdrew from the UNESCO. With such withdrawals it looked as if even the delicate strings that held Moscow to the Organization had been severed. With the defection of Yugoslavia from Stalin's orbit in 1948 the Soviet Union seemed to have lost all its lobbying powers within the Organization.

The year 1952, perhaps, marked the culminating point in the deteriorating situation of Soviet-UNESCO relations. In 1953 the unexpected death of Stalin signalled a possible reconciliation between Moscow and the UNESCO. The uneasy reconciliation came barely a year after the upheaval of 1953. In the wake of the general reappraisal of Soviet foreign policy which took place in the post-Stalin era the Soviet Union,

139

among other things, decided to bid for UNESCO membership. Committed to its policy of encouraging cultural diversity while encouraging universal membership, the UNESCO had no problems accepting the Soviet Union into its fold. However, before we go into any appraisal of Soviet participation in the UNESCO after 1954, we shall attempt a synthesis of the factors which, in our view, influenced her decisions between 1946 and 1954.

A leading American scholar John A. Armstrong has suggested three possible reasons for Soviet attitude[24] towards the UNESCO at this time:[25]
First. Financial and Material Aid.
Czechoslovakia and Poland probably joined the UNESCO counting on some material and financial aid in the reconstruction of their educational and cultural facilities. As it became apparent that the likelihood of obtaining large sums of money from the West with "no strings attached" was remote, their comments about the Organization became more hostile;
Second. Effect on World Opinion.
The broad spheres of UNESCO's activities made it inevitable that it would become involved to some extent in the formation of views on international affairs; its special interests indicated that its primary influence in this regard would be among intellectuals. The Soviet bloc countries increasingly met with failures in their efforts to use the platform of UNESCO for their propaganda purpose. They therefore became frustrated and this led to antipathy for the Agency;
Third. Internal Factors.
Potential influence of the UNESCO on the population of the Soviet satellite countries somewhat scared away the Soviets. The dangerous possibility for Soviet intellectuals to admire foreign states and their ideologies constituted a threat to the purity of the communist system. Consequently, a xenophobic campaign to shut out external influences was undertaken.

There is certainly much to be said in favour of the third argument put forward by Mr. Armstrong as to why the Soviet Union decided to shut its gates against the UNESCO. Even though the membership of the UNESCO is restricted to states and to such territorial units that may be admitted as associate members, there is no doubting the fact that the UNESCO was out to woo the various intellectual and cultural groups within the member states. Such a possibility understandably was not very palatable to the Kremlin rulers who replied to UNESCO's cosmopolitanism with ideological paternalism and close protectionism over Soviet intellectuals.

Between 1946 and 1954 the ideological hazards involved in any Soviet participation in the UNESCO outweighed any promisory political or economic gains that such a move might net for the Kremlin. And the not unexpected decision at this time was for the Soviet Union to stay outside the Organization. This decision was maintained until, in the Kremlin's views, new factors emerged which probably led to a radical change in the circumstances which had existed hitherto. This unexpected political somersault came in 1954 and in the next paragraph we shall be examining the role of such a decision on the entire strategy of Soviet foreign policy of peaceful coexistence.

Par. 2. *The mechanics of Soviet participation*

K. P. Rubanik, a leading Soviet ideological watchdog of the UNESCO scene was perhaps representing the Soviet position when in the Introduction to his monograph on the UNESCO he stated: "At the first stages of its existence, while the Soviet Union and other socialist countries were not represented, this Organization was actively used by Western countries in the attainment of their narrow goals. However, after 1954 the situation inside the UNESCO changed. The active foreign policy of the Soviet Union, the growth of its influence and authority on the international plane, the strengthening of the socialist system, the success of the national-liberation movements and the collapse of the colonial system of imperialism, the admission into the UNESCO of new independent states of Africa and a host of other factors led to a serious change in the balance of power inside the Organization."[26]

He saw the entry of the Soviet Union into the UNESCO in the spring of 1954[27] as sparking off a process of change within the Organization. It is this process of change that we hope to examine in this paragraph. We hope to examine Soviet participation in the UNESCO from two major angles—first, through its participation in the work of the General Conference; second, through the coordination of political issues arising within UNESCO with those characterizing the UN system as a whole. As a subsidiary source of our analysis we shall examine Soviet role inside the Executive Board as well as its secondment of Soviet citizens to the UNESCO Secretariat as international civil servants.

As if providing justification for Soviet entry into the UNESCO in 1954 after almost nine years of virtual boycott of the Organization, K. P. Rubanik tells us that "the entry of the Soviet Union into the UNESCO was dictated by its efforts to contribute to the attainment of international peace through the extension of the cooperation of all countries in the field of education, science and culture."[28]

There is no doubt, of course, that Soviet entry into the Organization in 1954 threw two immediate challenges to the UNESCO itself—the first challenge was to the dominant concept in the UNESCO at this time that the functions of the Organization are essentially non-political;[29] the second challenge was to the liberal and democratic principles upon which the Organization was founded.[30]

On the apolitical nature of the UNESCO the Soviet position has always been that "UNESCO is by the nature of its aims and functions a political organization, and not just an administrative union engaged in questions of narrow technical and special character."[31] Similarly, at the 13th session of the General Conference when the Australian delegate took the stand that a Soviet proposal calling for a discussion on "The task of the UNESCO in the strengthening of peace and peaceful coexistence and cooperation of states belonging to different socio-economic systems" was too political for the UNESCO to handle,[32] the Chief Soviet delegate seized the opportunity to present the official Soviet stand on the distinction between political and non-political questions. He stated, inter alia: ". . . It is impossible to draw a line between the political and non-political questions of the practical operation of the Organization. . . We can and ought to discuss problems of peace and peaceful coexistence and the role of our Organization in strengthening them."[33]

With such declarations inside the Organizations and such commentaries from the home front by Soviet scholars, the Soviet Union wished to make it known that she was not prepared to draw any line between what might be called political and non-political questions inside the UNESCO. As a result of this uncompromising Soviet attitude, the UNESCO has certainly become more political than it ever was before 1954. The Soviet Union has tabled before the General Conference of the UNESCO questions ranging from the principles of peaceful coexistence of countries with different socio-economic structures, disarmament, decolonization and racism, to such questions as the banning of war propaganda. Inside the General Conference itself "the Soviet Union seems to be using two kinds of orator. One is an academician who may indeed read a fiery piece about the October Revolution but who normally outlines a position with restraint and manifests a desire to cooperate. The other is a diplomatic functionary who lays down blistering barrages."[34]

The first political act of the newly admitted Soviet Union was its call at the 8th session of the General Conference in 1954 for a discussion of a banning of war propaganda by the western press. This was followed by a strong statement made by the Soviet delegate at the 9th session of the General Conference in 1956 in which he called for a condemnation of "the aggressive acts of the imperialist powers against Egypt". When the plenary session of the 9th Session of the General Conference (Nov. 21, 1956) was debating whether or not to include a joint Czechoslovakian-Bulgarian draft resolution on "imperialist aggression against Egypt" into its agenda, most western members maintained that such a question was "purely political"—a position which drew Soviet comment to the effect that "when we are told that we must not meddle with politics and must sidetrack a fact of aggression, this means that we are being invited to close our eyes to the fact that there is an attempt to return Egypt to the oppression of colonialism. And not only Egypt. Attack on Egypt constitutes a threat to other countries of the Middle East which have been liberated and continue to be liberated from colonial and semi-colonial dependenec."[34a] Similar confrontation was noticed between the Soviet political stand and the position of the supporters of a less political UNESCO at the 11th. session of the General Conference in 1960 when the question of disarmament and colonialism was being discussed; at the 13th session in 1964 during a discussion of the principle of peaceful coexistence and at the 14th session in 1966 in connection with the discussion of a Soviet draft resolution on "the tasks of the UNESCO in the execution of the decisions of the 20th session of the GA of the UN on the struggle against colonialism and racism."

Inside the principal organs of the UNESCO itself Soviet strategy has been geared predominantly towards three main questions—peaceful coexistence, disarmament and the liquidation of colonialism. Let us now examine in greater detail Soviet efforts along these lines.

The Soviet Union and Peaceful Coexistence

On the initiative of the Soviet Union acting in alliance with other socialist states, the UNESCO ever since 1956, devoted a certain amount of time and energy towards inquiring into the political, economic, philosophical and legal aspects of the principle of peaceful coexistence.

In November 1960 at the 11th session of the General Conference the Soviet delegation tabled a draft resolution on "Peaceful Coexistence and Cooperation of States with different socio-economic systems" in which she called for the adoption of the principle of peaceful coexistence as the basis of all UNESCO activities. The Conference ended up with the adoption of a resolution (Resolution No. 81)[35] which bore the same name and expressed the same ideas as an analogous Resulution adopted by the General Assembly of the United Nations (Resolution 1236-XII)— "Peaceful and Good Neighbourly Relations among States" and a second resolution on "Measures aimed at the Establishment and Strengthening of Peaceful and Good Neighbourly Relations between States".

In 1964 at the 13th Session of the General Conference the Soviet delegation insisted on the inclusion in the agenda of a special question on "The tasks of the UNESCO in the strengthening of peace, peaceful cooperation and peaceful coexistence of states with different social systems". The proposal drew heavy support from other socialist countries and from some neutral countries of the third world. After careful examination by the General Conference a joint draft resolution (put forward by nine states—USSR, Algeria, Dahomey, India, Iraq, Mali, Mongolia, United

143

Arab Republic, and Yugoslavia) with the same designation was tabled for discussion. This draft resolution drew heavy attack from some western countries particularly the USA who proposed an amendment calling for a replacement of the term "peaceful coexistence" with "peaceful and good neighbourly relations".

Western delegates put forward a three point argument to the effect that:

1. the question of peaceful coexistence is purely political and, therefore, it lies outside the competence of the UNESCO to discuss it;

2. the question of the codification and identification of the norms of peaceful coexistence lies within the exclusive competence of the United Nations Organization;

3. the UNESCO cannot go outside the framework of resolutions already adopted by the organs of the UN or by the organs of other international organizations.

The Soviet delegation fought back by arguing that under Art. 1 of the UNESCO Constitution "the purpose of the Organization is to contribute to peace and security by promoting collaboration among the nations through education, science and culture ..." and, therefore, the Organization certainly had powers to discuss political matters including questions of peaceful coexistence so long as this was essential towards the attainment of the aims and objectives of the Organization.

After a protracted debate between the socialist and western forces inside the Organization, the General Conference finally adopted a Resolution (retaining the original Soviet designation) on Nov. 6, 1964.[36] The Resolution as adopted called upon member-states to base their relations with one another on the principle of peaceful coexistence. From the Resolution itself the following principles of peaceful coexistence suggest themselves:

1. Mutual respect and mutual benefit;
2. Non aggression;
3. Mutual respect for sovereignty of each other;
4. Equality of states and respect for the territorial inviolability of each other;
5. Non-interference in the domestic affairs of each other;
6. Widening of the base for international cooperation;
7. Removal of international tension and the settlement of disputes through peaceful means as prescribed in the UN-GA Resolution 1236 (XII).

The General Conference called upon the executive organs of the UNESCO to abide by these principles in their day-to-day operations. As was expected the Soviets hailed the 13th session of the UNESCO General Conference as going down into history as having granted official recognition to the principle of peaceful coexistence between states with different socio-economic systems. However, whether or not we can say that the UNESCO, by adopting such a resolution, had finally settled the thorny question that constantly surrounds this principle of peaceful coexistence is highly doubtful. But at least the fact that the Soviet Union pushed the Organization into this tight corner represents a remarkable victory for Soviet strategy on the entire question.

Disarmament Question inside the UNESCO

Citing that section of the Preamble to the UNESCO Constitution which declares that "since wars begin in the minds of men, it is in the minds of men that the defense of peace must be constructed", the Soviet Union interpretes the competence of the UNESCO to cover possible discussion of disarmament questions particularly through the formation of such public opinion that would favour the cause of world disarmament.

Accordingly, in 1959 at the initiative of the Soviet Union the Executive Board in its 55th session adopted a Resolution (Resolution No. 5.2. A) on "The participation of the UNESCO in the activities of the UN aimed at complete and total disarmament". In this resolution the Executive Board directed the Director-General:

1. to continue to take all necessary measures which are considered favourable for the attainment of the aims outlined in the UN Resolution;
2. to report back to the Executive Board, as soon as the UN reaches any agreement on total and complete disarmament under an effective international control, on any such measures that the UNESCO, qua an international organization, can take to ensure the prompt implementation of such agreement;
3. to make such proposals to the Executive Board, as soon as this is possible, on the most effective use, for the attainment of the needs of the UNESCO in the field of education, science and culture, of any such resources that shall be released as a result of disarmament.[37]

In May 1962 at the initiative of the Soviet Union and Poland the 61st session of the Executive Board adopted a Resolution (Resolution No. 4.2.6) on "The examination of the economic and social results of disarmament".[38] The Board went on to express support for UN-GA Resolution 1516 (XV) and resolved to include on the agenda of the 12th session of the General Conference of the UNESCO (1962) a Report by the Director-General of the UNESCO on the question of the economic and social results of disarmament.

After a thorough examination of the Director-General's Report, the 12th session of the General Conference adopted a Resolution (Resolution No. 3.73) on the economic and social results of disarmament,[39] a resolution which in its turn was based on Resolution No. 891 (XXXIV) of July 26, 1962 as adopted by the ECOSOC of the United Nations. In its decision the General Conference adopted the position already taken by the group of Expert-Consultants of the UN and further authorized the Director-General of the UNESCO to inform the UN Secretary-General of his preparedness to furnish him with any such information and research findings within the competence of the UNESCO as may be required by the Secretary-General for further study of the economic and social results of disarmament.

At its 13th session in 1964 the General Conference of the UNESCO adopted a resolution jointly sponsored by the USSR and some other socialist countries (Resolution No. 3.255) on "Measures affecting the economic and social results of disarmament and research on problems of peace".[40] This resolution stressed the need to intensify UNESCO research in the fields of the economic and social results of disarmament.[41]

With the adoption of the Moscow Partial Nuclear Test Ban Treaty, the Soviet Union tried to swerve UNESCO activities in this direction. With the support of some neutral countries of Asia and Africa, the Soviet Union proposed to the 66th session of the Executive Board in 1963 and the latter after a long and acrimonious debate finally adopted a resolution (Resolution No. 9.3) on the "Tasks of the UNESCO in the encouragement of complete and total disarmament in the light of the Moscow Partial Nuclear Test Ban Treaty".[42] There is no doubt, of course, that with the adoption of such a resolution the UNESCO has certainly gone off the course originally carved out for it by its founding fathers. This is yet another manifestation of the impact of the Soviet Union on this Organization which was specifically founded to promote educational, scientific and cultural cooperation among its members.

UNESCO and the Question of the Liquidation of Colonialism

The third major line of action generally taken by the Soviet Union inside the UNESCO has been to fight for a complete and total liquidation of colonialism in all its manifestations. Such actions certainly were bound to draw heavy opposition from the Western member states many of which were colonial masters not too long ago. On the other hand such moves by the Soviet Union were bound to draw considerable sympathy from the "oppressed nations" of Africa and Asia who in collaboration with the socialist and the Latin American states constitute today a mechanical majority inside the Organization. The Soviet Union was, therefore, out to enlist the sometimes unpredictable support of these "political prostitutes".

Accordingly, at the 11th session of the General Conference of the UNESCO the Soviet delegation proposed the inclusion in the agenda a discussion of the "Declaration on the granting of independence to all colonial countries and peoples". The specific intention here was for the

UNESCO to grant official support to the UN-GA Resolution and to push the UNESCO into taking specific measures aimed at the liquidation of colonialism in education, science and culture. As was probably expected the delegates of USA, Great Britain, France, Australia etc. argued that it would be out of place for the UNESCO to discuss measures directed at decolonization as this was the exclusive prerogative of the United Nations Organization.

However, after a bitter and protracted debate the Conference on Dec. 12, 1960 adopted a Resolution (Resolution No. 8.2) on the "Role of the UNESCO on the granting of independence to colonial peoples and countries" without voting.[43] In this Resolution the General Conference proclaimed the following principles: equality of all nations and the right of nations to self-determination. The General Conference then went on to declare that colonialism in all its forms and manifestations ought to be liquidated and that the granting of freedom and independence to colonial peoples cannot be denied under the false contention that such territories have not attained a sufficiently high level of development in the social and economic, cultural and educational fields.

The 12th session of the General Conference sanctioned the decision of the 11th General Conference and instructed the Director-General to continue the study of the possible ill effects of colonialism in the fields of education, science and culture and to report back to the 13th session of the General Conference on his progress.

When the time came to hear the Progress Report by the Director-General of the UNESCO at the 13th session of the General Conference, the Soviet delegation seized the opportunity to level criticisms against the Chief Executive for dragging his feet on the implementation of the resolutions referred to above. At Soviet insistence the General Conference adopted a new resolution (Resolution No. 6.3) on "The Role of the UNESCO in the granting of independence to colonial peoples and nations". This new resolution only reiterated the basic position of the previous one but provided new grounds for executive action.

We can go on almost indefinitely to pinpoint politically-oriented draft resolutions which the Soviet delegation tabled before the General Conference of this otherwise technical organization. But at this point let us pause for a while and try to see to what extent this Soviet imposition of political approach has influenced the UNESCO itself. An analysis of UNESCO activities shows many instances in which the Organization took up resolutions, this time with very little direct influence from the Soviet delegation, which have open political tones.

This new trend probably came from the UN itself. Beginning from 1960 when the UN-GA adopted its historical Declaration on the granting of independence to colonial peoples and nations, the GA as well as the ECOSOC has tended to adopt recommendatory resolutions directed at the

UNESCO, among other specialised agencies of the UN, calling on them in effect to take practical measures aimed at the implementation of the political resolutions of the UN itself. A typical example of such political pressure from the UN was the adoption at the 20th session of the General Assembly of a resolution on "The implementation of the Declaration of the granting of independence to colonial peoples and nations". In this resolution the GA called on all governments and international organizations, including the specialised agencies of the UN, not to offer any help to the governments of Portugal and the Union of South Africa as a result of the colonial policies of these governments in Africa. Certainly this was a political resolution addressed to an otherwise non-political organization like the UNESCO. In fact, this recommendatory resolution of the UN-GA was adopted and carried out by the UNESCO.[44]

The practical implementation of this UN recommendation was the adoption by the General Conference of the UNESCO at its 14th session of a resolution (Resolution No. 11) in which it instructed the Director-General of the Organization not to render any help to the governments of Portugal, South Africa and to the illegal regime in Southern Rhodesia in the fields of education, science and culture. The resolution also directed the Chief Executive not to invite the governments of these countries to any such conferences of the UNESCO or, in fact, to any activities of the Organization if such invitation might entail the granting of technical aid, until such a time as these governments shall abandon their policy of colonial oppression and racial discrimination.

On the basis of this general directive by the General Conference the Executive Board dropped Portugal and Southern Rhodesia from its list of invitees to the 74th, 76th, and 77th sessions as well as from the list of participants at such important UNESCO discussions as: the Intergovernmental Conference of the UNESCO on the admission to higher education (Vienna, Nov. 1967); the consultation of government experts on the implementation of UNESCO agreements of 1949 and 1950 on the transfer of educational, scientific and cultural materials (Paris, Dec. 1967); and the Conference on general and technical education in Africa (Nairobi, July 1968). Similar political discrimination against the government of South Africa was demonstrated when the UNESCO jointly with the ILO decided to work out certain international recommendations on the socio-economic situation of teachers. At this joint conference the Union of South Africa, then an ILO member, was not allowed to participate (Paris, Sept. 21-October 5, 1966) because the UNESCO was entrusted with the task of sending out invitations and she deliberately left out the government of South Africa in accordance with her policy of non collaboration with the regime in South Africa.

When on Nov. 4, 1966 the UNESCO celebrated its 20th anniversary the Soviet Union seized the opportunity once again to force a highly political topic for discussion on the General Conference. At the insistence of the Soviet Union the question to be discussed was the contribution of the UNESCO to peace. In view of the significance of this topic it was discussed not only in the plenary session of the General Conference, but also at other working committees of the Conference. As expected there was a sharp confrontation between the socialist and western delegations especially as regards what the UNESCO could or could not do for peace.

In the heat of the debate over this question the Soviet delegation proposed a draft resolution on "The contribution of the UNESCO to peace"[45] in which she emphasized the deficiencies of the measures taken by the UNESCO Secretariat in the implementation of important General Conference and Executive Board resolutions on peace, peaceful coexistence and colonialism. The Soviet draft resolutions contained other such cardinal recommendations as:

1. in carrying out UNESCO program for 1967-1968 the Director-General should take into full consideration all such decisions of the principal organs of the Organization to the extent to which such decisions are geared towards maximizing the contribution of the Organization towards peace;

2. detailed plan for concrete actions by the various departments and information services of the Secretariat aimed at stepping up the contribution of the UNESCO towards peace in the two succeeding financial years;

3. a recommendation to convene in 1969-1970 a world congress of a wide representation of the scientific and cultural circles to discuss a suggested topic: "Science and culture in the defense of peace";

4. to hold a symposium on the topic "Ways of socio-economic development of mankind and the problem of peace"; and

5. the adoption of a draft convention on "The banning of the use of the mass communications media for the propagation of militarism, revanchism, and racial hatred".[46]

The Soviet draft resolution certainly sparked off a heated debate inside the General Conference over the idea of adopting any such resolution and most importantly over the language of the draft. In the long run an uneasy compromise was arrived at—a Declaration on "The contribution of the UNESCO to peace" was adopted by the General Conference. Soviet commentators have long dubbed the compromise draft of the Declaration as representing "liberal-bourgeois positions".[47]

The other suggestions put forward by the Soviet delegation were adopted in one form or another.[48] The adoption of the Declaration on "The contribution of the UNESCO to peace", despite the compromise positions which it contained, has since been hailed as a big victory for the "progressive, peace-loving forces" inside the UNESCO.[49]

With the adoption of this Declaration the UNESCO Secretariat immediately settled down to working out concrete plans for its materialization: in December 1967 a Conference of UNESCO experts was convened in Paris to discuss the question of the role of moral and civic education in the maintenance of peace. The outcome of the Conference was the decision to convene another conference in 1969-70 on the role of moral and civic education in the maintenance of international peace and brotherhood of nations. Special attention was granted to the role of humanitarian (social) sciences in the strengthening of world peace and as was expected a primary place was granted to the development of international law in the third world. This was certainly a nice opportunity for the Soviet Union to vie with the west for the minds of the youth of Africa. A series of seminars in international law was planned for Africa and the third world the first of which was held in Dar-es-Salam between August and September of 1967. A leading Soviet international lawyer, perhaps the Soviet Union's best salesman abroad, Professor G. I. Tunkin was invited to deliver two lectures—the normative functions of the UN family organizations and international law today and yesterday. As was probably expected Professor G. I. Tunkin seized the unique opportunity to present the Soviet view on the evolution, development, contents, and future of the law of nations, the law of "peaceful coexistence". There is no doubt that this was a moral victory for the Soviet Union—the fact that one of her best scholars could ride to the heart of the third world on a vehicle provided by the UNESCO to present a Soviet position was a great achievement in itself.

Having utilised the occasion of the 20th anniversary celebrations of the UNESCO to achieve certain foreign policy ends, the Soviet Union quietly waited for yet another golden opportunity to manipulate the UNESCO vehicle to its benefit. On the occasion of the 100th anniversary of V. I. Lenin's birth (1870-1970) the Soviet Union worked out a plan to involve the UNESCO in this world-wide celebration of the birth of its founder. At the 15th session of the General Conference of the UNESCO a resolution was adopted, of course, under Soviet pressure, (Resolution No. 3.12) to celebrate Lenin's anniversary.[50] Accordingly, the Organization went ahead and convened an international symposium in Finland on "Lenin and his ideas in the struggle for peace". The UNESCO Symposium at Tampere (Finland) undoubtedly provided an international forum for the Kremlin ideologists to preach to the whole wide world how peace-loving Lenin himself was and how dedicated to international peace the Soviet state itself was. The decison by the UNESCO to get involved officially in the celebration of Lenin's birthday is yet the greatest victory the Soviet Union has ever scored with the Organization. More plans may yet be in the making. Nobody knows. But whatever is the case the achievements so far are a grim reminder of the bitter fact that the Soviet latecomer to the UNESCO circle is now very deeply rooted inside the Organization. Her contribution to the budget of the Organization may be meagre,[51] her quota in the staffing of the UNESCO Secretariat may be hopelessly insignificant, her voice in the Executive Board of the Organization may be faint, but her impact on the entire outlook of the Organization is far from insignificant.

Another aspect in which the Soviet Union has consistently tried to influence UNESCO policies is in the sphere of admission of new members. Whereas Art. 2, parag. 1 of the UNESCO Constitution regulates the admission of UN members into the UNESCO, a different procedure is established for admitting into the UNESCO entities, other than dependent territories or groups of territories, that are not members of the UN by the time they apply for UNESCO membership. Art. 2, par. 2, stipulates: "Subject to the conditions of the agreement between this Organization and the United Nations Organization, ... states not members of the UNO may be admitted to membership of the Organization upon recommendation of the Executive Board, by a two-thirds majority vote of the General Conference." A combination of this provision with those of the other applicable sources of UNESCO law—Art. V, sect. 6; Sect. XVI of the Rules of Procedure of the General Conference of UNESCO—produces the following procedure for the admission of non-UN members into the UNESCO:

1. application to the Director-General of the UNESCO for membership (of the UNESCO) from a non-UN member shall be accompanied by a declaration by the applicant-state stating its determination to observe the provisions of the UNESCO Constitution and to carry out her obligations under this Constitution;

2. Recommendation in favour of admitting such an applicant shall come from the Executive Board;

3. The decision (to admit) by the General Conference of the UNESCO shall be taken by a two-thirds majority vote of the entire membership of the UNESCO. Such an applicant-state shall become a member of the Organization from the time the Director-General is informed by the government of the United Kingdom that it has received the instrument of ratification of the UNESCO Constitution from such an applicant. This new rule came into operation as from Dec. 10, 1962.

Under the old rule which operated between 1946 and 1962 an applicant state that was not a member of the UN had to direct its application for membership of the UNESCO first to the ECOSOC of the UN. Such application then had to go before the UNESCO only after a positive recommendation from the ECOSOC to that effect has been received. Such an arrangement granted the ECOSOC some veto power over UNESCO admission policy because, on the basis of Art. 2 of UN-UNESCO Agreement (prior to its amendment in 1962), the ECOSOC may recommend to the UNESCO to reject any such application and any such recommendation shall be accepted by the UNESCO. But if within six months from the time the ECOSOC receives such an application it shall fail to send in its recommendation to the UNESCO, the procedure provided under Art. 2 parag. 2 of the UNESCO Constitution shall be applied. The practical result of such admission procedure was that the UNESCO tended more towards admitting pro-Western countries. Thus, whereas the ECOSOC saw it fit to recommend South Korea and South Vietnam for admission to the UNESCO, it declined at its 20th session on Dec. 7, 1955 (by a 13-5 vote) to recommend the German Democratic Republic for UNESCO membership.[52]

At the 11th session of the General Conference of the UNESCO the Soviet delegation launched a strong attack against the "undemocratic procedure" for admitting non-UN members into UNESCO and tabled a draft amendment to this procedure "to set it on the democratic rails". The Soviet draft proposal[53] maintained that Art. 2 of the UN-UNESCO Agreement and Art. 93, par. 2 of the Rules of Procedure of the General Conference of the UNESCO impose un-necessary restrictions on the rights of the Executive Board and the General Conference with regard to the admission into the UNESCO of applicant-states that are not members of the UN. The draft resolution sought to request the General Conference to instruct the Director-General of the UNESCO to enter into consultations with the appropriate organs of the UN on the question of possible amendment of Art. 2 of the UN-UNESCO Agreement with a view to eliminating the necessity of seeking the recommendation of the ECOSOC before the UNESCO could act on the application of such applicants.

At this point it became very clear that the Soviet Union was trying to shut off the tap on Western influence over the UNESCO admission policy. At this time the Western powers apparently had a firm grip over the ECOSOC and this indirect control over UNESCO admission policy was exercised to the fullest in keeping out potential Soviet supporters from the Organization. Now the Soviets sought to fight this power of indirect veto right from its source—the ECOSOC.

As was expected most Western delegates very violently opposed the Soviet draft proposal. In the long run the legal committee of the General Conference by a majority vote decided that so long as the Soviet proposal for amendment of the UN-UNESCO Agreement did not entail any amendment to the UNESCO Constitution the committee saw no "legal obstructions" why it could not table such proposal before the 11th session of the General Conference. At this juncture circumstances forced a compromise on all parties—it was agreed that a draft proposal should be tabled before the Executive Board of the UNESCO instead.

The Executive Board at its 60th session in Nov. 1961 looked into the question and decided to amend the present admission procedure and instructed the Director-General of the UNESCO to enter into immediate talks with the competent organs of the UN with a view to amending Art. 2 of the Agreement between the Organizations. The Director-General was to report back to the 12th session of the General Conference on the outcome of such talks with the UN.[54]

The recommendation of the Executive Board on the need to amend Art. 2 of the UN-UNESCO Agreement was adopted by the ECOSOC at its 33rd session and by the legal committee of the 12th session of the General Conference of the UNESCO. The Soviet delegate in his testimony before the legal committee of the 12th session of the General Conference put forward four "legal reasons" why he thought Art. 2 of the UN-UNESCO Agreements should be repealed:

1. it conflicted with the legal status of the UNESCO as an autonomous of the Organization;
2. it imposed unnecessary restrictions on the rights of the General Conference of the UNESCO and, ipso facto, on the rights of the member states of the Organization;
3. it lowered the authority and prestige of the UNESCO on the international plane; and
4. a majority of other specialised agencies of the UN had long maintained full independence from the UN particularly with regard to their admission policy and there was no reason why the UNESCO should continue to be tied to the apron strings of the UN.[55]

On Dec. 10, 1962 the General Conference unanimously (with 2 abstentions) resolved to amend the procedure for admitting applicant-states that were not members of the UN and subsequently instructed the Director-General to sign a Protocol with the Secretary-General of the UN repealing Art. 2 of the UN-UNESCO Agreement.[56] Corresponding amendments were introduced into Art. 93 (paras. 1 and 2) of the Rules of Procedure of the General Conference of the UNESCO.

No doubt the adoption of such a resolution by the General Conference of the UNESCO marked a moral victory for the USSR. The aim, of course, was to open the gate of the UNESCO to these communist applicant-states whose support the Soviet hoped to enlist inside the Organization. However, the Soviets soon realised that the transfer of the veto on admission from the ECOSOC to the Executive Board would not resolve all her problems. Under the new procedure the positive recommendation of the Executive Board was still necessary before the General Conference could handle any such application.

Realising how difficult it would be to get a positive recommendation out of the Executive Board in view of the considerable influence which the western powers still wielded inside this body, the Soviets proposed yet a watering down of the powers of the Executive Board over such admission policy. The Soviet delegation proposed the following amendments to the new procedure:

a) the Executive Board should only report to the General Conference on any such application it should receive without accompanying it with any recommendation—positive or negative;

b) the General Conference should resolve to admit such applicant by a simple majority vote instead of the two-thirds majority requirements under the 1962 procedure.

These Soviet amendments were rejected by 35 votes against 22, with 11 abstentions. This is where the battle stands today. The Soviet Union has certainly pushed the UNESCO to great lengths—the admission procedure since 1962 definitely represents a big change even though the Soviets still fall short of their ultimate goal—the admission into the UNESCO of these communist halves of the partitioned countries of Europe and Asia. However, with the admission of Peking to the UN in November 1971 UNESCO moved to expel the Nationalist Chinese delegation and granted the Chinese seat in the Organization to the Peoples' Republic of China.

Now that the manipulation of Art. 2, par. 2 produced a far-from-total victory for Moscow, the Soviets decided to woo the third world—this time by focussing attention on Art. 2, par. 3. Art. 2, par. 3 of the UNESCO Constitution provides that "Territories or groups of territories that are not responsible for the conduct of their international relations may be admitted as associate members by the General Conference by a two-thirds majority of members present and voting, upon application made on behalf of such territory or group of territories by the member or other authority having responsibility for their international relations..."

The institution of associate membership in international organizations is a recent innovation in the law of international organizations and it did not find its place in the UNESCO Constitution untill 1951 when at the 6th session of the General Conference a decision was taken to incorporate Art. 2, par. 3 into the Constitution. Whereas this was a partial recognition of the limited autonomy enjoyed by these dependent territories, the UNESCO Constitution still reserved to the administering authorities the right to apply for such membership on behalf of these territories.

The incorporation of the status of associate membership into the UNESCO Constitution in 1951 remained a dead letter until 1954 when at the 8th session of the General Conference, at the request of Great Britain, the first set of associate members were admitted and these included: Gold Coast, Sierra-Leone, Borneo, Northern Borneo, Sarawak, Singapore and the Federation of Malaya which constituted one group, Barbados, Dominica, Grenada, Trinidad, and Jamaica—these constituted yet another group. By the end of 1959 the list had grown to include Nigeria, Kuwait, and Somalia. After 1960 there was a wave of decolonization and many former colonies gained independence thus becoming, in their own right, full-fledged members of the UNESCO. This left the British Eastern Caribbean Group, Qatar and Bahrain as the only associate members as of Nov. 1, 1968.

With the adoption of the 1960 GA Resolution calling for the granting of independence to all colonial peoples the Soviet Union took up the issue inside the UNESCO and sought to propose ways through which the Organization could give effect to the demands of this resolution. She drew up a two-stage program: stage 1—to upgrade the status of associate membership by granting to the remaining associate members more rights and responsibility within the UNESCO structure. This constituted the program-minimum. The program-maximum called for a complete liquidation of the discriminatory status of associate membership as, in the opinion of the Soviet Union, this was a shameful edifice to colonialism.

Accordingly, at the 11th session of the General Conference the Soviet delegation tabled a resolution calling for a radical change in the status of associate membership.[57]

In the draft resolution the Soviet Union put up the following arguments:

1. the existence of a category of members dispossessed of any voting power is a vestige of the shameful system of colonial past;

2. in the resolution of this question the General Conference should take into consideration the democratic principle of equality of states and the right of all nations and peoples to self-determination;

3. the General Conference should grant immediate effect to the UN Declaration on the granting of independence to all colonial peoples and nations by condemning colonialism in all its manifestations;

4. subsequently, the General Conference should upgrade all the remaining associate members to full members.

When the question of the admission of new associate members stood before the plenary session of the General Conference on Nov. 15, 1960 the Soviet delegate remarked that she would like to see Ruanda-Urundi, Mauritius, Tanganyika and other applicant-territories inside the UNESCO "not as associate members dispossessed of voting power, but as full-fledged members possessive of all rights and powers which are granted to member-states of the Organization in accordance with the Constitution". The Soviet statement went on to present the by-now famous concept of popular sovereignty in the following passage: "The continued retention in the Constitution and in the practices of the UNESCO of the distinction between full-fledged member states and associate members not only does not correspond to the demands of the principle of equality of states and the right of all nations to self-determination which are solemnly proclaimed in the UN Charter, but also constitute a serious deviation from this principle. All nations are equal in their right—this equality is not a gift to the peoples, but rather is a right inalienably rooted in national sovereignty."[58]

The Soviet draft resolution, as unpalatable as it may have been to the western delegations, raised very serious questions which were bound to win the sympathy of the member states of the UNESCO who only yesterday were colonies. These newly liberated member states were in majority within the Organization and it was this group that the Soviet Union was out to woo.

However, the western powers were alive to the political risks that might be involved in any open opposition to this Soviet draft resolution—for example, any open opposition to the "delicate ideas" which this resolution contains would immediately alienate the third world. The only way left to the Western bloc was to attack the resolution from the point of view of procedure—they argued that its adoption would involve an amendment to the Constitution of the UNESCO and under the Rules of Procedure such proposals ought to be sent in to all member states 6 months prior to the opening of the session in which it ought to be discussed. The Soviet proposal, it followed, could not be discussed at this 11th session of the General Conference. The Soviet delegation was talked into accepting a compromise solution to the effect that her proposal should be tabled before any of the subsequent sessions of the General Conference. At this point the heat was taken out of the Soviet proposal and the question was immediately buried there and then. Since the 11th session the question has not been raised again by any of the parties. But at least the Soviet Union demonstrated some "concern" for the cause of the "oppressed peoples of the third world".

On the third front the Soviet Union, at its convenience, had raised now and again the question of Chinese representation in the UNESCO—a question which was very closely tied up with the dilemma of Chinese representation in the United Nations Organization itself. Now that UNESCO has voted to seat the Peking delegation instead of the Taiwanese, thanks to a similar decision by the UN in November 1971, this political football over Chinese representation has been snatched from the Soviets.

In conclusion we can only say that Soviet achievements on the membership front are only symbolic—the German Democratic Republic, North Korea and North Vietnam continue to remain outside the UNESCO, Nationalist China continues to hold fast to the Chinese seat, while the retention of the associate membership status in the UNESCO Constitution seems likely to remain.

The next phase of Soviet political game inside the UNESCO is its attempt to "democratise" the election procedure and the distribution of seats in the Executive Board of the Organization. As of the Nov. 15, 1962 amendment "the Executive Board shall be elected by the General Conference from among the delegates appointed by the member states and shall consist of thirty members each of whom shall represent the government of the state of which he is a national. . ." (Art. V, par. I) This procedure remained in force until the 15th session of the General Conference in 1968. Until 1968 members of the Executive Board were elected for four years and under the provision of Art. V, par. 3 "members of the Board shall serve from the close of the session of the General Conference which elected them until the close of the second ordinary session of the General Conference following that election. They shall be immediately eligible for a second term, but shall not serve consecutively for more than two terms. Half of the members of the Board shall be elected every two years".

The strengthening of the role and importance of the Executive Board after 1952 led to a corresponding change in the status of its members. At the 8th session in 1954 the General Conference adopted a resolution (Resolution No. 11.1.2) to amend the Constitution (and the Rules of Procedure of the Executive Board) according to which a member of the Board should represent the government of the state of which he is a national. Prior to this amendment members of the Executive Board were elected in their own capacity and executed their functions according to the directives issued by the General Conference. Such a manifestation of "individualism" in the Executive Board was considered to be in disaccord with the intergovernmental character of the Organization hence the change.

However, whereas the change was welcomed in Moscow most Western observers regretted it. In fact, a French commentator, Professor Claude-Albert Colliard went to the extent of condeming the 8th session of the General Conference for this regressive change and expressed his deep regret at such a move.[59] Such a change in the powers of the Executive Board certainly carried with it a corresponding weakening in the powers of the Director-General who in his dealings with the Board members was constantly aware that he was dealing with the representatives of sovereign states. The Executive Board had now grown from its former status as adviser to the Director-General to that of a regulating influence on the powers of the Director-General. In the words of Walter H. C. Laves and Charles A. Thomson "the Board had become a body of instructed government representatives whose actions tended to be more consistent with the policies of member states. Closer contact had been achieved between the headquarters staff and member states."[60]

Art. V, par. 2 of the UNESCO Constitution requires that "in electing the members of the Executive Board the General Conference shall endeavour to include persons competent in the arts, the humanities, the sciences, education and the diffusion of ideas, and qualify by their experience and capacity to fulfil the administrative and executive duties of the Board. It shall also have regard to the diversity of cultures and a balanced geographical distribution." As of 1968 the strict application of these principles netted only three seats for the socialist camp—USSR, Hungary, and Rumania out of a total of 30 seats. This, of course, left Moscow very dissatisfied. There was a loud cry from both the socialist camp and from the third world[61] to increase the number of seats on the Executive Board. At the same time the numerical advantage jointly held by the socialist and the neutral countries inside the Executive Board was cause for great concern in the west and efforts were being made to devise formulae to reduce the influence of the Executive Board.[62]

At the 77th session of the Executive Board in Oct. 1967 a decision was taken to the following effect:

a) it was desirable to increase the number of seats in the Executive Board from the then 30, to 32 or 34, depending on the choice to be made by the General Conference;

b) to recommend to the General Conference to reduce from 8 to 6 years the maximum length of time during which a member of the Executive Board can remain in office;

c) to request the Director-General to inform all member states of these draft amendments (in accordance with Art. XIII of the Constitution) six months in advance of the opening of the 15th session of the General Conference.

At the 15th session two decisions were taken:

a) to increase the number of seats on the Executive Board to 34,

b) not to incorporate any amendments to the Constitution of the Organization. At the same session of the General Conference, Academecian S. L. Tikhvinskii, a corresponding member of the Academy of Sciences of the USSR, was elected to represent the USSR on the Executive Board.

Yet another aspect of Soviet 'bor'ba' (struggle) inside the UNESCO is in the area of the selection of those non-governmental (international and national) organizations which shall be granted consultative status with the UNESCO. Under the provision of Art. XI, par. 4 "the UNESCO may make suitable arrangements for consultation and cooperation with non-governmental international organizations concerned with matters within its competence, and may invite them to undertake specific tasks. Such cooperation may also include appropriate participation by representatives of such organizations on advisory committees set up by the General Conference."[63]

Whereas most of the Western countries represented in the Executive Board would insist on granting to pro-western non-governmental organizations the higher category of consultative status—A and B, the Soviets naturally would like such status also granted to many communist-front organizations. For quite a long time the Executive Board refused to grant any form of consultative status to what the Soviet camp called "democratic organizations". But with time and hard bargaining things tended to change in favour of this Soviet position—such organizations as the World Federation of Trade Unions now enjoys consultative status category A with the UNESCO, whereas the World Federation of Scientific Workers at the 70th session of the Executive Board was upgraded from consultative status category C to the more prestigious status B—this also at the insistence of the Soviet representative. In the Spring of 1966 at the 72nd session of the Executive Board also at the insistence of the Soviet lobby consultative status category A was granted to the World Federation of Related Cities; at the 1967 76th session of the Executive Board despite strong opposition from the US delegate the Board decided to grant consultative status category B to the International Democratic Federation of Women. For eight years this Federation of Democratic Women had sought consultative status with the UNESCO but had always been turned down by what the Soviets termed the "pro-American majority on the Executive Board". At this 76th session it was also decided that in 1968 the application for promotion to consultative status B from the World Federation of Democratic Youth, and the International Organization of Radio and Television should be tabled for discussion. Prior to 1968 these two organizations were listed under category C.

In June 1968 at the 78th session of the Executive Board these two organizations as well as the World Federation of Trade Union of Educational Workers were granted consultative status category B. However, at this same session two Soviet-sponsored candidates for consultative status category B—the International Association of Democratic Jurists and the International Federation of Journalists—were turned down.

Much to the distaste of many western delegates to the UNESCO many communist-front organizations, with the support of the lobbying power of the Soviet representative inside the Executive Board, have come to be granted one form of or other consultative status with the UNESCO. This certainly could not have happened a decade or two ago when Soviet influence inside the Organization was still at its lowest.

Now that the Soviet Union seems sure of its lobbying power inside the Organization it has decided to carry on the war for consultative status with the Organization to cover new dimensions—it has now launched a strong attack against the granting of consultative status to what it terms "CIA-financed non-governmental organizations". At the 76th session of the Executive Board the Soviet delegate seized the opportunity to issue the following statement: "In the recent past it has come into the open that the Central Intelligence Agency of the United States of America is granting financial support to certain non-governmental organizations which cooperate with the UNESCO. In actual fact many organizations which enjoy consultative status category A, B, or C with the UNESCO receive help and are financed by the CIA [e.g.] the International Confederation of Teachers' Organizations, the World Youth Assembly, the

International Confederation of Students, the International Commission of Jurists, the Congress for the Freedom of Culture, etc... Some of these organizations also receive aid from the UNESCO. As a result of this we find a strange situation—the UNESCO indirectly helps to bear the financial burden of the CIA. It is time to call a halt to the granting of UNESCO aid to such organizations".[64]

Since through Soviet influence most communist-front organizations have come to be granted consultative status category A, B, or C with the UNESCO, and since some of these organizations, ipso facto, receive aid from the UNESCO,[65] and bearing in mind that the US government is the largest single contributor to the budget of the UNESCO, we find ourselves in the ridiculous situation of accepting the bitter fact that the US government is indirectly providing funds for these communist-front organizations. What else could be more comforting to the Soviet Union than to see its arch ideological enemy—the US government—making financial contributions towards a pro-Soviet cause.

As for the battle for top Secretariat posts in the UNESCO all we can say at this moment is that the Soviet Union is very disappointed over the present composition of the Organization's Paris apparatus. As of July 15, 1967, argues K. P. Rubanik,[66] of the top 56 posts in the UNESCO 21 went to just three countries—France, Great Britain, and Switzerland. The office of the Director-General of the Organization has been held consecutively be representatives of Great Britain (1946-1948), Mexico (1948-1952), USA (1953-1958) and Italy (1958-1961). On Nov. 14, 1962 René Maheu (French) was elected to a six-year term as Director-General of the UNESCO. In view of what K. P. Rubanik terms the "pro-Western composition of the UNESCO's Central Apparatus in Paris" he adds a note to the effect that "the General-Directorate of the UNESCO must take the most radical measures to enhance the representation of the Soviet Union and other socialist countries in the apparatus of the UNES-CO."[67] Western observers cannot but take consolation in the fact that Soviet representation in the central apparatus of the UNESCO is far from domineering and the day is still far away when a Soviet Director-General shall be imposed on the Organization. The threat of any possible "sovietization" of the UNESCO Secretariat remains very remote. But for how long the situation will remain like this is anyone's guess.[68]

Soviet Union and UNESCO Conventions (International Agreements)

In the Introduction to this chapter we dealt very briefly with the legal aspects of the conventions and international agreements adopted by the UNESCO under the provisions of Art. IV, par. 4 of the Constitution. Here we hope to examine in fuller details the attitude of the Soviet Union towards UNESCO conventions in general (including the present position

160

of Soviet doctrinal international law on the legal nature of UNESCO conventions) and on the basis of this we shall attempt to analyse the Soviet attitude to the individual conventions so far adopted by the UNESCO.[69]

We might begin by stating very briefly the present position of Soviet doctrinal international law on the juridical nature of these conventions and international agreements. The salient points of this doctrine are as follows:

1. The Constitution of the UNESCO is not sufficiently explicit on the juridical nature of these conventions and international agreements as it leaves us in the dark as regards the nature of obligations these conventions create for members of the Organization. However, two articles in the Constitution—Arts. IV and VIII—tend to throw some light on these questions.[70]

2. All conventions so adopted by the General Conference are subject to ratification by the member states. "This requirement testifies to the fact that the juridical nature of such legal acts of the UNESCO in essence is not different from the juridical nature of international treaties entered into at diplomatic conferences. In both cases these international acts create an obligation for states only if and when ratified by these states."[71] The requirement under the Constitution of the UNESCO that these conventions be ratified by member states means that the adoption of the convention, per se, by the General Conference does not automatically create any concrete obligations vis-à-vis the respective member states of the Organization.

3. There is no doubt at all that to these conventions that are adopted by the General Conference shall be applied the established norms and the generally recognised principles of international law. Parties to these conventions are states, i.e. subjects of international law. These conventions are international treaties and, ipso facto, are sources of international law.[72]

4. However, the granting to the General Conference of the UNESCO of this type of normative function does not mean that the General Conference of the UNESCO possesses any form of international legislative powers.[73]

5. Nevertheless, it would be wrong to absolutise the assertion that the adoption of a convention by the General Conference of the UNESCO does not create any form of obligation for member states. Under the provision of Art. IV, par. 4 each member state shall submit such conventions to its competent authorities within a period of one year from the close of the session at the General Conference at which they were adopted. Art. VIII also requires member states to report periodically to the Organization on its laws, regulations, and statistics relating to educational, scientific and cultural life and institutions and on the actions taken upon the recommendations and conventions referred to in Art. IV, par.

4. In addition to the mandatory annual reports member states are required to present special reports on the state of their domestic laws with regard to conventions and recommendations adopted by the General Conference of the UNESCO.

Elaborating on the 'locus standi' granted by domestic laws to international treaties and agreements, Professor F. I. Kozhevnikov states: "All international treaties are at the same time acts of state authority having normative significance. The distinction between them and internal laws is eliminated in the sense that a treaty which is declared for general notice is converted into a law which makes it binding upon all citizens of the given state."[74] Addressing this general postulate to the situation in Soviet law, K. P. Rubanik states: "This situation to the same extent applies to international conventions adopted by the UNESCO. All the UNESCO Conventions that are ratified by the Soviet Union have the same force as national law."[75]

Let us now direct ourselves to the question of the Soviet attitude towards international conventions or international agreements adopted by the UNESCO. UNESCO started a practical exercise of its normative functions under Art. IV, par. 4 only in 1949 and ever since then she has adopted quite a few conventions and international agreements among which we have:

1. Agreement for facilitating the international circulation of visual and auditory materials of an educational, scientific and cultural character (with Protocol of signature and Procès-Verbal of deposit of the model form of certificate provided for in Art. IV of the Agreement) Dec. 10, 1948. The Agreement came into force on August 12, 1954 after 10 states had ratified it. As of April 1, 1968 there were only 19 ratifications including that of the US in 1966. Of the socialist states only Yugoslavia ratified it.

In the Soviet view[76] the Agreement has certain "major weaknesses"— the provision for compulsory ICJ adjudication under Art. IX, par. 1 and the fact that the right of states to denounce the Agreement is provided for only after the expiration of three years from the time the Agreement comes into force (Art. XIII). Accordingly, the Soviet Union refused to ratify it.

2. Agreement on the Importation of Educational, Scientific and Cultural Materials (with Annexes A, B, C, D, E, and a Protocol) of June 17, 1950. This Convention was adopted at the 5th session of the General Conference of the UNESCO and came into force on May 21, 1952. As of April 1, 1968 there were already 53 ratifications by members of the UNESCO. The Agreement seeks to regulate the importation of books, newspapers, journals, official documents, periodicals, catalogues and illustrated publications by the UN and the Specialised Agencies, artistic paintings, and scientific apparatus. The Soviet Union refused to ratify this Convention

162

because, as it contends, "accession to such an agreement has been rendered useless by the fact that Soviet domestic laws already lift all custom duties on the importation of those materials covered by the Agreement."[77]

This is hardly a convincing reason why the Soviet Union refused to ratify this Convention. An examination of her politics of ratification vis-à-vis ILO Conventions shows that she has ratified some Conventions of the ILO even though the specific provisions of such conventions have been adequately taken care of in Soviet domestic laws. Certainly in doing so she puts other considerations into play.[78]

3 and 4. Convention concerning International Exchange of Publications (Dec. 3, 1958) and the Convention concerning the Exchange of Official Publications and Government Documents between States (Dec. 3, 1958). These Conventions were adopted at the 10th session of the General Conference of the UNESCO on Dec. 3, 1958. Representatives of the socialist camp, notably the USSR, Czechoslovakia, Poland and Hungary, took an active part in the preparation of these conventions. As of April 1, 1968 there were already 22 ratifications of the International Exchange of Publications Convention. "Wishing to encourage the development of wide international cooperation in the area of book exchange", the Soviet Union ratified this Convention in 1962. As of April 1, 1968 there were 24 accessions to the Exchange of Official Publications and Government Documents Convention including that of the Soviet Union. It should be recalled that the Soviet Union took an active part in the preparation of these Conventions—a fact which probably goes a long way towards explaining why she finally ratified them.

5. Convention against Discrimination in Education.

This Convention was originally proposed by the Soviet Union. The Soviet delegate as well as the delegates of the Ukraine, Belorussia, Poland, Czechoslovakia, and Bulgaria took an active part in the preparation of this Convention at the Paris meeting of government experts in June 1960. The Convention was adopted at the 11th session of the General Conference of the UNESCO on Dec. 14, 1960 and it came into force on May 22, 1962 after ratification by 3 states. After the 1954 Hague Convention for the Protection of Cultural Property in the event of Armed Conflict this Convention presents the "greatest political and legal interest" to the Soviet Union.

The Convention requires, among other things, the abrogation of all types of administrative and legislative regulations which tend to impose discriminatory standards on access to education (Art. 3), calls for free and compulsory primary education and requests member states to make secondary and higher education to be reasonably accessible to all (Art. 4). The Soviet Union fought strongly against an attempt to impose compulsory ICJ adjudication on parties to the Convention. Under the compromise solution arrived at in Art. 8 of the Convention, the consent of both parties to any such disputes shall be sought and received before the dispute can go before the ICJ.

As of April 1, 1968 there were 40 signatories and these included the signatures of all the socialist member states of the UNESCO. One can say that this Convention was conceived by and born to forces favourable to the Soviet Union. The US government refuses to ratify this Convention on the ground, inter alia, that the federal structure of the Union and the autonomy which US universities enjoy would militate against any implementation of the provisions of such a Convention.

6. Universal Copyright Convention (with Appendix Declaration relating to Art. XVII and Resolution concerning Art. XI) of Sept. 6, 1952. The idea of a universal copyright convention was conceived inside the UNESCO long before the 1952 Conference as a result of the disquieting fact that there existed at the time two different copyright conventions—the Berne Convention of 1886 and the 1948 Washington Convention. In the view of the UNESCO a universal copyright convention would serve as a bridge linking these various regional conventions. Accordingly, at the Geneva Inter-governmental Conference in September 1952 a Universal Copyright Convention was adopted. The Convention came into force on Sept. 16, 1955 after it had been ratified by 12 states. As of April 1, 1968 there were 55 ratifications to the Convention and these included those of Cuba, Czechoslovakia and Yugoslavia.

Once again the Soviets rejected the idea of the imposition of compulsory ICJ adjudication which was inserted into Art. XV and the prohibition of any sort of reservation to the Convention under Art. XX. These two "dilutions of state sovereignty" are enough to keep the USSR at an arm's length from the Convention. Similarly, the Soviets contended that the provision in Art. XVII of the Universal Convention to the effect that the "present Convention" does not in any way affect the provisions of the Berne Convention nor does it affect the obligations arising out of that Convention "reduces to zero any effect that this Universal Convention has". As expected the Soviet Union remains outside this Convention.

7. Convention for the Protection of Cultural Property in the Event of Armed Conflict (with Regulations for the Execution of the Convention) of May 14, 1954.

This Convention occupies a central place in the system of law on warfare and is closely associated with the Hague Conventions of 1899 and 1907.

The Soviet Union very willingly ratified this Convention, thus becoming a party to it. While recognising the significance of this Convention, however, it must be pointed out that Moscow's willingness to ratify it was partially dictated by the Convention's apparent apolitical nature and not necessarily because of the place it occupies in the network of laws on warfare.

164

The Soviets, on the other hand, have been quite vocal on the question of the need for an international regulation of war propaganda, particularly among the younger generation. While on the one hand rejecting the idea that "wars originate in the minds of men", the Soviet government has gone all the way to show its concern for the need to root out from the minds of all men the idea that wars are a necessary instrument of national policy. To this end the Soviet delegation tabled a draft convention on the banning of war propaganda. The draft convention stressed the need to bring up the younger generation and to inculcate into the older citizens of all countries the spirit of peace and international friendship. So far, however, this Soviet aspiration has not yet been realised and the UNESCO does not seem to be prepared to give it the priority that the Soviet government intended for it.

Whereas the Soviet call for the adoption of an international convention to regulate war propaganda is only a part of her by-now too familiar peace offensive, her interest in having an international convention adopted to grant equivalent status to foreign diplomas and university certificates is intended to remove any future discrimination by western countries against holders of Soviet diplomas as these number in the thousands today.[79]

Between 1956, when the UNESCO began its quasi-legislative function with regard to the adoption of recommendations, and today, the Organization has adopted quite a number of recommendations, for example, the Recommendation concerning the International Standardization of Educational Statistics (Dec. 3, 1958); Recommendation against Discrimination in Education (Dec. 14, 1960); Recommendation concerning the International Standardization of Statistics relating to Book Production and Periodicals (Nov. 19, 1964); Recommendation on the means of prohibiting and preventing the illicit export, import, and transfer of ownership of cultural property (Nov. 19, 1964); Recommendation concerning the Status of Teachers (Oct. 5, 1966), etc. Obligations of members vis-à-vis these recommendations are those provided in Art. VIII of the Constitution— the requirement to report periodically to the Organization on the state of the domestic laws with regard to the question discussed in these Recommendations.

A perusal of these conventions and international agreements to which the Soviet Union is a party portrays the following picture: the Soviet Union will not ratify any international agreement or convention unless all or some of the following legal and political criteria are fulfilled:

1. The Soviet Union and at least some other socialist countries must have taken part in the preparation of these conventions. It is this pre-adoption participation in the drafting and negotiation of a convention that determines whether or not there is any likelihood of Soviet ratification of the Convention. Since the Soviet doctrine of international law sees any inter-

national agreement as a coordination of the wills of the participating states, Soviet "will" cannot be assumed to have been reasonably coordinated into the often antagonistic wills of the bourgeois West if she did not take part in the 'bor'ba i ustupki' (struggle and concessions) that invariably take place at this negotiating stage.

2. Nothing in the convention or international agreement should be capable of being interpreted to mean a dilution of Soviet state sovereignty. This in essence means that there should be no provision requiring compulsory ICJ adjudication in disputes affecting the interpretation or application of the convention or international agreement; there should be no absolute prohibition of the right of the parties to declare a reservation to any particular provision of the convention; too much emphasis must not be placed on international control as a means of guaranteeing observance of such convention.

3. Nothing in the convention or international agreement shall be construed to conflict with Soviet public order. Under Soviet domestic law any international agreement to which the Soviet Union is a party has the force of law in the Soviet Union and should it conflict with another Soviet law of the same status (in most cases it has the status of a federal statute), priority should be granted to the international agreement. But under the public order clause in Soviet treaty practices the Soviet Union will never ratify any treaty or convention which conflicts with her socialist public order.

When these three criteria are satisfied there is reasonable expectation that the Soviet Union will probably ratify the convention or international agreement in question.[80]

In conclusion we can only say that the Soviet Union has come a long way toward making the UNESCO what it is today—the Organization is certainly more political than it ever was before the admission of the Soviet Union in 1954.

In 1967 the Institute of World Economics and International Relations of the Academy of Sciences of the USSR sponsored a research study on the contemporary situation in the various specialised agencies of the UN.[81] The study divides the history of the UNESCO into three periods: the first period runs from 1946 until the Soviet Union joined the Organization in 1954. At this time, says the study, membership of the Organization was dominated by capitalist countries of the West and a handful of economically underdeveloped countries. The result of such imbalance was that "the imperialist states headed by the United States in essence determined the policy of the UNESCO and used it for the attainment of their own narrow goals."[82]

Stage 2 runs from 1954 to 1960 i.e. from the time the USSR, Ukraine and Belorussia joined the Organization and ending with the mass entry into the UNESCO of "yesterday's colonies". During this time we notice a gradual formation within the Organization of two diametrically opposed camps—the democratic and the reactionary. If in the first period, according to the findings of the study, the UNESCO engaged itself in trivial matters that had nothing to do with international peace and security, in the second stage internal pressure from the democratic forces within the Organization was brought to bear upon the UNESCO to make her handle questions of urgency to world peace and to peaceful coexistence.

The mass entry into the Organization by the newly independent states of Africa sparked off the third stage in the history of the UNESCO. The study suggests that with the admission of these new African members and with closer cooperation amongst members of the socialist caucus a psychologically favourable atmosphere has been created to make it possible for the Soviet Union to table its peaceful coexistence menu before the Organization.[83]

The internal struggle between the pro-communist and the pro-Western forces inside the UNESCO continues. But whereas the prospects of an immediate "sovietization" of the Organization are still very slim it will certainly do the West good to bear in mind that the Russians are slowly but surely on the forward move.

1. The injection of Lord Atlee's reference to "the minds of men" into the Constitution of the UNESCO was intended to stress such factors as ignorance, denial of democratic principles and Nazi racial doctrines as the causes of World War II. But as we shall find out later on in the chapter the Soviets originally picked up quarrel with this phrase, only to turn around later on to use it to justify certain actions inside the Organization.

2. UNESCO, qua an instrument for promoting international cooperation in the fields of education, science and culture is the creature of history in the sense that before 1945 there had been attempts to encourage cultural interchange but all such efforts had been "unsystematic, often unconscious of itself, casual, slow-moving, individualistic." See Howard E. Wilson (ed.), "National Programs of International Cultural Relations". International Conciliation, No. 462, June 1950, p. 304. For a detailed historical analysis of efforts that preceded the creation of the UNESCO see W. H. C. Laves and C. A. Thomson, UNESCO, Bloomington 1957, pp. 8-18; see also George N. Shuster, UNESCO—Assessment and Promise, N.Y. 1963.

3. Of the 51 states which signed the UN Charter at San-Francisco all were present at the London Conference except seven—Ethiopia, Costa Rica, Honduras, Paraguay, USSR, Belorussia, and the Ukraine. The Conference delegates included such dignitaries as Britain's Prime Minister, Clement Attlee, his Education Minister, Ellen Wilkinson; former French Prime Minister Léon Blum, etc. Gilbert Murray and Sir Albert Zimmern—both keen students of International Relations provided the intellectual background to the Constitution.

4. UNESCO, Preparatory Commission, Conference for the Establishment of the UNESCO, London 1945 (London 1946), p. 87. Statement by Etienne Gilson.

5. 1945 London Conference, pp. 54, 43, 85, 27, 22, etc.

6. It is true that opposition to the work of the UNESCO came both from the communist countries and from the United States. But whereas in the case of the former opposition came from those who controlled the governments, in the United States opposition was centered in the number of "professional" patriotic groups—these included, for example, the American Legion, Zionist Organizations, the Public School Authority in the City of Los Angeles, and from the Catholic Church which saw the UNESCO as a subversive Organization in view of its communist membership. See Walter H. C. Laves and Charles A. Thomson, UNESCO—Purpose, Progress and Prospects, Bloomington 1957, at pp. XIX-XX; see also George N. Shuster, UNESCO—Assessment and Promise, N.Y. 1963, at pp. 69-75.

7. See Julian Huxley, UNESCO—Its Purpose and its Philosophy, Washington, Public Affairs Press, 1947. For a detailed debate on the question of a philosophy for the UNESCO, see Basil Karp, The Development of the Philosophy of the UNESCO (unpublished Ph.D. dissertation, University of Chicago, 1951, pp. 50-63).

8. It should be recalled that prior to the defection of the Yugoslav regime from the Stalin-controlled communist orbit in 1948 the international communist order acted almost in ideological and philosophical unison.

9. UNESCO, General Conference, First Session, pp. 38-41.

10. UNESCO—General Conference, First Session, pp. 38-41. However, the Marxists were not alone in their condemnation of the Huxley philosophy. Richard McKeon recalls that "Hindus, Thomists, and dialectical materialists, pragmatists, positivsits and idealists, whether inspired by like desire to avoid dogma and particularism or by their own aspirations to universality and their own convictions of adequacy and the truth, could see no particular advantage in Dr. Huxley's formulation of a philosophy for UNESCO; nor any reason for omitting it from the list

of philosophies to be excluded". See Richard McKeon, A Philosophy for the UNESCO, Philosophy and Phenomenological Research, vol. III, No. 4, June 1948, p. 576; see also Harold Stanley Thames, "An Analysis of Representative Ideological Criticism of the UNESCO in the United States, 1946-1954", (unpublished Ph.D. dissertation, Duke University, 1955).

11. A yet stronger argument against the Huxley doctrine came from the Head of the US delegation, William Benton who argued that world peace could not rest on any single political philosophy or religious faith. UNESCO, he maintained, was pledged to cultural democracy, "a democracy of mind and spirit in which every culture shall be free to live and develop in itself and in the great community of common culture... Free men do not fear ideas; free men are not afraid of thought; free men are eager to confront the differences and rich varieties that life presents, and to determine for themselves the things they take as true. This, from the beginning, has been the path of freedom". See UNESCO, General Conference, 1st Session, p. 64.

However, in the final analysis the General Conference adopted the attitude, as had the Preparatory Commission that the Huxley statement represented his own personal views and not those of the Congress.

12. See ILO Conventions—Table of Ratifications, January 1, 1970, published by the International Labour Office, Geneva.

13. Vide infra for a detailed analysis of the Soviet attitude towards individual conventions and international agreements that have so far been adopted by the UNESCO.

14. Throughout the London Conference which resulted in the adoption of the UNESCO Constitution "hope was repeatedly expressed that the Soviet Union, which had contributed so much to winning the war, might find it possible to join the UNESCO". See speech by US Congressman Chester E. Marrow of New Hampshire in the House of Representatives, Nov. 26, 1945. Congressional Record, vol. 91, Part 8, 79th Congress, 1st Session, at p. 10998. It has even been suggested that "the reason why the term 'scientific' appears in the Organization's title was not primarily because exchanges of scientific information were deemed desirable... Rather it was believed that the language of science was the medium in which conversations with the Russians would prove possible." See George N. Shuster, UNESCO—Assessment and Promise, N.Y. 1963, p. 6.

The London Conference in addition even reserved a seat for the USSR on the Executive Committee of the Preparatory Commission. However, following the ratification by the USSR in 1954 of the UNESCO Constitution George N. Shuster, Chairman of the US National Commission for UNESCO issued a statement recalling the indifference and hostility shown to the UNESCO since its foundation by the Soviet Union. The statement also pointed out certain violations by the Soviet government of basic UNESCO principles with regard to human rights and to the "perversion of education, science and the arts for political purposes". He noted that Soviet membership in the UNESCO would provide an "unparalleled opportunity for a world audience to contrast Soviet promises and Soviet performance". US National Commission for UNESCO, "Statement by Dr. George N. Shuster", June 29, 1954. Document NC/(54)7, p. 2 (mimeographed).

15. The relevant section of the Treaty of Versailles which was incorporated into the Covenant of the League of Nations and subsequently into the Constitution of the ILO granted automatic membership of the ILO—a sister-institution of the League of Nations—to League members and this fact sparked off a doctrinal controversy over the Soviet relationship with the ILO between 1919 and 1934. Vide supra at chapter two.

16. However, since neither party took issue with the implications of Art. 2, par. 1 in relation to Soviet-UNESCO relationship prior to 1954, we shall on our part

let the sleeping dog lie. The error may well have been the result of bad draftsmanship rather than a manifestation of the real intentions of the founding fathers of the Organization.

17. Under the provision of Art. XIV "the English and French texts of this Constitution shall be regarded as equally authoritative". The French text reads: 'Les Etats Membres de l'Organisation des Nations Unies possèdent le droit de faire partie de l'Organisation des Nations Unies pour l'Education, la Science et la Culture'. See UNTS vol. 4, 1947, 52:275.

17a. The Russian text of Art. 2, parag. 1 reads (in transliteration): 'Priem v chleny IuNESKO otkryt dlia gosudarstv-chlenov OON'. In this case the word 'otkryt' (is open) compares favourably with the French 'possèdent le droit de faire partie' (posseses the right to become a party) as both phrases suggest some form of action on the part of the applicant state.

18. Our conclusion to the effect that Art. 2, par. 1 of the UNESCO constitution presupposes automatic membership for UN members in the UNESCO is buttressed by the provision of Art. 2, parag. 5 which provides that "members of the Organization which are expelled from the UN Organization shall automatically cease to be members of this Organization". Cf. also the close affinity between UN membership and the exercise of the rights of membership of the UNESCO in Art. 2, par. 4 of the UNESCO Constitution.

19. Vide supra for an examination of this philosophy.

20. See J. Huxley, UNESCO: Its Purpose and its Philosophy, Preparatory Commission of the UNESCO, UNESCO/C/6, Sept. 15, 1946, p. 7.

21. See G. I. Tunkin, Ideologicheskaia Bor'ba i Mezhdunarodnoe Pravo, Moskva 1967. See chapter I for a detailed analysis of this concept.

22. It should be recalled, however, that the Soviet press was completely silent on this question and there was no direct way of ascertaining what the official Soviet position was on the issue. But as Yugoslavia at this time was Russia's best spokesman in the West, there is every reason for us to believe that the ideological argument put up by the Yugoslav delegate against the concept of synthetic ideology for the UNESCO met with the approval of Moscow, if not directly dictated from the Kremlin.

23. N. Evgenev, New Times, March 29, 1950.

24. "Soviet attitude" in this context is intended to cover the attitude of the whole of Eastern Europe at this time.

25. John A. Armstrong, "Soviet attitude towards UNESCO", International Organization, vol. 8, 1954, No. 2 at pp. 217 et seq.

26. K. P. Rubanik: Mezhdunarodno-Pravovye Problemy IuNESKO, Moskva 1969 at p. 4.

27. The USSR deposited its instrument of acceptance of the UNESCO Constitution on April 21, 1954; while the Ukrainian and the Belorussian Soviet Socialist Republics both deposited their instrument of acceptance on April 30, 1954.

28. K. P. Rubanik, Mezhdunarodno-Pravovye Problemy IuNESKO, Moskva 1969 at p. 5.

29. At the first session of the GA and at the third session of the ECOSOC the question of passing on to the UN of some of the non-political functions and similar operations of the LN was discussed. The GA and the ECOSOC regarded as non-political all questions dealing with economic, financial and social matters, as well as questions of health statistics, demography, etc. This enumeration of the so-called non-political functions included the operations of the International Organization for Intellectual Cooperation—the immediate predecessor of the UNESCO. This distinction between political and non-political operations has since remained with the UNESCO.

30. A Western commentator then wrote that the "entry into the UNESCO of

the USSR with its authoritarian communist ideology may threaten the quasi-monopoly of the liberal democratic countries and face UNESCO with the need of reappraising the assumptions on which it at first proceeded". See Harold Stanley Thames, "An Analysis of Representative Ideological Criticism of the UNESCO in the United States, 1946-1954", (unpublished Ph.D. dissertation, Duke University, 1955) pp. 282-283. Quoted by W. H. C. Laves and C. A. Thomson, UNESCO—Purpose, Progress, Prospects, Bloomington 1957 at p. 51.

31. K. P. Rubanik, Op. cit. pp. 7-8.

32. See UNESCO, Acts of the General Conference, 13th. Session, Paris 1964, p. 748.

33. Ibid., p. 861.

34. George N. Shuster, UNESCO—Assessment and Promise, N.Y. 1963, p. 14.

34a. IZVESTIIA, Nov. 25, 1956.

35. See UNESCO, Acts of the General Conference, 11th Session, Paris 1960, Resolutions, p. 70.

36. UNESCO, General Conference 13th Session, Resolutions, 13C/Resolutions (prov) Paris Dec. 18, 1964, pp. 139-140. The US and other Western countries subsequently withdrew their amendments to the draft resolution.

37. UNESCO, Executive Board 55th Session, Resolutions and Decisions, 55/Ex/Decisions, Paris Dec. 15, 1959, pp. 7-8.

38. UNESCO, Ex. Board 61st Session, Resolutions and Decisions, 61 Ex/Decisions, Paris July 15, 1962, pp. 6-7.

39. UNESCO, Acts of the General Conference, 12th Session, Paris 1962, Resolutions, pp. 46-47.

40. UNESCO, General Conference 13th Session, Resolution 13C/Resolutions (prov), Paris Dec. 18, 1964, p. 85.

41. UNESCO Program for 1965-1966 provided for the following positive steps in this direction:
1. the UNESCO Secretariat was to encourage disarmament research;
2. UNESCO was to offer its help to the European Center for the coordination of scientific research and documentation in social science (Vienna) in the conduct of research into such fields like "the economics of disarmament", "the sociology of disarmament", "disarmament and public opinion", "disarmament and education", "disarmament and scientific research", etc. See UNESCO Draft Program and Budget for 1965-1966, chpt. 3.2—Social Science, Sect. III.

42. UNESCO, Ex. Board 66th Session, Resolutions and Decisions, 66 Ex/Decisions, Paris Nov. 12, 1963, p. 32.

43. UNESCO, Acts of the General Conference, 11th Session, Paris 1960. Resolutions, p. 71.

44. See UNESCO, Ex. Board 72nd Session. Later decisions of the UN and the Specialised Agencies which were of interest to the UNESCO, Paris March 31, 1966 at p. 2.

45. See UNESCO Doc. 14C/DR 11 (P), Oct. 21, 1966.

46. See UNESCO Doc. 14C/DR 11 (P), 21 Oct. 1966.

47. K. P. Rubanik, Mezhdunarodno-Pravovye Problemy IuNESKO, Moskva 1969 at p. 15.

48. See UNESCO, General Conference 14th Session, Paris Dec. 30, 1966, p. 115.

49. K. P. Rubanik, Op. cit. at p. 17.

50. V. I. Lenin, 1870-1970. Lenin's birthday (April 21) is a public holiday throughout the Soviet Union even though offices and all public enterprises are open as on ordinary days. The celebration of the 100th anniversary of the founder of the Soviet state in April 1970 marked a culminating point for a preparation which went on throughout the Soviet Union right from 1967 when the Soviet state had just finished celebrating its golden jubilee.

51. As of 1961-1962 financial year Soviet Union's contribution to the budget of the UNESCO was raised from its pre-1961 level of 15.02% to its present level of 15.37% of the UNESCO annual budget.

52. Of the ideologically partitioned countries today only three sections—West Germany, South Korea and South Vietnam—are members of the UNESCO while the other three communist halves are not—German Democratic Rebublic, Democratic Republic of Vietnam, and the Korean Peoples' Democratic Republic.

53. See UNESCO, General Conference 11th Session, Draft Resolution tabled by the Soviet delegation for changes in the procedure for admitting non-members into the UNESCO, Paris Nov. 14, 1960.

54. See UNESCO Ex. Board 60th Session, Resolutions, Paris Dec. 22, 1961, p. 22.

55. See UNESCO, Acts of the General Conference, 12th Session, Stenographic Reports, p. 800.

56. UNESCO, Acts of the General Conference, 12th Session, Resolutions Paris 1962, pp. 98 et seq.

57. See UNESCO, General Conference, 11th Session. Draft Resolution, No. 130, Paris Nov. 14, 1960.

58. UNESCO, Acts of the General Conference, 11th Session, Stenographic Reports, p. 100.

59. See Claude-Albert Colliard, Institutions Internationales, at p. 540.

60. Walter H. C. Laves and Charles A. Thomson, UNESCO—Purpose, Progress and Prospects, Bloomington 1957 at p. 305.

61. In 1967-1968 Asia had three seats, Latin America—six, Africa and Arab East —nine, Western Europe and North America—eight seats.

62. For example, at the 76th and 78th sessions of the Executive Board Switzerland called for a replacement of the equitable geographical distribution principle with the "equitable representation of professions" in the Executive Board, while Brazil called for the setting up of a permanent consultative committee to be attached to the Directorate-General—an attempt to switch powers from the Executive Board to a new organ. All these proposals were rejected.

63. The General Conference approved Directives concerning UNESCO's relations with international non-governmental organizations at its 11th Session (11C/ Resolutions, p. 85); see also 14/C Resolutions, p. 104.

There are three categories of consultative status: A, B, and C, with the first two categories—A and B—carrying more rights and privileges. Status A calls for close consultation and cooperation between the UNESCO and the non-governmental organization; status B calls for just the exchange of information and consultation; while status C merely calls for the exchange of information between the UNESCO and the non-governmental organizations. As of 1966-1967 there were 25 organizations with status A, 118—with status B, and 105—with status C.

64. See UNESCO Doc. 76 Ex/SR 1, 17, July 12, 1967 at p. 135. The Peace Corps has also from time to time come under Soviet fire inside the Organization.

65. In 1947, for example, UNESCO granted subventions to non-governmental organizations totalling $291,000; in 1956 the total was $633,200 or approximately 6% of the total expenditure for that year. See UNESCO Doc. 9C/5, pp. 272-273. Ever since then the amount of money spent by the Organization on subventions to non-governmental organizations has increased considerably. However, after some sharp criticism of UNESCO's subvention policies new criteria have been devised for granting subventions. See UNESCO Doc. 9C/Resolutions, pp. 74-79.

66. K. P. Rubanik, Op. cit. p. 138.

67. Ibid. at p. 139.

68. "Today the principle of geographical distribution is dominant. Member states are entitled to representation in proportion to their respective contributions

to the budget. In practice this means, for example, that virtually no candidates can now be presented by West-European countries other than the Federal Republic of Germany (which obtained membership in the Organization at the relatively late date of 1951), because the number appointed earlier exceeds the quotas of these states. In contrast, the Russians and their satellites have the right to make a goodly number of nominations". George N. Shuster, Op. cit. p. 16.

It, therefore, looks like Western domination of the UNESCO Secretariat continuously is becoming a thing of the past, while possible Soviet "take over" hangs over UNESCO's future.

69. In Chapter 2 above we attempted a similar analysis with regard to ILO conventions. Vide supra.

70. K. P. Rubanik, Op. cit. p. 104; see also by the same author: 'Mezhdunarodnye Soglasheniia, Konventsii i Rekommendatsii IuNESKO', SEMP 1961, pp. 294-306.

71. K. P. Rubanik, Mezhdunarodno-Pravovye Problemy IuNESKO, Moskva 1969, p. 141.

72. K. P. Rubanik, Op. cit. p. 141.

73. K. P. Rubanik, Op. cit. p. 141.

74. F. I. Kozhevnikov, 'Nekotorye Vosprosy Teorii i Praktiki Mezhdunarodnogo Dogovora, 2 SGP 1954, p. 74.

75. K. P. Rubanik, Op. cit. p. 149.

76. K. P. Rubanik, Op. cit. p. 150.

77. K. P. Rubanik, Op. cit. p. 151.

78. Vide infra.

79. A few years ago holders of American university degrees were grossly discriminated against by countries that had adopted the English educational system. Today things are not as bad for holders of such US degrees as these countries have come to look upon these "cheap American degrees" with less suspicion. It is the intention of the Soviet Union to prevent the possible application of this "American treatment" to the holders of Soviet university degrees in the future.

80. All the three criteria are not of equal significance in Soviet practice. The third and the second criteria are crucial whereas the Soviet Union is somewhat flexible on the application of the first criterion.

81. See Spetsializirovannye Uchrezhdeniia OON v Sovremennom Mire (ed. by G. I. Morozov), Izdatel'stvo 'Nauka', Moskva 1967.

82. Ibid., p. 62.

83. See Spetsializirovannye Uchrezhdeniia OON v Sovremennom Mire (ed. by G. I. Morozov), Moskva 1967. (The Specialised Agencies of the UN in the Contemporary World).

CONCLUSIONS

The Soviet state as it was conceived in 1917 and as it continues to operate today is a political organization that is deeply committed to ideological struggle. It is this distortion of objective reality known as ideology that has characterised Soviet foreign policy right from its inception. However, the relationship between state ideology and Soviet behaviour on the international plane is neither constant, consistent, readily apparent nor easily ascertained or even ascertainable. But whereas the ideology of world communism (za pobeda kommunizma vo vsem mire) is the chief determinant factor for all Soviet global strategy, it would be basically incorrect to think that the Soviet Union sometimes is incapable of rational behaviour. Commenting on the apparent incompatibility of state ideology and rational behaviour by the Soviet state, Zbigniew Brzezinski stated: "There is a tendency in the West to view ideology as something irrational and to counterpoise it against pragmatism and empiricism... It would appear that ideology is not incompatible with rational behaviour once the basic assumptions are granted. While these assumptions may or may not be rational, they are at least so far removed from immediate concerns that they do not produce a conflict between the ideology and a rational approach to reality."[1]

Since policy in international organizations is a facet of overall Soviet foreign policy, we shall try to evaluate the role of the policy of peaceful coexistence in the determination of Soviet general strategy inside international organizations. The policy of peaceful coexistence, as we have attempted to show above (see Chpt. 1), has been the theoretical basis upon which Soviet attitude towards any particular international organization is founded. In analysing the Soviet attitude towards two different international organizations or, as is sometimes the case, in evaluating the Soviet role inside one and the same organization, we have sometimes tended to observe some inconsistency between the basic theory of the policy of peaceful coexistence and its practical application. Such "inconsistency" is only apparent. The fact remains that whereas the policy itself provides the basis for overall Soviet attitude inside these organizations, any particular application of its contents shall be modified to suit the "different historical circumstances" of the time. It is this act of political surgery that Soviet foreign policy makers have treid to perform in all the incidents that we have so far examined.

Commenting on this apparent inconsistency in the theory and practice of peaceful coexistence in Soviet foreign policy, former Soviet Premier N. S. Khrushchev once wrote: "We live at a time when Marx, Engels, and Lenin are no longer with us. If we act like children, who compose words letter by letter, we are not going to get very far. Marx, Engels and Lenin created immortal works that will live down the ages. They showed mankind the way to communism. And we are following it firmly. Taking Marxist-Leninist theory as a basis, we must think for ourselves and study life thoroughly, analyze the contemporary situation and draw conclusions of benefit to our common communist cause.

"One must not only know how to read, but must also understand correctly what one reads, and know how to apply it to the concrete situations of our time, to take account of the existing situation, of the actual balance of forces. A political leader who does so shows that he is not only able to read, but also to creatively apply revolutionary theory. If he does not, he is like the man of whom people say that 'he reads books with his eyes shut' ".[2] In other words, what the Soviet Union does inside these organizations is to read the doctrine of peaceful coexistence "with the eyes open and not shut". This in effect means that the doctrine of peaceful coexistence is not a dogma but a platform for action.

The Soviets have certainly demonstrated alacrity and dexterity in their manipulation of this political platform. Founded in 1917 by Lenin, or as some might interject—long before 1917, officially promulgated in 1920 by the Foreign Affairs Commissar Chicherin, and developed thereafter in Soviet government and party documents and in the documents of international conferences of communist and workers' parties, the policy of peaceful coexistence provided the basis for Soviet participation in the San Francisco Conference of 1945 which resulted in the creation of the United Nations. Determined to join forces with other countries in order to save the succeeding generations from the scourge of war, resolved to cooperate with many other states in the promotion of peaceful and good neighbourly relations among nations, the Soviet Union became a member, and for that matter an original member, of the United Nations, qua an international organization for the maintenance of international peace and security. The preliminary bargaining which preceded the 1945 San Francisco Conference showed that the Soviet Union placed highest her demand, as a prerequisite for her participation in any such international organization, for adequate constitutional safeguards for her state sovereignty and the retention of the great power veto inside the Organization.

Even though the very concept of great power veto was first suggested by the United States at the Yalta Talks as a means of making the final draft of the UN Charter palatable to the US Congress,[3] the Soviets eventually seized upon this veto power and made their continued membership of the Organization dependent upon its retention or abandonment.

Soviet membership of the United Nations marked the first grand application of the policy of peaceful coexistence with regard to a universal international organization. The half-hearted accession by the Soviet Union to the Covenant of the League of Nations in 1934 was, perhaps, only a partial rehearsal for the full dive which was to come in 1945. Since the Soviet Union, at this time Soviet Russia, did not participate in the preliminary manoeuvres which led to the creation of the League of Nations, and bearing in mind the highly political nature and clubbish character of the League, no serious observer at that time had really expected the Soviets to remain long inside this union. As was expected, the break came in 1939 when the Soviet Union was expelled from the League for its attack on Finland. This act of expulsion from the League drove the Soviets back again behind their iron curtain from which they refused to come out until 1945.

The attitude of the Soviets towards the International Labour Organization (ILO) has been explored above (see Chpt. 2). Initial Soviet hostility towards the ILO was most probably due to the latter's close affiliation with the "imperialist League of Nations". The same relationship existed between the Soviet Union and another sister-institution of the League—the Permanent Court of International Justice—which the Soviet Union consistently regarded as an "international organ of imperialist justice".

The UN experiment prepared the grounds for Soviet entry into many other universal international organizations. In 1947 she acceded to the constituent instruments of the Universal Postal Union (UPU), the International Telegraphic Union (ITU), and the World Meteorological Organization (WMO). These organizations were founded first as Administrative Unions in 1874, 1865 and 1878 respectively, but when they became UN Specialised Agencies in 1947 the Soviet Union became an original member in all of them and since then she has remained inside these organizations.

In 1948 the Soviets decided to flirt with the World Health Organization (WHO) only to realise after barely one year of membership of that Organization that the time was not yet ripe for such a move. (See Chpt. 3). Consequently, the Soviet Union pulled out in 1949 and did not come back until 1957. When the International Maritime Consultative Organization (IMCO) was founded in 1958 the Soviets became an original member of it. The same thing happened in 1956 when the International Atomic Energy Agency (IAEA) was founded in Vienna. In 1954 the Soviets came back to the ILO from which they were expelled in 1939. In the same year (1954) the Soviets joined the United Nations Educational Scientific and Cultural Organization (UNESCO).

The Soviet delegation was on its way to the Chicago International Civil Aviation Conference of 1944, which eventually resulted in the setting up of the International Civil Aviation Organization (ICAO) when it was recalled only in Winnipeg. Consequently, the Soviet Union remained outside the Organization and continued to do so until very recently.[4]

Even though the Soviets took so long time to decide upon joining the ICAO, it should be recalled that this Organization bears marked similarity to most of the other universal international organizations of which the USSR is a member today—all of them deal with international cooperation in purely technical fields. On the other hand the Soviet Union nurtures deep suspicion for another group of international organizations— the Bretton-Woods Group. This group includes the International Bank for Reconstruction and Development (IBRD), the International Finance Corporation (IFC), the International Development Association (IDA), and the International Monetary Fund (IMF). The Soviet Union participated in the preparatory conferences (1943, 1944) which led to the establishment of the IMF. The Soviet delegate even signed the Final Act of the IMF on July 22, 1944. But thereafter no ratification was forthcoming as the Soviet Union decided to stay out of the Organization. Since then Soviet attitude towards all the Bretton-Woods Institutions has been to regard them all as "departments of international finance of the US government". The weighted voting system inside these organizations has particularly drawn heavy barrage from Soviet commentators and the prospects of the Soviet Union joining any of these financial organizations in the immediate future are very slim.

This leaves us with the Food and Agricultural Organization of the United Nations (FAO) which the Soviet Union continues to boycott until this day because of what Soviet officialdom describes as the Organization's "imperialist and colonialist food and agricultural policies" towards the third world. All these scattered incidents lead us to the following general conclusions with regard to Soviet attitude towards international organizations in general:

1. The Soviets, in their choice of universal international organizations, prefer organizations with professed technical functions to those with even the slightest taint of political aims, even though in Soviet doctrinal international law the difference between technical and political international organizations is almost completely obliterated. However, it is this consideration that has made it possible for the Soviet Union to retain its membership in such organizations as the ILO, IAEA, UNESCO, WHO, UPU, ITU, WMO, IMCO, and the ICAO.[5] All these organizations profess to operate in the highly illusory field of "purely technical cooperation" while laying claims to apoliticism. One really needs to follow up the debates within the various organs of these international organizations to come to the more realistic conclusion that the question of in-

ternational educational, cultural or scientific cooperation, or even the problems of international postal and telecommunications exchanges, not to mention the highly sensitive areas of international labour or health legislations, are no less political than the task of maintaining international peace and security which the so-called political organizations are designed to carry out. The fact that the Soviets decided to participate in the ILO or in the ICAO, for example, does not mean that Moscow necessarily accepts all that these Organizations stand for. Far from it. It is only a political investment with some reasonable expectations of some proportionate returns.

2. The Soviet Union has maximum distrust for all international financial arrangements. The Soviet ruble is certainly not yet in a position to fight any pitched battle with the combined forces of the dollar, the sterling, the franc, the yen, and the mark. As a result of this the tendency is for the Soviet Union to look upon the Bretton-Woods Institution as a mighty financial weapon in the hands of the imperialist West. The doctrine of peaceful coexistence would appear to discourage any East-West confrontation on such un-equal terms.

3. Before the Soviets accept to participate, in any tangible form, in a political international organization of East-West cooperation she must first see to it that the following precautionary measures are taken: there should be full respect for the sovereign equality of the member states, there should be no imposition of the compulsory jurisdiction of the International Court of Justice over intra-organizational relations, and, most importantly, in order to guarantee these two elements, it is desirable that the Soviet Union itself participate in the drafting and preparation of the constituent instrument of the organization in question.[6] The insistence on the retention of the great power veto is a peculiarity of Soviet-UN relations.

All these factors are the result of a direct and practical application of the doctrine of peaceful coexistence the great goal of which is the imposition, sooner or later, of 'Pax Sovietica' on the whole world. The general strategy of the policy of peaceful coexistence, as it seems to us, is to prepare the ground for the eventual evolution of a 'Civitas Gentium Maxima' founded on the global victory of communism—a state of affairs which the Soviets consider as "the childhood of mankind" (kommunizm est' detstvo chelovechestva).

It is remarkable to note, however, that Soviet attitude towards international organizations underwent a significant change in the post-Stalin era. During the early stages of the existence of the Soviet state, her attitude towards international organizations was born in revolution, rooted in ideology and reinforced by bitter anti-war experiences. This attitude guided Soviet relationship with the League of Nations and the United Nations at the initial stage. It is no secret that the Soviets joined the

United Nations in 1945 as an act of accommodation rather than of conviction. Always paramount in Stalin's mind was the security function of the UN, qua an international organization, whereas the economic and social functions were basically ignored.

For example, during Stalin's time the Soviets were highly sceptical of the functions of the ECOSOC of the UN whose activities the Soviets sought to restrict to mere deliberations. The Soviet Union abstained from the International Refugee Organization and nourished deep suspicion for the International Trade Organization. In those few instances in which she saw it fit to participate in any international economic operation of the UN she insisted on the retention of what has come to be known as the "escape clause"—i.e. the Soviet Union supported the idea of extending technical assistance and economic aid to the underdeveloped areas but with the qualification that such assistance must not endanger the sovereignty or independence of the recipient state. This qualification provided excuse for subsequent Soviet non-participation in these operations. The Soviet Union was opposed to all forms of international investment as was evidenced by its total boycott of all the international lending institutions, like the Bretton-Woods Institutions. Even though she was a member of the Technical Assistance Committee of the ECOSOC, the Soviet Union did not participate in the UN Expanded Program for Technical Assistance on the ground that the Program was tailored to meet the requirements of Washington rather than the needs of the recipient nations of Africa, Asia and the Arab East. The final result of such policy was that during Stalin's time the Soviet Union did not spend "one red ruble" on UN efforts to promote the economic development of the underdeveloped world.

But the big re-appraisal of Soviet foreign policy, particularly towards international organizations, came after the death of Stalin. The significant changes that were introduced into Soviet foreign policy at this time included:

1. A decision by the Soviet government to court the third world. The Soviets now realised the potential political power that lay in the third world. There was at this point a switch from a continental-oriented strategy to a global one.

2. The abandonment of the two-camp thesis which tended to lump the neutral countries with the imperialist West. In February 1956 the 20th Congress of the CPSU enunciated the concept of a "zone of peace" to supplement the already existing socialist and imperialist camps.

3. The Soviets decided to break off from the self-imposed isolationism of Stalin's era and to go all out to the West to seek new ideological frontiers. The attitude of the Soviet government towards any participation in the staffing of international secretariats underwent a most radical change after 1953—from a position of absolute neglect to that of super-

activism. As far back as 1920 Lenin in his "Left-Wing Communism, An Infantile Disorder" had castigated those communists who disputed the need to participate in bourgeois parliaments, pointing out that participation "not only does not harm the revolutionary proletariat, but actually helps to prove to the backward masses why such parliaments deserve to be dispersed; it helps their successful dispersal and helps to make bourgeois parliamentarians 'politically obsolete'."[7] He ridiculed those communists who, out of their "superrevolutionariness", repudiated participation in bourgeois parliaments. He called on all communists to make "all the necessary practical compromises, to manoeuver, to make agreements, zigzags, retreats, and so on" in order to disrupt the stability of traditional bourgeois institutions and ipso facto prepare the grounds for further communist advances.

A few months later, in August 1920, the second Congress of the Communist International adopted a series of Lenin-inspired "theses", one of them being "The New Epoch and the New Parliamentarism" in which it stated that "each communist member of parliament must remember that he is not a "legislator", but a party agitator sent into the enemy's camp in order to carry out Party decisions".

In a little over three decades later the Soviet government decided to apply to her relationship with international organizations those tactics that were originally evolved by Lenin for application to national parliaments—Soviet delegates were now to participate in bourgeois-dominated international secretariats with a view to fighting the bourgeois influence in such institutions "from within". Ever since then the Soviet Union has decided to participate in certain universal international organizations while, however, retaining to itself the right to stay entirely out of some of them. The Soviet Union now decided to evoke its right to participate in the staffing of the secretariats of those international organizations of which she was a member.

It was on the basis of this new approach that Premier Nikita Sergevich Khrushchev on September 23, 1960 in the General Assembly of the United Nations, launched a frontal attack on the distribution of posts in the UN Secretariat. Disillusioned with UN activities in the Congo, he called for a more equitable re-apportionment of posts inside the UN Secretariat by tabling his famous "troika formula": "It is necessary that the executive agency of the United Nations should reflect the actual situation now existing in the world. The UN includes member-states of the military blocs of the Western powers, Socialist states and neutral countries. This would be absolutely fair and we would be better protected against the negative phenomena which have been observed in the work of the UN; particularly during the recent developments in the Congo.

"We consider it wise and fair that the UN's executive agency should appear, not as one person—the Secretary-General—but should consist of three persons invested with high confidence of the UN—representatives of the states belonging to the three basic groupings already mentioned.

". . .Briefly speaking, we think that it would be wise to replace the Secretary-General. . . by a collective executive agency of the UN which would consist of three persons, each representing a definite grouping of states. This would provide a definite guarantee against the activity of the UN's executive agency being detrimental to one of the groupings of states."

Khrushchev's demand that the UN Secretariat be re-organised has long since been extended to other international organizations in which the Soviet Union participates. In the past Stalin downgraded the value of these international secretariats in the promotion of Soviet interests. For example, since Soviet Union's main interest in the UN was in the security functions of the Organization, she felt the veto was enough to protect this interest and, therefore, did not care to encourage Soviet nationals to seek employment with the UN Secretariat.[8] Right until 1960 the Soviets virtually ignored international secretariats—the big turn came with Khrushchev's troika speech at the United Nations General Assembly and it has been suggested that the immediate cause of this foreign policy reappraisal was the bitter experience of the Congo crisis—the Soviets came to appreciate the political weight of the Secretariat as a complement to the veto right in the Security Council.

There is another possible factor that led to Soviet insistence on the troika formula—by this time many Afro-Asian countries were being admitted into these international organizations and naturally these new members called for an equitable share of the secretariat posts. The Soviet Union wished to capitalise on this Afro-Asian sentiment. Ever since then the troika formula has remained the cornerstone of Soviet formula towards international secretariats.

However, in 1962 a Soviet commentator went yet further than the original Krushchev's troika blueprints. M. Volodin, in an article in the influential Soviet current affairs Journal—International Affairs[9]—called for an immediate extension of the troika formula to all other organs of the UN including the Security Council, the ECOSOC, the International Court of Justice, and in the election of the post of President of the General Assembly and Chairman of its main Committees.[10] The Soviets now sought to be granted the opportunity to second their political lieutenants to these international agencies. Voicing Soviet attitude towards the entire question of international civil service, Premier N. S. Khrushchev in an interview granted to Mr. Walter Lippmann stated that he "would never accept a single neutral administrator. Why? Because while there are neutral countries, there are no neutral men. You would not accept a communist administrator, and I cannot accept a non-communist administrator."[11] Questioned as to whether he believed that one Secretary-General can act with equal regard for the interests of the socialist, neutral and capitalist countries during a press conference in New York on Sept. 24, 1960, he replied with an old saying: "There are no saints on earth and there never have been. Let those who believe that there are saints keep their belief; we have no faith in such fables."[12]

If, however, at the initial stages of this Soviet onslought on the West, the program-minimum was to obstruct the effective functioning of these international institutions, today Soviet tactics inside these organizations have taken on an offensive posture thus driving the Western bloc nations for the first time to resort to defensive manoeuvres. There is no doubt at all in our mind that the Soviets have won many ideological and political pitched battles with the West inside these organs, but the war continues. The end of this war of attrition is not immediately in sight and the final outcome of it is a subject for political speculation.

It may be too early to assess the impact of the admission of the Peoples' Republic of China into the UN and subsequently into the various UN Specialised Agencies but our brief observation of Communist Chinese behaviour in the various organs of the UN, notably the General Assembly and the Security Council, would lead us to the tentative conclusion that Soviet bargaining position with the West on principal issues that came before these Organizations and notably her political image before the eyes of the nations of the third world are bound to suffer a set back. For the Western powers the admission of Peking into the various Organizations of the UN family provides a golden opportunity for a thorough re-appraisal of the present allignment of voting patterns inside these organs.

NOTES

1. Z. Brzezinski, "Communist Ideology and International Affairs", Journal of Conflict Resolution (Sept. 1960), pp. 110-111. This article is also included in the author's stimulating collection of essays on ideology and power in Soviet politics, N.Y. 1962.

2. N. S. Khrushchev, On Peaceful Coexistence, (Moscow, Foreign Languages Publishing House, 1961), p. 247.

3. President Roosevelt proposed the great power veto as a possible way of making the contemplated UN Charter acceptable to the US Congress as he feared he might suffer the same defeat from the Congress as President Woodrow Wilson did in 1919 with regard to the Covenant of the League of Nations.

4. After over twenty-five years of close observation and deep heart-searching the Soviet Union finally decided to join the ICAO in 1970.

5. Partial suggestions as to why the Soviets prefer the purely "technical" international organizations to political ones are given in the concluding paragraphs of Chapters 2, 3, and 4.

6. The Soviet Union places more or less emphasis on each of these considerations in her determination of which non-political international organizations she ought to participate in.

7. V. I. Lenin, Left-Wing Communism, An Infantile Disorder, Moscow, Foreign Languages Publishing House, 1950, p. 74.

8. One estimate states that out of more than 1.000 professional staff members at the UN Headquarters, other than linguists, Moscow never had more than 15 serving in any particular year during Stalin's period. By 1956 only 25 out of 1,163 were Soviet nationals. See Alvin Z. Rubinstein, The Soviets in International Organizations, Princeton 1964, at p. 258.

9. M. Volodin: "UN in a changed world", International Affairs, No. 9, Sept. 1962.

10. Ibid. at p. 7.

11. New York Herald Tribune, April 17, 1961.

12. The Soviet "no saint" dogma is not without a precedent in Western practice—In a report reviewing the administration of the League Secretariat two experts noted in a minority opinion that "so long as there is no superstate and, therefore, no international man, an international spirit can only be assumed through the cooperation of men of different nationalities who represent the public opinions of their respective countries". See Sydney D. Bailey, "The Troika and the Future of the UN", International Conciliation, No. 538 (1962), at p. 21.

SELECTED BIBLIOGRAPHY

Part I. *Anglo-American and West European Sources (In English and French)*

American Bar Association: Peaceful Coexistence, A Communist Blueprint for Victory, Chicago 1964.

Armstrong, John A.: The Soviet Attitude towards UNESCO, International Organization, vol. 8, 1954, No. 2.

Baade, Hans W. (ed): The Soviet Impact on International Law, N.Y. 1965.

Bailey, Sydney D.: The Troika and the Future of the UN, International Conciliation, No. 538, 1962.

Barghoorn, Frederick Charles: Soviet Foreign Propaganda, Princeton, N.J. 1964.

Barghoorn, F. C.: The Soviet Cultural Offensive: The Role of Cultural Diplomacy in Soviet Foreign Policy, Princeton Univ. Press 1960.

Beguin, B.: Le Tripartisme dans l'OIT Genève 1959.

Beguin, B.: ILO and the Tripartite System, International Conciliation, May 1959, No. 523 at 405-448.

Beloff, Max: The Foreign Policy of Soviet Russia (2 vols.), N.Y. 1947.

Benton, W.: Progress Report on the UNESCO, Congressional Records, March 18, 1964, p. 5465.

Berkov, R.: The WHO: A Study in De-centralised International Administration, Geneva 1957.

Berman, Harold J.: Law as an Instrument of Mental Health in the U.S. and Soviet Russia, U. Pa. L. Rev. 109:361 Jan. 1961.

Boudreau, F.: International Cooperation in Public Health Prior to the Establishment of WHO, Lancet, June 1958.

Briggs, H. W.: Power Politics and International Organization, 39 AJIL 1945, 664-679.

Broches, A.: International Legal Aspects of the Operations of the World Bank, 98 Hague Recueil 1959-III.

Brzezinski, Z.: Communist Ideology and International Affairs, Journal of Conflict Resolution, Sept. 1960.

Calderwood, Howard B.: The WHO and Regional Organizations, 37 Temple Law Quarterly, No. 1, 1963-64.

Calves, Jean-Ives: Droit International et Souveraineté en URSS, Cahiers de la Fondation Nationale des Sciences Politiques, 48 Paris 1953.

Dallin, Alexander: The Soviet Union at the United Nations: An Inquiry into Soviet Motives and Objectives, N.Y. 1962.

Davis, Kathryn: The Soviets at Geneva, Geneva Librairie Kundig 1934.

Demay, Bernard: L'URSS et l'Organisation Internationale, Paris 1951 (Mimeo).

Department of State (USA): Soviet Violation of Treaty Obligations: Document submitted by the Department of State to the Senate Committee on Foreign Relations, Department of State Bulletin, 18:738-744, June 6, 1948.

Evans, L. H.: Some Management Problems of UNESCO, International Organization, 1963 vol. XVII, No. 1, p. 81.

Fernbach, Alfred P.: Soviet Coexistence Strategy, Washington D.C. 1960.

Fischer, G.: La caractère tripartite de l'Organisation, AFDI, 1955.

Fitzmaurice, Gerald (Sir): The Law and Procedure of the ICJ—International Organizations and Tribunals. 29 BYIL 1952.

Florin, Joseph: La Théorie Bolsheviste du Droit International Public, XII Revue Internationale de la Théorie du Droit, 1938.

Freeman, Joseph: The Soviet Worker—An account of the economic, social and cultural status of labour in the USSR, N.Y. 1932.

Fuller, C. D.: Lenin's attitude towards an International Organization for the Maintenance of Peace. 1914-1917, 64 Pol. Sc. Quarterly 245-261, June 1949.

Gallagher, M: The WHO: Promotion of US and Soviet Foreign Policy Goals. Chicago 1963.

Gardner, Richard N.: "The Soviet Union and the United States", The Soviet Impact on International Law (ed. by Hans W. Baade) Oceana N.Y. 1965.

Gardner, Richard N.: The Soviet Union and the United Nations, 29 Law and Contemporary Problems, 845-857, 1964.

Ginsburgs, George: The Soviet Union and International Cooperation in Legal Matters: The Current Phase—Civil Law, 53 Iowa Law Rev. 1020, April 1968.

Goodman, Elliot R.: Soviet Design for a World State, N.Y. Col. Univ. Press 1960.

Gross, Leo: Was the Soviet Union expelled from the League of Nations? 39 AJIL, 35-44, 1945.

Grzybowski, K.: Soviet Public International Law—Doctrines and Diplomatic Practice, Leyden Durham N.C. 1970.

Grzybowski, Kazimierz: International Organizations from the Soviet point of view. 29 International and Contemp. Problems 882-895, 1964.

Grzybowski, K.: The Socialist Commonwealth of Nations: Organizations and Institutions, New Haven, Yale 1964.

Hazard, John N.: Cleansing Soviet International Law of anti-Marxist Theories, 32 AJIL 244-252, April 1938.

Hazard, John N.: The Soviet Concept of International Law, 33 PASIL 33-40, 1939.

Hazard, John N.: The Soviet Union and the World Bill of Rights, 47 Col. Law Rev. 1095-1117, Nov. 1947.

Hazard, John N.: Pragmatic View of the New International Law, 57 PASIL, 79-83, 1963.

Hazard, John N.: Socialist Law and the International Encyclopaedia, 79 Harv. Law Rev., 278-302, 1965.

Hexner, Ervin: The Soviet Union and the International Monetary Fund, 40 AJIL 1946, 637-640.

Hislop, R. I.: The United States and the Soviet Union in the ILO, Michigan 1963.

Huxley, Julian Sorell: UNESCO: Its Purpose and its Philosophy, Washington, Public Affairs Press, 1947.

ILO: The Trade Union Movement in Soviet Russia, Studies and Report, Series A, No. 26, Geneva 1927.

ILO: Trade Union Situation in the USSR, Geneva 1960.

ILO: Trade Union Rights in the USSR, Studies and Reports, New Series, No. 49, Geneva 1959.

ILO: The Trade Union Situation in the US, Geneva 1960.

Ivanova, Z. P. and Kriuchkova, V. S.: International Public Organizations, Washington, D.C. 1962 (Joint Publications Research Trans.)

Jacobson, H. K.: Labour, the UN and Cold War, International Organization, Winter 1957, vol. 11, No. 1, pp. 55-67.

Jacobson, H. K.: The USSR and ILO, International Organization, 1960, No. 3.

Jenks, Wilfred C.: Coordination in International Organizations—An Introductory Survey, XXVII, BYIL 29, 1951.

Jenks, W. C.: Unanimity, the Veto, Weighted Voting, Special and Simple Majorities and Consensus of Modes of Decisions in International Organizations, McNair Collection, 48.

Karp, Basil: The Development of the Philosophy of the UNESCO (unpublished Ph.D. Dissertation) Univ. of Chicago 1951.

Kelsen, Hans: The Communist Theory of Law, London 1955.

Kulski, W. W.: The Soviet Interpretation of International Law, 49 AJIL 1955, No. 4.

Landy, E. A.: The Effective Application of International Labour Standards, International Labour Review, Nos. 4-5, pp. 346-363.

Leaves, H. and Thomson, A.: UNESCO: Purpose, Progress, Prospects. Bloomington, 1957.

Legal Note: The US Reservation to the Constitution of the WHO, 44 AJIL 122, 1950.

Lerner, Warren: "The Historical Origins of the Soviet Doctrine of Peaceful Coexistence", The Soviet Impact on International Law (ed. by Hans W. Baade) Oceana, N.Y. 1965.

Lipson, Leon: "Peaceful Coexistence", The Soviet Impact on International Law (ed. by H. W. Baade) Oceana N.Y. 1965.

Lusignan, G. de: L'Organisation Internationale du Travail (1919-1959) Paris 1959.

McKeon, Richard: "A Philosophy for the UNESCO", Philosophy and Phenomenological Research, vol. III, No. 4, June 1948.

McMurray, Ruth and Lee, Muna: The Cultural Approach, Chapel Hill, 1947.

McWhinney, Edward: Peaceful Coexistence and Soviet Western International Law, Leyden 1964.

McWhinney, Edward: "Soviet and Western International Laws and the Cold Wars in the Era of Bipolarity: Interblock Law in a Nuclear Age", 1 Can. YBIL 40-81, 1963.

Morawiecki, W.: Institutional and Political Conditions of Participation of Socialist States in International Organizations—A Polish Review. International Organization, vol. XXII, No. 2, 1968.

Morawiecki, W.: Some Problems Connected with the Organs of International Organizations, International Organization vol. 19, No. 4, 1965.

Osakwe, C. O.: The International Legal Status of Universal International Organizations, (unpublished Ph.D. dissertation, Moscow State University, Moscow. June 1970).

Osakwe, C. O.: Izmenenie Uchreditel'nykh Aktov Universal'nykh Mezhdunarodnykh Organizatsii (The amendment of the constituent instruments of universal international organizations), SGP No. 7, 1970.

Osakwe, C. O.: "The Concept and Forms of Treaties concluded by International Organizations", in Agreements of International Organizations and the Vienna Convention on the Law of Treaties (edited by Professor Karl Zemaneck), NY/Vienna 1971.

Osakwe, C. O.: Contemporary Soviet Doctrine on the Juridical Nature of Universal International Organizations, 65 AJIL No. 3, July 1971.

Panhuys, H. F. van (et alt.): International Organization and Integration—A Collection of Texts of Documents Relating to the UN, its Specialised Agencies and Regional International Organizations, Leyden 1968.

Patkin, A.: The Soviet Union in International Law, Proceedings of the Australian and New Zealand Society of International Law, Melbourne 1935, vol. I.

Pethibridge, R.: "The Influence of International Politics on the Activities of Non-Political Specialised Agencies—A Case Study", The Journal of Political Studies Association of the United Kingdom, 1965, vol. XIII, No. 2.

Prince, Charles P.: Current Views of the Soviet Union on the International Organization of Security, Economic Cooperation and International Law: A Summary. 39 AJIL 450-485, 1945.

Prince, Charles P.: The USSR and International Organizations, 36 AJIL 425-445, 1942.

Prince, Charles P.: Legal and Economic Factors affecting Soviet Russia's Foreign Policy, Am. Pol. Sc. Rev. 38:656-669, 876-894, Aug./Oct. 1944.

Ramundo, Bernard A.: The (Soviet) Socialist Theory of International Law. Washington, D.C. Institute of Sino-Soviet Studies, The George Washington University, 1964.

Ramundo, Bernard A. : Peaceful Coexistence—International Law in the Building of Communism, Johns Hopkins Press, Baltimore 1967.

Rashba, Evesey, S.: Materials Relating to Soviet Doctrines and Practices of International Law, N.Y. NYU Law School 1953, 2 vols. (Mimeo).

Rubinstein, Alvin Z.: "The USSR and the IMCO: Some Preliminary Observations", US Naval Institute Proceedings LXXXV, No. 10, Oct. 1959, pp. 75-79.

Rudzinski, Alexander W.: "Soviet Peace Offensives", International Conciliation, No. 490, April 1953, pp. 177-225.

Schlesinger, Rudolph: Soviet Legal Theory—Its Social Background and Development, London 1945.

Schlesinger, Rudolph: Soviet Theories of International Law, Soviet Studies, vol. 4, No. 3 1953.

Schwebel, Stephen M.: The United States assaults the ILO 65 AJIL No. 1, Jan. 1971.

Sharp, Walter R.: The New World Health Organization, 41 AJIL 509-530, No. 3 July 1947.

Shuster, George N.: UNESCO—Assessment and Promise, N.Y. 1963.

Sigerist, Henry E.: Socialised Medicine in the Soviet Union, N.Y. 1937.

Sigerist, Henry E.: Medicine and Health in the Soviet Union, N.Y. 1947.

Simpson, S.: The ILO in 1940, 35 AJIL 359-363, April 1941.

Taracouzio, T. A.: International Cooperation of the USSR in Legal Matters, 31 AJIL 55-65, 1937.

Taracouzio, T. A.: The Soviet Union and International Law, N.Y. 1935.

Thames, Harold Stanley: "An Analysis of Representative Ideological Criticism of the UNESCO in the United States: 1946-1954" (un-published Ph.D. Dissertation) Duke University 1955.

Thomas, Jean: UNESCO, Paris 1962.

Thorp, Willard L.: New International Programs in Public Health, 40 Amer. Journal of Public Health, Dec. 1950.

Toynbee, Arnold and Israel, Fred L.: Major Treaties of Modern History (1648-1967), vol. II, N.Y. 1967.

Tripp, Brenda M. H.: UNESCO in Perspective, International Conciliation, No. 497, March 1954.

Triska, Jan F.: The Soviet Law of Treaties, 53 PASIL 294-301, 1959.

Triska, Jan F.: Soviet Treaty Law: A Quantitative Analysis. 29 Law and Contemporary Problems, 896-909, 1964.

Triska, Jan F. and Slusser, Robert M.: A Calendar of Soviet Treaties (1919-1957), 1959.

Triska, Jan F. and Slusser, Robert M.: The Theory, Law and Policy of Soviet Treaties, Stanford 1962.

Walline, P.: La Crise de l'Organisation du Travail, Revue des deux mondes, Paris 1. VIII. 1959.

Wilson, Howard E. (ed.): "National Programs of International Cultural Relations", International Conciliation, No. 462, June 1950.

Yakobson, Sergius: "World Security and Regional Arrangements—Soviet Position", 44 PASIL 15-22, 1950.

Yemin, Edward: Legislative Powers in the UN and the Specialised Agencies, Leyden 1969.

Part II. *Soviet Sources (Transliterated from Russian into English using Library of Congress Transliteration System)*

Afanacieva, O: Kratkaia Istoriia Ligi Natsii, Moskva 1945.

Aleksandrov, N. G. (ed.): Zakonodatel'stvo o Trude—Kommentarii, Moskva 1953.

Blishchenko, I. P.: K. Voprosu o Printsipakh Othnoshenii Gosudarstv s Mezhdunarodnymi Organizatsiiami, SEMP 1964-1965.

Bobrov, R. L.: Iuridicheskaia Priroda Organizatsii Ob'edinennykh Natsii, SEMP 1959.

Bobrov, R. L.: Osnovnye Problemy Teorii Mezhdunarodnogo Prava, Moskva 1968.

Boguslavskii, I. M. and Rubanov A. A.: Pravovoe Polozhenie Inostrantsev v SSSR, Moskva 1962.

Borisov, K. G.: K. Voprosu o Regulirovanii Nauchno-tekhnicheskogo Sotrudnichestva v Sovremennom Mezhdunarodnom Prave, SEMP 1966-67.

Durdenevskii, V. N. and Krylov, S. B.: Mezhdunarodnoe Pravo—Uchebnik, Vypusk I, Moskva 1946.

Ganiushkin, B. V.: V.O.Z., Moskva 1959.

Ivanov, L. N.: Liga Natsii, Moskva 1929.

Ivanov, S. A.: M.O.T. i Profsoiuznue Prava v Kapitalisticheskikh Stranakh (red. A. E. Pasherstnik) Moskva 1959.

Ivanov, S. A.: Problemy Mezhdunarodnogo Regulirovaniia Truda (red. S. L. Zius), Moskva 1964.

Ivanov, S. A.: Primenenie Mezhdunarodnykh Konventsii o Trude, SEMP 1958.

Ivanov, S. A.: Voprosy Predstavitel'stva v Mezhdunarodnoi Organizatsii Truda, SEMP 1961.

Ivanov, S. A.: International Labour Conventions and the USSR, International Labour Review, vol. 93, April 1966, p. 401.

Khrushchev, Nikita S.: On Peaceful Coexistence, Moscow (Foreign Languages Publishing House) 1961.

Klepacki, Z. M.: "Attempt at defining an International Organization", Pánstwo i Prawo (Polish) with Summaries in English, French and Russian.

Korovin, E. A.: Sovremennoe Mezhdunarodnoe Publichnoe Pravo, Moskva 1926.

Korovin, E. A.: Mezhdunarodnoe Pravo Perekhodnogo Vremeni, Moskva 1924.

Korovin, E. A.: Ustav OON i Mirnoe Sosushchestvovanie, SEMP 1960.

Korovin, E. A.: Otkritoe Pis'mo ot 5 maia, 1935 goda, 4 SGP 1935, p. 71.

Korovin, E. A. and Ratner L.: Programma po Mezhdunarodnomu Publichnomu Pravu, Moskva 1963.

Kozhevnikov, F. I. (ed.): Sovetskoe Gosudarstvo i Mezhdunarodnoe Pravo, Moskva (IMO) 1967.

Kozhevnikov, F. I. (ed.): Kurs Mezhdunarodnogo Prava (six vols.), vol. 5 Moskva 1969.

Kozhevnikov, F. I. (ed.): Uchebnik Mezhdunarodnogo Prava, Moskva (IMO) 1964.

Kozhevnikov, F. I.: Uchebnik Publichnogo Mezhdunarodnogo Prava, Iurizdat, Moskva 1947.

Kozhevnikov, F. I.: Nekotorye Voprosy Teorii i Praktiki Mezhdunarodnogo Dogovora, 2 SGP 1954.

Kral, K.: Short Encyclopaedia of the International Trade Union Movement (Translated from Czech), [Kratkaia Entsiklopediia Mezhdunarodnogo Profsoiuznogo Dvizheniia], Moskva 1963.

Kukarenko, F.: Rassmotrenie Iuridicheskikh Voprosov vo Vsemirnoi Meteorologicheskoi Organizatsii v 1961 godu, SEMP 1962.

Kukarenko, F.: Rassmotrenie Iuridicheskikh Voprosov v IuNESKO v 1961 godu, SEMP 1962.

Kukarenko, F.: Rassmotrenie Iuridicheskikh Vosprosov vo V.O.Z. v 1961 godu, SEMP 1962.

Kurilin, N.: Mezhdunarodnyi Valiutnyi Fond, Moskva 1967.

Lazarev, M. I.: Antikommunizm i Mezhdunarodnoe Pravo, 7 SGP 1968.

Lenin, V. I.: Left-Wing Communism, An Infantile Disorder, Moscow, (Foreign Languages Publishing House) 1950.

Levin, D. B.: O Poniatii i Sisteme Sovremennogo Mezhdunarodnogo Prava, 5 SGP 1947.

Levin, D. B. (ed.): Mezhdunarodnoe Pravo—Uchebnik dlia Iuridicheskikh Vuzov, Moskva (Iuridicheskaia Literatura) 1964.

Levin, D. B.: Osnovnye Problemy Sovremennogo Mezhdunarodnogo Prava, Moskva 1958.

Lukashuk, I. I.: Mezhdunarodnaia Organizatsiia kak Storona v Mezhdunarodnykh Dogovorakh, SEMP 1960.

Malinin, S. A.: Iuridicheskaia Priroda i Pravovoi Status Spetsializirovannykh Uchrezhdenii OON, 11 SGP 1958.

Mikhailov, V. S.: Mezhdunarodno-Pravovye Formi Sotrudnichestva Sotsialisticheskikh Gosudarstv v Oblasti Zdravookhraneniia, 1 SGP 1963.

Mikhailov, V. S.: Vozniknovenie i Razvitie Mezhdunarodno-Pravovykh Form Sotrudnichestva Gosudarstv v Oblasti Zdravookhraneniia, SEMP 1961, p. 282.

Minasian, H. M.: Sushnost' Sovremennogo Mezhdunarodnogo Prava, Rostov-na-Donu, 1962.

Minasian, H. M.: Pravo Mirnogo Sosushchestvovaniia, Izdatel'stvo Rostovskogo Universiteta, 1966.

Modzhorian, L. A.: Sub'ekty Mezhdunarodno-Pravovoi Otvetsvennosti, 12 SGP 1969.

Modzhorian, L. A.: O Sub'ektakh Mezhdunarodnogo Prava, 6 SGP 1956.

Modzhorian, L. A.: Sub'ekty Mezhdunarodnogo Prava, Moskva 1958.

Modzhorian, L. A.: O Sub'ektakh Mezhdunarodnogo Prava, Moskva 1948.

Molodtsov, S. V.: Pravilo Edinoglasiia Postoiannykh Chlenov Soveta Bezopasnosti—Nezyblemaia Osnova OON, 7 SGP 1953.

Morozov, G. I.: (ed.): Spetsializirovannye Uchrezhdeniia OON v Sovremennom Mire, Moskva 1967.

Morozov, G. I.: Organizatsiia Ob'edinennykh Natsii, Moskva 1962.

Morozov, G. I.: Mezhdunarodnye Organizatsii—Nekotorye Voprosy Teorii, Moskva 1969.

Negin, M.: IuNESKO, Moskva (IMO) 1959.

Rokovskii, Kh. G.: Liga Natsii i SSSR, Moskva 1926.

Rozanov, L. L.: "Nekotorye Problemy Zdravookhraneniia i Deiatel'nost' V.O.Z.", Spetsializirovannye Uchrezhdeniia OON v Sovremennom Mire (ed. by G. I. Morozov) Moskva 1967.

Rubanik, K. P.: Proval v IuNESKO Kolonizatorskoi Zatei Portugalii, 5 SGP 1967, pp. 133-136.

Rubanik, K. P.: Mezhdunarodnye Soglasheniia, Konventskii i Rekommendatsii IuNESKO, SEMP 1961, p. 294.

Rubanik, K. P.: Mezhdunarodnopravovye Voprosy na Sessiiakh Rukovodiashchikh Organov IuNESKO, 1960-1965, SEMP 1964-1965.

Rubanik, K. P.: Mezhdunarodno-Pravovye Problemy IuNESKO, Moskva 1969.

Sevetskoe Gosudarstvo i Pravo: Peredovaia Stat'ia: Novyi Shag v Razvitii Sovetskoi Sotaialisticheskoi Demokratii, 3 SGP 1958.

Shibaeva, E. A.: Spetsializirovannye Uchrezdeniia OON, Moskva 1962.

Shibaeva, E. A.: Spetsializirovannye Uchrezhdeniia OON, Moskva 1966.

Shibaeva, E. A.: Iuridicheskaiia Priroda i Pravovoe Polozhenie Spetsializirovannykh Uchrezhdenii OON, (Avtoreferat Doktorskoi Disser-
tatatsii) Moskva 1969.

Shibaeva, E. A.: Mezhdunarodnopravovye Formy Organizatsii i Deiatel'-
nosti Spetsializirovannykh Uchrezhdenii OON, SEMP 1964-65.

Shkunaev, V. G.: M.O.T., Vchera i Sevodnia, Moskva 1968.

Shurshalov, V. M.: Osnovnye Voprosy Teorii Mezhdunarodnogo Dogovora, Moskva 1959.

Talalaev, A. N.: Iuridicheskaia Priroda Mezhdunarodnogo Dogovora,
Moskva 1963.

Talalaev, A. N.: Fal'sifikatsia Sovetskoi Teorii Mezhdunarodnogo Prava
i Printsipov Mirnogo Sosushchestvovaniia, 11 SGP 1966, p. 104.

Tokareva, P. A.: Pravovye Voprosy Spetsializirovannykh Uchrezhdenii
OON, 2. SGP. 1967.

Tunkin, G. I.: Printsip Mirnogo Sosushchestvovaniia—General'naia
Liniia Vneshnepoliticheskoi Deiatel'nosti KPSS i Sovetskogo Gosudarstva, 7 SGP 1963.

Tunkin, G. I.: The Legal Nature of the UN, 119 Hague Recueil 1966-III.

Tunkin, G. I.: Remarks on the Normative Function of Specialised Agencies, Revista Española de Derecho Internacional, vol. 21, April-June
1968.

Tunkin, G. I.: Teoriia Mezhdunarodnogo Prava, Moskva 1970.

Tunkin, G. I.: Sorok Let Sosushchestvovaniia i Mezhdunarodnoe Pravo,
SEMP 1958.

Tunkin, G. I.: Uspekh Politiki Mirnogo Sosushchestvovaniia, SEMP
1962.

Tunkin, G. I.: Bor'ba Dvukh Kontseptsii v Mezhdunarodnom Prave, 11
SGP 1967.

Tunkin, G. I.: Osnovy Sovremennogo Mezhdunarodnogo Prava, Moskva 1956.

Tunkin, G. I.: Ideologicheskaia Bor'ba i Mezhdunarodnoe Pravo, Moskva 1967.

Usenko, V. L.: Problemy Teorii Mezhdunarodnoi Organizatsii (A Review
of G. I. Morozov's Mezhdunarodnye Organizatsii—Moskva 1969)
12 SGP 1969, p. 155.

Ushakov, N. A.: Sub'ekty Sovremennogo Mezhdunarodnogo Prava,
SEMP 1964-65.

Ushakov, N. A.: K Voprosu a Prave "Veto" v OON, SEMP 1959.

Veral'skii, M. et alt.: Problemy Mezhdunarodnogo Finansovogo Prava,
1 SGP 1967.

Vladimirov, V.: M.O.T., Moskva 1959.

Volodin, M.: "UN in a changed world", International Affairs, No. 9, Sept. 1962.

Zadorozhnyi, G. P.: 'Vliianie Oktiabr'skoi Revoliutsii na Progressivnoe Razvitie Mezhdunarodnogo Prava', (Soobshchenie na Nauchnoi Konferentsii Iuristov-Mezhdunarodnikov, posveshchennoi Oktiabr'skoi Revoliutsii), SEMP 1968, pp. 364-365.

Zhdanov, A. A.: O Pravovom Statuse Sluzhashchikh Mezhdunarodnykh Organizatsii, SEMP 1964-1965.

Part III. *Basic Documents*

1. Charter of the United Nations Organization.
2. Constitution of the UNESCO.
3. Constitution of the ILO and Standing Orders of the International Labour Conference, International Labour Office, 1963 Edition, Geneva.
4. Programma Kommunisticheskoi Partii Sovetskogo Soiuza (Program of the Communist Party of the Soviet Union) Politizdat, Moskva 1965.
5. Konstitutsiia (Osnovnoi Zakon) SSSR. [Constitution (The Fundamental Law) of the USSR.]
6. UNCIO Documents, vols. 1-15, San Francisco 1945.
7. Osnovy Zakonodatel'stva Soiuza SSR i Soiuznykh Respublik o Trude (The Fundamental Principles of Labour Legislation of the USSR and the Union Republics) adopted by the Supreme Soviet of the USSR, July 15, 1970. See Vedomosti Verkhovnogo Soveta SSSR, No. 29 (1531) July 22, 1970.
8. Kodeks Zakonov o Trude (Labour Code of the USSR).
9. Ustav Profsoiuzov SSSR (Rules of the Trade Unions of the USSR) adopted at the 12th Congress of the AUCCTU, March 27, 1959, Moskva Profizdat, 1959.
10. WHO—Basic Documents, 31st Edition, Geneva, April 1970.

INDEX